# THE

# COLONIAL FARM

A Memoir of Family and Community

# Books by Wanjirũ Warama

## Alone in America Duology:

Unexpected America
Entangled in America

## Standalone:

Years of Shame (a 3-story novella)
Beyond Conscious Self (a two-story novella)
The Colonial Farm
The Native Daughter

## Short stories

NEW BEGINNING: Why Religion Never Appealed to Me Until…

## Anthology:

Why Religion Never Appealed to Me Until… (Personal Essay – San Diego Writers and Editors Guild 2023 Anthology)

# THE

# COLONIAL FARM

## Wanjirũ Warama

Athomi Books
San Diego, California, USA

Wanjirũwarama.com

United States of America – December 2024

Library of Congress Control Number: 2024924277

ISBN:  Print: 978-1-954423-08-4

E-book: 978-1-954423-09-1

Cover Design by ebooklaunch.com

Cover Image by Wanjirũ Warama

First Edition

Published by Athomi Books
8064 Allison Ave, #684, La Mesa, California, 91942
United States of America

# DEDICATION

The Colonial Farm is dedicated to the first generation of Warama sons and daughters, born and raised under the inhumane shadow of a colonial yoke, and who lived to witness and experience the responsibilities, challenges, and joys of self-determination.

*Map of Kenya and its Neighbors*

# TABLE OF CONTENTS

# Author's Note

The nonfiction stories in this book span the period from late 1959 to January 1965. My family and our community witnessed or experienced them firsthand, except for incidents I have referenced from historical accounts.

Quotations come from my recollections, reconstructed dialogue, and eyewitness statements from relatives and others. I have translated from Gĩkũyũ or Kiswahili to English, unless otherwise quoted from reference sources.

I use actual names except in a handful of cases where my community and I did not know the individuals' names or where the names proved hard to pronounce and, over time, faded from collective memory.

Readers should note that Kenya, like the rest of Africa, is culturally diverse and complex. This book, however, covers only a small part of my family's story and that of my Gĩkũyũ community.

For historical context, readers should also know that the Bantu communities of the Meru, Embu, Mbeere, and Tharaka—close cousins of the Gĩkũyũ—were also drawn into the conflict between the Mau Mau and the colonizers. Still, this book is a family memoir focused mainly on my family, other Gĩkũyũ farmworker peasants, and Kikuyuland, the epicenter of Mau Mau activity.

*Wanjiru Warama*

# Chapter 1

# The Whisper

For the first time in my life, in mid-1959, before I turned thirteen, shame settled within me when I realized I had a fool for a father. Worse still, I belonged to a helpless people, brave only within the safety of their temporary homes.

But I did not arrive at that thought all at once.

It came to me slowly, during Kenya's turmoil that had led to our four impromptu relocations that Baba, the head of our household, had no say in. And to top it all, a whisper.

The seven of us children sat around the three-stone hearth in Mami's house one evening, waiting for supper. The fire cracked softly, and an occasional puff of smoke wafted away while we swiped it off our faces. Mami stirred the pot and kept the spatula aside. Nothing in her manner suggested anything unusual until she spoke.

She had great news.

She could not resist sharing it with us before consulting with Baba.

None of us asked who had told her. We were used to her social ways. Mami always seemed to know things before anyone else. She sniffed out adult village gossip and whispers and kept us children informed.

"Kamunge is selling the farm," she said.

That part did not surprise us. We had already heard that one.

Then came the whisper.

"Kamunge," she said, "has offered your father twenty-five acres of land."

Some of us gasped. Others stared, mouths open.

For a moment, none of us spoke.

Then came the chatter—wild, scattered, incredible. Our sheltered minds strained to grasp possibilities far beyond anything we had known. We needed time for the news to settle.

That evening, no one complained that Mami took too long to cook.

We sat with our thoughts.

At least, I did. My mind tumbled and marveled at the epic lifestyle changes that awaited our family, a lifestyle I had never associated with Africans. In colonial Kenya, we lived in a world that had trained us not to expect or dream of such worldly riches.

The helplessness that gripped my family and the Gĩkũyũ community still lingered heavily over us. The British colonizers had crushed the Mau Mau freedom fighters with bombs and modern weapons, hunted them in Mt. Kenya and Nyandarua forests and other hideouts, detained and hanged many, and left others broken, starved, or dispossessed.

The rest of us still lived under watch on colonial farms, segregated in town neighborhoods, or in fenced villages in the *Native Reserves*.

People had learned to endure.

They longed for peace, for time to breathe, and take stock.

It had been months since Kamunge, the British landowner, ordered us to move yet again.

It was our fourth move.

Each time, my parents hurriedly built the same stick-and-mud circular houses arranged around a courtyard. Like in our last fenced village, my family's homestead ended up tucked at the back of the village.

Change did not affect adults only; it affected us children, too. The move added another half-mile to our two-mile walk to school. Now in grade three, my class had begun learning English and civics. Like my siblings, I focused on school the best I could, while the adults settled into their routines under a dull, war-worn fatigue.

Nothing in our lives suggested other changes.

Until that whisper.

By then, windowed, Kamunge had grown old. I remember him in khaki shorts, a white shirt, a bucket hat, and sandals, moving gingerly about the farm as if everything within it were part of his being.

In a way, it was.

And now he had to move, not just from his colonial house set on a ten-acre homestead, but from "his" country as well, and especially the farm that had defined his family's lives for decades. He and his son's family prepared to transfer the farm's title to a new owner, pack, and return to England.

But before Kamunge left, he planned to settle the unfinished business between him and Baba.

They went way back. Long before Kamunge became a wealthy landowner, he had been a young, inexperienced farm manager, newly arrived from England. At the time, Baba was on the run from ruthless, colonial militia officials in Nyeri. Work on that farm, answerable to only one man, had become his refuge.

In those early days, before money and power hardened the lines between them, the two men had sometimes worked side by side, though even then each knew his place.

Now they were both old men.

One had become a rich landowner.

The other remained a worn-out peasant.

And yet, the whisper said Kamunge had offered Baba twenty-five acres of land for retirement after more than thirty years of loyal service. Kamunge either wanted to ease his conscience or to share in his windfall.

That night, my mind wandered.

I imagined what the offer meant to my family.

We knew that precious, temperate land well. It lay just beyond the dirt road behind our new homestead. It consisted of six or seven acres of coffee bushes heavy with cherries, and the rest open, bushy country, waiting.

My family had worked that land for pay. But now, everything changed in my mind. In my imagination, we owned the land, like a mzungu (white) family.

Baba would build a large concrete house with a red-tiled roof and a wraparound veranda. He and Mami would sit there and drink tea, like Kamunge and his European friends.

We would replace our rough wooden benches and stools with soft furniture.

We would wear colorful, ready-made clothes, and each of us would have a second school uniform.

We would even wear shoes!

The thought alone filled my heart with pride.

I did not think about the work required to run such a farm.

Only the life it promised.

The next day passed.

And the next.

I waited.

Baba was not a man anyone hurried. He ruled our family with quiet authority, a reserved dictator whom no one questioned openly.

Still, I believed he would speak.

In my mind, he had already accepted the land.

I waited for him to say the words that would change everything.

# Chapter 2

# Mother's Impossible Burden

Baba did not speak the next day.

Or the day after that.

With each passing evening, the whisper that had set our imaginations ablaze settled into something harder to bear: suspense. Only Baba could end it.

We children spent our evenings in nyũmba, Mami's house, where life followed its usual rhythm of cooking, eating, and chatter. Baba spent his evenings in his thingira, the traditional circular mud-and-thatch cottage that served as his private domain. After work, and after settling his goats in their cottage, he waited for his mug of tea, the one he drank every morning and evening.

Mami made it with mathache, the severely skimmed milk from the quart Kamunge provided long-term workers as part of their employment. It was thin, but it was something.

One evening, instead of sending one of us children to take Baba his tea as she always did, Mami took it herself.

That alone told me the matter of the land had become too large for her to sit with in silence.

Before she left, she instructed my brother Joseph and me—the oldest children at home—to watch her simmering pot.

Mami was gone for nearly half an hour.

When she returned, she said nothing.

That silence told me more than words could.

For her, a naturally sunny and talkative person, saying nothing meant her mission went against what she hoped. Perhaps Baba did not want to discuss the land while he mulled on how to tackle it, I thought.

Based on her history, I knew she wouldn't just wait.

"I'll talk to him," she usually quipped if we doubted Baba would accept our request. After twenty-three years of marriage, she knew how to approach him. She had learned when to prod, when to soften, and when to circle a matter patiently until he lowered his guard. More often than not, when she prepared herself well, she could make him reconsider even a decision he had already settled in his mind.

So she delivered tea again.

And then once more.

Only later did she tell us how the first conversation had gone.

She had handed Baba his tea, sat on a low bench, and begun carefully.

"Is it true what I hear about the coffee farm?" she asked.

"What farm?" Baba said, eyeing her as if surprised that she knew.

"That I hear Kamunge gave you."

"What would I do with a coffee farm?"

"Did you say that to him?"

"Yes," Baba said. "That's exactly what I asked him."

"Did he say anything?"

"He told me to think about it."

"I wanted to know," Mami said after a controlled pause, "instead of hearing it secondhand."

Then she let the matter rest and turned to other family concerns.

But she had not let it rest in her heart.

She waited a day or two before she approached him again.

That was her way when something mattered deeply. She needed time to gather herself, to keep anger from spilling ahead of sense.

The second attempt got her nowhere.

On the third try, she dropped caution altogether.

She sweet-talked him, cajoled him, reasoned with him, and finally begged him to accept the land.

He had made up his mind.

He was not taking it.

Back in nyũmba, Mami sat with her defeat like a woman carrying a load too heavy to set down. She mused about women's helplessness. We children, her loyal allies, listened, eyes on her, sober, without comment.

There was nothing to say or do.

In our world, such a decision belonged to Baba alone.

And Mami, for all her spirit and sharpness, had been raised within the same Gĩkũyũ traditions and colonial rules as everyone else. A wife did not go around her husband and negotiate with a man, let alone a white landowner—not if she wished to remain respectable, and not if she wished to leave her husband's authority intact.

Kamunge, like other colonizers, never dealt with a woman directly, even if her husband stood nearby. If he wished to address a female worker, he spoke to her husband or to an overseer. The husband would then turn to the wife and say, *Nĩwaigua ũrĩa mũnene auga?*—Did you hear what the boss said?

That was the order of things.

And everyone lived inside it.

Still, later I thought of how close Mami came to breaking that order and wished she had.

She often told us, "The neck never overtakes the head," when Baba made a decision she disliked.

But this was one of the few times when the neck might have saved the whole body.

If she had gone to Kamunge herself to ask for the land, she would have risked shaming Baba and becoming the talk of the village. She might have been called a disobedient wife, a woman who ruled over her husband's homestead.

Or she might have saved us.

But that thought did not come to her then.

Or if it did, she could not bring herself to follow it.

That evening, as she cooked ugali and collard greens and spoke of her failure, a heaviness settled around the hearth.

We lowered our voices in case Baba overheard us.

I was not yet thirteen, but I already knew, deep inside me, that he had made a grave mistake.

Why, I wondered, did Kamunge not simply force him to take the land? Give it to him outright instead of offering it?

If the title had been placed directly in Baba's hands, I believed, without a shred of doubt, he would have accepted it without question, and even thanked Kamunge.

That thought kept a sliver of hope alive in me.

A useless hope.

But as the days passed, even that began to fade.

Kamunge had his departure to think about. He had eased his conscience and had no reason to stand over Baba and rescue him from his lack of foresight.

And so the matter slipped away.

Over the following months, Mami mentioned the land now and then, and each time the old regret stirred in us. But nothing came of it.

For years afterward, I carried that loss in my mind—not only the land itself, but everything I believed it might have given us: the security, the dignity, the beautiful life I had already built around it in my imagination.

As I grew older—through school, through work, through the ordinary burdens of life—that loss never fully left me.

Decades later, my brother would buy a small piece of that same land. When I visited his family in 2022, I joined his coffee pickers and picked coffee cherries again.

My fingers remembered what my mind had long tried to forget, while a tinge of regret I thought had long gone resurfaced.

All those years, I mourned that land without ever asking myself the question that mattered most:

Why had my father refused it?

# Chapter 3

# The Colonial Cult

As I spent years mourning the coffee farm, I remained blind to the question that mattered most: Why had my father turned it down? It took writing about the whisper to finally ask why.

The answer remained locked inside Baba until his last breath.

Now, in old age, I am no longer surprised by his decision. But I still marvel at the inner workings of a man who, as a small boy, had watched the British invade and crush his people, burn homes, maim men, women and children and animals screaming in the chaos, and drive away livestock to feed their troops. And as if that were not enough, he had also watched them take the land.

As a grown man, Baba suffered in the colony in other ways. He endured insults, slights, and the daily humiliations that came with being African in British Kenya. The British even conscripted him into World War I. He was lucky to return home alive, though little more than a skeleton. His only brother never returned, and no word about where he might have perished.

And still, after all that, Baba spent decades helping build the wealth of another man.

He watched Kamunge rise from a poor young Englishman into a rich and secure landowner, while he himself remained a peasant earning a pittance.

So why would such a man refuse A tiny fraction of that farm?

I have turned that question over in my mind many times.

Perhaps Baba thought the land offer was so improbable that Kamunge was testing him.

That would not have been far-fetched. A few years earlier, Kamunge had refused to give him transportation to take a gravely sick child and his wife to the hospital. How could such a man suddenly offer him twenty-five acres of land? Baba may have suspected a trap where I, in my childish innocence, saw only fortune.

If he misunderstood the offer and lost Kamunge's favor, he risked more than embarrassment. He risked losing his job. Then, an old man with no job prospects and with a young family, he risked shelter, and the only refuge he and his family had known for decades. That was too much of a gamble.

Or perhaps, once Baba understood the offer was real, he still could not imagine himself as a landowner.

That may sound foolish to anyone who has never lived under domination long enough for it to settle into the bones. But by then, my father had lived so many years inside the colonial hierarchy that he may have seen such ownership as something meant for white men, not for the likes of him. Kamunge had land. Baba had labor. That was the order of things. As Carter Godwin Woodson said, "When you control a man's thinking, you do not have to worry about his action."

And even if Baba's mind had stretched far enough to accept the possibility, practical barriers stood in the way.

A coffee farm was not just land. It required labor, upkeep, transport, and money. To make use of it, Baba would have needed workers to till the land and pick coffee cherries. He would have needed access to processing, storage, transport, and sale.

But Kenya was still a British colony, and Africans were barred from growing or marketing coffee and other cash crops or becoming members of organizations such as the Kenya Coffee Board. To profit from such land, Baba needed capital and a hush-hush backing of a white man intermediary. He had none of those things.

So perhaps the offer looked less like liberation to him than another burden he could not carry.

As a child, I did not understand such details.

All I saw was loss.

I had already imagined the coffee bushes as ours. I had already furnished the house Baba would build and put shoes on our feet.

But if all Baba had ever known was oppression, how could he have looked beyond the next month's wages, the next school fee, the next bag of maize? How could a man trained by hardship to survive one season at a time suddenly think like a landowner? Let alone imagine that the British Empire itself might one day crack and give way to independence?

When Baba left his homeland and found work on Kamunge's farm, that farm became his refuge. It shielded him, to some degree, from the colonial government's demands and from the crushing burden of taxes that pushed even unemployed African men into labor on European farms. There, he kept his head down and raised his family without causing a ripple.

Year after year, decade after decade, the colonial system did its work.

It wore down not only his body and self-worth but also his imagination.

By the time Kamunge made his offer, Baba had lived so long under domination that he could no longer imagine himself or his family as anything other than farmhands.

That was the true power of colonialism.

Not only did it take land and labor, but it also taught the dispossessed to expect so little.

That decision shaped our lives for years.

Not because twenty-five acres would have turned us overnight into aristocrats. It would not have. My parents would likely have built another mud-and-thatch homestead, grown food, and continued working for wages to pay for school fees, clothes, medicine, and transport. But with title to that land, our family would have stood differently in the world. When independence came, and the rules changed, that land might have become the foothold from which everything else launched.

Instead, the opportunity passed us by.

And for a long time, I blamed only Baba.

Now, I understand that his refusal was not simply stubbornness. It was the harvest of a life lived under a colonial system designed to shrink a man's worth and a sense of what he could dare to claim.

*

"Kamunge" was a nickname. His workers either did not know his real name or could not pronounce it. He was an Englishman who arrived in Kenya after his countrymen had completed the invasion and divided the land according to colonial and racial privilege. The temperate lands termed "white highlands" went to whites. Crown lands belonged to England. Missionaries received their share. Indians received plots for commercial and residential use in towns. Africans got pushed into Native Reserves.

Kamunge, perhaps with little to hold him in England, bought himself a one-way steamship ticket to Mombasa and came in search of a life. Though only modestly educated, he possessed the one qualification that mattered most in a British colony and that Baba lacked: whiteness. That alone opened doors to land, opportunity, and security.

He first worked as a farm manager. Later, he bought his own land. Once he established himself, he returned to England to find a wife willing to trade predictability for colonial comfort: a big house, native servants, and the promise of prosperity in "untamed" Kenya. Together, they raised a son and enjoyed the fruits of the empire as respectable landowners.

By colonial standards, Kamunge counted as one of the "good" employers. He never beat his workers. But he lived well and supported a system that had stolen land, subordinated a people, and made men like Baba believe that servitude was natural.

That was the world in which Baba learned to survive.

And survival, in such a world, did not always look like courage. Sometimes it looked like obedience.

Sometimes it looked like fear.

And sometimes it looked like refusing the very thing that might have changed your life.

*

Kamunge did not fuss over Baba's refusal.

He had his own future to focus on.

After living most of his adult life in Kenya, England had become a place of memory more than belonging. He had not returned there since fetching his bride, whose remains he would now leave behind in Kenyan soil. He dreaded the move and spoke of it often to Baba.

According to Baba, Kamunge had not wanted to sell the farm. But his only son, whom we called Kang'oro, and his family had sensed what we villagers could not yet fully name: the winds of independence were beginning to blow. They wanted out. So Kamunge faced a choice—follow his son back to England, or remain alone in the colonial house with only his German shepherd and his memories.

In one of their last conversations, he confided in Baba.

"I'm leaving because of my family," he said. "But I'm afraid of the weather in England. I know the cold will kill me."

As it turned out, he was right.

England had no mercy for an old man who had spent most of his life in the tropics. He caught pneumonia halfway through his first winter and died not long after. I do not know where his son buried him, but I doubt they brought his body back to Kenya to rest beside his memsahib.

Baba heard of Kamunge's death from his new employer and quietly went back to work.

By then, the land was gone.

And so was the chance.

# Chapter 4

# The Farm Boys

Major Miller stepped into Kamunge's farm as if he had always owned it. When I first saw him, striding at a distance, he had the same build as Kang'oro, Kamunge's son—about five-foot-eight, slightly soft and stocky—and dressed much the same in khaki shorts, a white short-sleeved shirt, and tan safari boots. Unlike Kamunge, he rarely wore a hat. I never learned exactly when he and his family moved into the colonial house a quarter of a mile east of our village.

Village rumors said the British government had bought the farm from Kamunge and awarded it to Major Miller for his service in World War II. To us, the title "Major" and his limp were proof enough. In Solai, white men with war titles owned the farmland in every direction. After each world war, the British rewarded their senior veterans with African land, and our corner of the district filled with Majors as if war itself had planted them there.

We soon learned that Major Miller and Memsahib—as he called his wife in front of employees—had a son in boarding school in England, as many European families in Kenya did. Their children often began at white-only schools in the colony and were then sent "home" to England, even though Kenya was the only home they really knew. That was how the settler world kept itself tied to Britain, generation after generation.

Major Miller kept all Kamunge's former workers, and Memsahib oversaw the domestic staff. Karani, the head "boy," led the household help. He and his family lived east of our homestead. He had two wives—Esther and Dina—who stayed home, either because Karani earned enough or because, as Tiriki women, they did not do the kind of field labor Agĩkũyũ women did.

Karani wore a long white kanzu, a pointed cap, and a neatly fitted apron. He cooked, cleaned, laundered, served, and did whatever else the Millers' household required, helped by a junior "boy." Several fieldhands worked around the compound and garden as well. The man who tended the orchard, with one or two helpers, was known simply as Shamba Boy—garden boy.

I knew the English meaning of "boy" because we had begun learning the language in school, but I never connected that word to the Millers' "boys." Like everyone else in the village, I took it to mean a senior servant, almost a profession, like driver or overseer. But we never saw Agĩkũyũ men do housework on the farms—such work was dismissed as women's work. Yet somehow, under white authority, it seemed fitting enough for Karani to become a houseboy. That was one of the quiet distortions of colonial life: words and roles took on different shapes depending on who held power.

\*

The coffee factory stood between our village and the Millers' residence. Their compound covered about ten acres, with Jumatatu Mountain rising to the east and Tindaress River banks to the south. The colonial house sat behind a manicured lawn and flower beds bordered by bougainvillea and thick ornamental bushes. Its wide, gateless entrance left a person feeling exposed and watched.

North of the house, near the entrance, stood a sprawling barn where the Millers stored farm equipment—the tractor and trailer among it—and a mountain of sacks of coffee, wheat, and maize awaiting shipment.

Between Jumatatu Mountain and the house lay a two-acre orchard. Its fame had reached us long before I ever saw it for myself.

Once I did, I understood.

Its bounty tempted even the most obedient child.

For us children, there were only two choices: swallow our greed in silence as we feasted with our eyes, or trespass and snatch a few fruits and hope the gardener had gone, or Major Miller's German shepherds did not catch our scent.

The third choice had died with the lost lands. Our parents could not plant fruit of their own. Colonial law forbade Africans from growing certain perennial plants and cash crops, lest they compete with the landowners. Even fruit had become a mark of power.

*

At first, Major Miller drove around the plantations and appeared at job sites daily. He met with Baba and arranged the next day's work. Later, once he familiarized himself with the farm, his appearances became less frequent. It was during one of those encounters that he told Baba Kamunge had died.

After decades of association with Kamunge, Baba mourned quietly, perhaps thinking of his own mortality. The rest of the village, and our family too, took the news more lightly. It became another piece of gossip to pass from one mouth to another.

That was the little power we had over the lives that governed ours. Otherwise, we came with the farm and remained under the whims of whoever owned it.

Even as a child, I understood that my father, like the others, had no say in the matter.

It was a terrible thing for a child to know and quietly absorb.

# Chapter 5

# The Drifters

When Kamunge owned the farm, and we lived in our first fenced village, he sent a lorry to the Baringo area two or three times during the coffee-picking season to fetch Tugen seasonal workers. They came standing, stacked like maize ears on the roofless lorry.

Everyone on the colonial farms had a place—by tribe, by job, by what the landowners believed they were suited for. The Tiriki and Luo often worked as domestic servants. The Tugen came as herdsmen or seasonal laborers. My people, the Agĩkũyũ, did most of the fieldwork and much of the running of the farms. Indians thrived as shopkeepers. And the whites, of course, owned the land and ruled over it all.

For the Tugen workers, Kamunge had built clusters of camp-like circular mud-and-thatch cottages outside our fenced village. He crammed ten or more men into each and had them returned to Baringo once the coffee season ended.

After Major Miller took over, he stopped bringing in Tugen seasonal workers for coffee-picking. But the new owner who bought the second half of the farm—the side with the larger coffee plantations, a man I would only years later learn was Mr. Patel of Patel General Store—continued to bring them. Some of those men crossed the river and drifted over to Major Miller's side, looking for work. No one accused him of poaching them because they came of their own free will.

Tall and skinny, with reddish checked cloths tied across their midriffs and another over their shoulders, they all looked alike to us children. No one could say exactly who had slipped away from the neighboring farm.

Major Miller left it to Baba, as nyabaara, to find accommodation for the drifters who had no family or friends on the farm. He lodged some of them in the old workers' camp, pairing them with other single men. Sometimes, before he placed them, he brought them to our homestead, where they shared his thingira and ate Mami's food.

They were not supposed to stay long.

A few days, perhaps.

A week at most.

But one group of three lingered for weeks and weeks.

That was when Mami's patience began to fray.

Bringing strangers into our home irritated her mainly because Major Miller offered no compensation, and the men themselves had nothing to contribute toward their keep. If it had been left to Mami, the three lodgers would have gone hungry.

She hardly had a moment to rest as it were. She rushed home from the coffee plantation or the factory or stopped by our small employer-provided garden to gather what she needed for the evening meal. Then she had to feed the children—some of them hungry teenagers—Baba, his three guests, and herself.

After the men sensed Mami's displeasure, they stopped entering our courtyard alone. Instead, they hovered at a neighbor's porch and kept watch until Baba came home from work, his great gray coat slung over his shoulder. Within minutes of his arrival, they appeared in our courtyard as if beckoned by the imminent smell of tea.

That only made the tension in our household worse.

"Do you have food these men can eat?" Baba would ask Mami.

"My children are hungry too," Mami would answer. "And I don't know when they'll eat."

Other times, she answered him with silence.

She rattled dishes, clicked her tongue, and snorted each time Baba asked her for tea or food for the men. Her nyũmba now stood closer to thingira than it had before, and Baba's ears were sharp enough to catch even quiet conversations not meant for him. He knew harmony had left his homestead.

From then on, before asking Mami for anything, he would first ask the nearest child, "Is your mother busy?"

Our answer was always the same.

"Yes."

This went on for about three months.

Then one evening, the men never came.

No one ever saw them again.

We never learned whether Baba had quietly arranged their departure or whether they had simply drifted on in search of better luck. Whatever the case, he never again brought drifters to our household.

Besides, by then, we children were nearing our pre-teens and old enough to work on the plantations ourselves, so Major Miller had less reason to keep extra seasonal labor around.

*

The Tugen men lived like homeless people. The employer gave them a gallon of maize flour each on Saturdays and, now and then, a quart of skimmed milk. That was supposed to sustain them. We barefoot children, who looked like little vagrants ourselves, when not in school uniform, sometimes encountered a gaunt Tugen man crouched on his haunches, hand stretched out, saying, "Nguno."

One afternoon, a man near our homestead stretched his hand toward me and said it again.

"Nguno."

I skipped away, munching whatever I had in my hand, without once wondering what it meant for a grown man to beg food from a child. I simply concluded that begging must be the Tugen way of life.

If we children kept pestering Mami for something, she would say, "You beg just like the Tugen."

One day, one of them got back at us.

Or so my family believed.

Mami returned from work and entered her bedroom to find her wooden storage trunk—with its brass corners—frisked and emptied of most of its contents. All our best clothes were gone. She never mentioned whether any money had been taken, especially not the cash she called *mbia chia ũtukũ mũũru*—money for a bad night, emergency money—because she did not want us children to know where she hid it.

Our household blamed the Tugen for the break-in. No one paused to consider that the thief had simply walked in. We left our doors ajar from dawn to dusk, closed them only after nightfall, and only locked up—sliding the wood on the door brace—once we were going to bed.

But we never blamed our own carelessness.

And we never changed our open-door ways.

# Chapter 6

# Education For Girls

On the farms, most families owned little, worked for small wages, and survived on tiny plots of land the employer allowed them to cultivate. From those meager earnings, many fathers struggled to send at least one son to school. Daughters were, in most cases, left out. It was said there was no point in "wasting" money educating girls who would marry and leave.

That had been the fate of my three half-sisters.

But by the late 1950s, something changed.

Baba allowed my sister Tabitha and me to go to school.

I never knew exactly why he changed his mind. Perhaps he saw other fathers beginning to do the same. Perhaps he had softened with age. Or perhaps it was because I cornered him one day and offered to give up eating goat meat for a year if he enrolled me in school. I doubt he could bear his little girl suggesting he could not afford both my schooling and a bit of meat.

*

At thirteen, I passed the year-end test and moved to grade four, the senior class. That was when teachers began speaking about the common entrance exam—the test that would decide who might go on to the few boarding schools set aside for Africans and who would return to the fields. Most of us already knew what that meant.

Pass, and you might escape.

Fail, and you joined your parents in farm labor.

My older brother David had already gone far beyond what most children achieved. He had completed thirteen years of schooling, most of it at boarding schools, including Kijabe Full Primary School and Kabete Technical School, far from home. To us, he was already among the educated.

Being male and much older than I was, he remained a mystery.

We knew little about his life except that it was different from ours.

And that difference mattered.

As a girl, I doubted I could ever be like him.

But I still held onto the idea of going to a boarding school, even if I could not picture what such a place looked like.

I only knew this: I wanted a different life. A better life than farm labor

Mami had already trained me for the life that awaited most girls. I started as a babysitter trainee at six. By age ten, I could care for a baby almost as well as an adult.

I knew what my future looked like if I did not pass that exam.

And I did not want it.

It was not education itself that I longed for.

I did not know what educated women did. I had never seen one.

What I wanted was escape.

By thirteen, I was already doing heavy labor.

I carried firewood on my back, worked around the house, picked and hauled coffee cherries, and labored on weekends and school holidays—work that often pushed my small, undernourished body beyond its limits. We ate poorly, especially during dry seasons or when Mami was too exhausted to cook enough food for all of us.

That life was already closing in on me.

On the farm, education determined everything.

Those who had it, like our teachers, wore clean clothes, did lighter work, and earned more.

Those who did not labored harder and earned less.

I wanted to move from the side I was on.

David had shown me what his side looked like.

At age eight, I noticed that when he came home from school, my parents never asked him to do manual labor. At most, Baba sent him on errands. Whatever hard work he had once done belonged to a time before he joined boarding school in grade five.

Education had lifted him out of it.

My neighbor Wachuka gave me another glimpse.

She attended a boarding school and returned home during holidays as a changed girl. She kept to herself and did not mix with us village girls. She did no fieldwork, either

But as a female, she did not idle the way David did.

Her mother gave her what I considered comparatively cushy work—sweeping, washing, cooking.

Still, I believed her life would be different in the end.

She would finish school, marry an educated man, and live in town. She would hire girls like me—uneducated village girls—to help raise her children and do her domestic work.

That was how I understood the world.

Education meant: No more farm labor. Good food. Clean clothes. Shoes on my feet.

Nothing more.

And that was enough.

Sometimes I thought of Aunt Julia, Baba's only surviving sibling. Because she wrote letters to him, I believed she did not do manual labor like Mami. I had never met her or known what work she did. But Baba spoke of her with admiration—*Julia wa Maitũ*—Our Mother's Julia.

Maybe, I thought, I could be like her.

It took three more years to learn that a woman could work on a non-manual job right there on the farm.

# Chapter 7

# Child Labor

My siblings and I complained about hard work, but the hardest hit were the children whose fathers could not afford school fees (twenty-two shillings per pupil per year from 1956) or saw no reason to educate future farmhands. Those children worked full-time. They dug, weeded, and picked coffee cherries alongside adults for eight to nine hours a day, six days a week. Some landowners even used boys as domestic trainees. Karen Blixen of *Out of Africa* fame was one of them.

When wheat matured, before it was ready for harvest, landowners employed young boys to guard acres and acres of plantations. The boys flailed their arms and chased birds away with hollers, rocks, and slingshots under the scorching sun, without lunch or water, until they went home in the evening.

Before tractors became common in the mid-1950s, Kamunge used ox-drawn plows. A driver sat on a small trailer, barking orders or cracking a bullwhip to keep the animals moving. In front of the oxen walked a skinny boy, no more than ten or twelve, dressed in a cloth tied on one shoulder or a shirt down to his knees, without pants, gripping the leather reins.

Sometimes the whip caught him instead of the animals.

Occasionally, the oxen bolted.

The boy had to hang on, barefoot, sprinting through grass and thorny scrub, at risk of being trampled or bitten by a snake.

"I would have to be dead and buried," Mami used to say, "for my child to work as a reins-boy."

Like other fortunate children who attended school, my siblings and I worked on Saturdays and during school holidays. Just like the non-school children, we worked, gardened, or picked and hauled coffee cherries just like the adults.

We also weeded for pay.

When coffee bushes matured and their branches spread, the rows narrowed, and tractors could no longer pass between them. The land had to be cultivated by hand. During the off-season, those of us strong enough to swing a hoe joined casual laborers in the plantations. Unfortunately, Major Miller offered the work when weeds had already taken over, making it far more difficult.

Although I wanted to earn money, I rarely went. I was barely four and a half feet tall, and sometimes the weeds reached to my waist. It was like hacking through a stubborn little forest.

The few times I went, I partnered with my brother Joseph, who was two years older than I was. Each of us carried a medium-sized hoe on our shoulder as we left home at dawn—before even a sip of water or food—determined to finish our share before the equatorial sun grew unbearable.

Alan Kĩbuĩ, Wachuka's father and in charge of casual workers, assigned rows of coffee bushes—mĩhari—to workers as they arrived.

The early morning dew made the work harder. Wet weeds clung to clumps of soil and stuck to our hoes. Every few swings, the hoe became too heavy, and we had to stop and scrape the mud away with our fingers or the heels of our thumbs.

One day, by the time we finished, I was so exhausted that I didn't care whether we had done the work perfectly. I left it to Joseph to handle whatever weeds Alan pointed out during inspection.

I never dug those coffee rows again.

And it so happened, I gave up on the coffee farm that Baba had turned down.

Non-Gĩkũyũ people never dug weeds at the coffee plantations. I remember seeing only one Tugen man attempt that work. He abandoned his row halfway through, too exhausted to continue, even if it meant losing his pay.

Mami never sent us to do jobs where we would be paid only if we finished.

Now I wonder why I volunteered for such punishing work when we never kept any of the money we earned. Even when we picked coffee cherries, we handed the money to Mami at the factory without a second thought.

She controlled the household income, except for Baba's wages. She paid for everything we could not grow—clothes, transport, medicine, sugar, cooking oil, soap.

Baba paid for school fees, uniforms, and any other expenses.

It never occurred to us that, from about age thirteen, we children (except for David, who had spent his teenage years in boarding schools) were paying for much of our own upkeep.

We complained about chores at home and about working in our garden, but we worked eagerly at anything that brought in money.

My only payoff is that I learned about money by watching Mami budget hers.

Seated on a low bench in the sitting area, she divided her shillings into small piles—one for sugar, one for oil, one toward our home clothes savings, and so forth. Sometimes she delayed one purchase so another could be met first.

That was how my mother ran our household.

# Chapter 8

# Living off the land

Our garden, a narrow strip of land among similar terraced strips, stretched for at least a hundred yards. Taking care of it was a family affair. Baba passed by after work to break up clumps of soil or weeds until dusk, but he left the planting to Mami and us children. On Saturdays and school holidays, Simon, Joseph, and I accompanied her to the garden. My sister Tabitha stayed home to mind the three younger children, while Gĩthũi and Morry took the goats out to graze.

The garden fed us, but it needed coaxing to do so.

Because my parents had overworked the land for years, we tried to help it along with manure. At first, we used what we could gather from our goats' cottage. When that ran out, we collected dry cow manure from the cattle pen near the cow dip and carried it in sacks on our backs. It was smelly, fluffy, and light, which took little effort.

At one point, inspired by Tindaress Primary School, we even tried composting. That experiment died quickly. It took too much labor and too long to produce enough manure for even a small plot.

Even with the cow manure, we had to carry too many sacks to spread over our strip of land. So Mami improvised.

To use less manure, she and Simon dug holes in neat rows across the width of the garden, sometimes using sisal string to keep the line straight. Joseph followed behind with a small sack of manure, dropping in two fistfuls per hole and mixing it with the soil.

I followed him with a smaller kîondo (a sisal-woven basket) tied around my waist like a pouch, one-third full of maize seeds. I dropped two or three seeds into each hole, then covered them by pushing the dugout soil with my hands. When I got tired, I kicked it in with the heel of my big toe so I would not have to bend.

Only the maize received that kind of treatment.

The rest—beans, peas, black-eyed peas, white-eyed peas— had to fend for themselves on whatever goodness remained in the soil or the manure their roots could reach, and grow quickly before the maize overshadowed them.

To plant those short-season crops, we tied little kîondos around our waists, scooped holes with the point of a panga (machete), dropped in three or four seeds, and patted the soil shut with the blade.

Once you got the hang of it, you could move surprisingly fast.

Mami treated the tomato and vegetable garden behind our homestead with chicken manure—two tablespoonfuls per hole sufficed, as the manure was most potent. If one put more, it could burn the seeds, she said.

\*

Although my siblings and I hated the labor involved in growing our food, we did not mind cultivating after school.

That part gave us freedom.

During weeding season, after classes let out, we passed through our garden in our school uniforms. On the way, before we trailed off to our respective gardens, we socialized with our schoolmates, away from adults. My siblings and I cultivated at our own pace and returned home just before dusk.

Still, the work itself was relentless.

Two rounds of weeding usually brought a crop to harvest, and it often seemed as if the weeds drew more nutrients from the soil than the food plants did. By the time we finished the first round, the second one was already waiting.

During cultivation, Joseph and I trailed behind Simon and Mami. Baba weeded after work. To quiet our complaints and squeeze the last labor out of us, Mami measured a strip of land for each of us—a smaller one for me, a larger one for Joseph. She made it clear that we were not leaving until we finished.

That was all the motivation we needed.

In my hurry, I sometimes uprooted a plant along with the weeds. When that happened, I quickly dug a little hole and buried the plant. It was rare for a gardening session to end without at least one dead plant. Mami never caught me even once. I suspect my siblings had accidents too, but we all kept quiet about them.

When we finished our share, Mami or Simon inspected it.

It baffled me that I always seemed to leave behind a few tiny islands of weeds.

The same thing happened when I swept the floor or courtyard. It baffled me that no matter how carefully I worked, a patch of dirt always appeared afterward as if by mockery. This never happened when Mami swept.

At the garden, I thought my misery came only from too much work. I did not yet know about heat or dehydration.

Every inch of my exposed skin felt sun-scorched, assaulted by millions of tiny needle pricks. The loosened soil burned the soles of my feet. I stepped this way and that with my toes raised, complaining under my breath.

When I was little, and Mami took me along while she worked on the coffee plantation, she at least carried water and food, and the baby and I sat in the shade. But in our own garden, we rarely carried refreshments, and there was not a single patch of shade on those strips of land. On our way home, we walked halfway parallel to Tindaress River and almost never stopped to drink. To this day, I do not know how we survived that heat with hardly more than one drink of water a day and did not become seriously ill.

One afternoon in my teen years, I became so hot and tired that nausea rose in me as I hoed. Beads of tears slipped down my cheeks.

Joseph, too, looked miserable, his sullen face twisted with fatigue. But as a teenage boy, neither he nor anyone else expected him to cry. Simon, already a young man by then, kept working without joining in our childish complaints.

It never occurred to Joseph and me that we could defy Mami and simply abandon our portion and walk away. There wasn't much she could have done for us besides getting angry. But as one who never held her anger, she would have felt guilty by the time she arrived home, for having assigned us too large a piece of land.

But like our teachers and most parents around us, our parents had trained us to be obedient, timid children. We did what we were told.

So we stayed.

My tears of exhaustion did not move Mami one bit.

She called it laziness.

"You'd better do well in school," she said, "if you frown at this type of work."

I must have looked pitiful, because Simon stopped his work twice and looked at me. Finally, he stopped digging altogether and turned to Mami.

"Why don't you let them finish their portions some other day?" he asked.

Mami paused. Then she relented, but not without conse-
quences.

Joseph and I could finish our weeding later, during our free
time, but not in the main garden where our delay might endanger
her crops. Instead, she sent us to dig in another place—a forsaken
patch of land no villager cared about.

That was how mercy came into our household, just like on the
farm: not as release, but as relocation.

# Chapter 9

# The Forsaken Land

Kamunge never sent a tractor to plow the forsaken land. People had to dig the hard ground themselves. Mami got our plot dug last, like an afterthought. And after the first round of cultivation, she gave most of her energy to our regular garden and left this one to fend for itself with only occasional visits.

Cancerous grass crowded the crops, siphoning off their strength. The maize grew stunted, half the normal height, with tiny ears barely worth picking. Even the wild pigs ignored it and pushed farther inland to raid the regular gardens instead.

The worst enemy on that forsaken patch was thangari.

It crawled and spread underground in a web of roots, colonizing the soil like a living conspiracy. If you dug it out and missed even a tiny shoot, it soon started a clan of its own. To kill it properly, you had to dig deep and pull out every root, shake off every bit of soil, spread it in the sun, turn it over again days later, and then burn the heap. Even then, one was never quite sure. It seemed capable of rising from the dead.

People in the village spoke of thangari the way they spoke of a sneaky, incurable disease.

As punishment for the share I had failed to finish, Mami assigned me to remove thangari from the uncultivated part of that forsaken land. She sent Joseph elsewhere so we would not waste time talking. To adults of that era, an isolated child worked best.

I made the three-mile round trip three times.

Each time, I spent more than two hours bent over that stubborn ground, digging and shaking and hauling weeds until my back and limbs felt heavier than my body could bear.

On the last day, determined not to return a fourth time, I overworked myself.

When I finally finished, I dug a shallow trench, laid the hoe inside it, and covered it with weeds for the next unfortunate soul who would have to use it. Then I began my trek home. I dragged myself, exhausted, lonely, and too drained to feel even the relief I had expected.

Instead of relief, a different misery rose in me.

As I walked, I began to think of the orphaned Tugen boy who had once led oxen by the reins while the man conductor whipped the animals from behind. My mind told me I was no different from him.

The thought undid me.

Large tears began to slide down my cheeks. I did not wipe them.

By the time I reached the Solai–Subukia road bridge, my tears had mostly spent themselves. I looked right and left before crossing, just as Tindaress Primary had drilled into us.

And then I remembered another day on that same path.

Subukia/Solai Road Bridge-Still the same—October 10, 2022

I had been much younger, walking behind Mami from our main garden while she carried a heavy kĩondo of produce, and I trailed after her with a smaller one. Just east of the bridge, after we crossed the road, she suddenly stopped and held me back.

"We have to wait," she said softly. "A snake is crossing."

"Where? Can I see?" I asked.

"Let's get out of the way," she said as we stepped back. "It can't hear, but it can sense us."

I tried peering around her, but the path ahead was choked with tall wiregrass and bushes. I could not see the snake itself, only the brush shaking as it moved along.

We waited as if we were at a railway crossing.

"It's going on a hunting expedition," Mami said.

After it passed and we continued on, she told me that kind of snake hunted small animals and, if hungry enough, could swallow a child my size.

On the day of the forsaken land, alone and preoccupied, I had forgotten that snake incident.

As I crossed the bridge in my misery, I realized how thirsty I was. I hungered for one thing: water.

To reach the river, I turned right onto a narrow footpath that wound through tall grass, weeds, and bushes before dropping toward Tindaress River under a canopy of creepers and small trees that let in almost no light. It felt like entering a cave.

That was when the snake stories came back to me.

Footpath top left. The cave is somewhere in there - October 10, 2022.

People said predatory snakes stretched themselves across dense branches or overhangs and dropped onto prey that passed below. Years before I was born, one had spat into Baba's eyes from above the threshold of his thingira when he looked up after hearing a rustle. For two terrible months, he feared he would go blind and be unable to provide for his family.

Now I looked up into the canopy.

Nothing. All clear.

Still, I stepped carefully into the cool, dim clearing, where only loose brown mulch and a few weak weeds clung to the ground. The drop in temperature felt like walking out of blazing heat into shade at dusk. I followed the narrow path down to the water.

Across the river, the opposite bank was thick with brush and large rocks. Upstream, beyond the thicket, I could hear the river's gurgles and swooshes loud enough to drown a scream. But where the water opened into view, it softened into a cheerful flow over gravel and small stones.

I paused for only a moment, captured by the river-like symphony of noises and the coolness.

But alone in such a setting unsettled me.

I refocused, squatted quickly, scooped up water in my palms several times, and drank.

A few steps from the river, I glanced toward a giant rock that jutted outward to form a cave-like shelter, large enough for several people to crouch beneath.

And there, under the rock, was its lone resident.

A giant python lay coiled in a heap, beautiful in shades of brown and beige, with droppings by its tail that looked like goat pellets.

I gasped and froze.

For several seconds, I could do nothing but stare while my heartbeat pounded through my ears.

I had seen many snakes in my life, every size and color, typical of the African savanna in those days. On my way home from my first trip from the forsaken plot, I had seen five snakes in one day, a record—from a tiny one-footer to a four-footer.

But I had never seen anything the size of what lay before me. Could it rise if it sensed me? Pounce? Coil around my skinny fourteen-year-old torso? Break my ribs and snuff the life out of me?

It could break the ribs, but I doubted it could swallow me. I was older now, bigger than the child Mami once warned about.

But again, the snake was bigger too.

That thought gave me the energy I had lacked all afternoon.

I tiptoed and crossed the overhang. The moment I reached the open brush, I ran and ran.

I ran as if a predator was after me.

Only when I was safely back on the main footpath did I slow down.

At a distance, I wished Joseph had been there with me. He was a born comedian who always found a way to turn danger into a story. I could almost hear him telling me to run ahead while he threw a stone to rile up the snake before sprinting out.

But without Joseph's embellishments, even the python failed to hold my mind for long.

My thoughts slid back to my misery.

Desperate to get back at Mami for putting me through that gloom, a thought came to me.

I had seen how pitiful she looked at a suffering child; it occurred to me that I might use tears to my advantage. If she saw my wet, gloomy face, I knew her heart would ache, and she would feel guilty for sending me to that forsaken plot.

In my family, guilt had a look.

That look was as close to an apology as anyone ever got

Earlier, the tears had come without effort. That was what I expected. Decision made, I got myself worked up to get them flowing. But now, despite scrunching my face and letting out puffs of breath, nothing came out.

I squeezed my eyes shut. Fluttered my lids. Thought pitiful thoughts.

Still nothing.

Then I remembered I had not washed my face at the river. The dried tear tracks still clung to my cheeks. They would have to do, as long as I kept my misery alive until I reached home.

"What happened?" I imagined Mami asking.

I planned to pout and refuse to answer.

But when I reached home, no one noticed my dry trails or my pout.

Or if they did, they ignored them.

That hurt more than I expected.

For a little while, I brooded and convinced myself that nobody in my family cared what happened to me.

Then, with no better choice, I drifted back into the household chatter, and before long, my misery dissolved into the ordinary noise of home.

I never even told them about the giant snake.

# Chapter 10

# Modern Fertilizer

After Major Miller settled in, he learned of our "outdated" fertilizer, the free and healthy manure we used. In his second year before the rains, he introduced commercial fertilizer. The exciting news spread throughout the village about the *caring* landowner and the modern method that would help grow a bountiful crop.

When the planting season arrived, women placed orders through their husbands for the number of bags of fertilizer they required; most families needed only one twenty-pound bag. Major Miller would deduct the cost from their husbands' monthly wages.

When Mami ordered our bag, she mentioned people said a person needed only a small scoop of fertilizer per hole. That was the last I heard about the scoop.

When she brought the bag home and opened it, there was no scoop inside. She used an old paint gallon.

She liked the modern fertilizer because we no longer needed heaps of manure. We liked it too, because beside her, none of us dealt with fertilizer again.

Mami stored the fertilizer in a corner of the granary, where she also kept our dry foods and, occasionally, a tray of cooked *mataha or mũkimo* that we ate over several days. None of us mentioned anything about that setup.

From then on, she carried to the garden what she needed for the day in a small sack and scooped it herself. Half a scoop of her hand per hole sufficed. I now suspect, besides the cost, she feared we might use too much of the bluish/white granules and *burn* her seeds.

Every planting season, she complained of *burned* hands before she added a comment about the potent fertilizer. With the manual labor her callused hands handled, they could have taken any abuse short of a knife or machete cut. But they couldn't take the fertilizer's abuse. Tiny blisters cropped up on the tips of her fingers, around the nails, and on her knuckles. After she washed in the evening before bed, she lathered her hands with *Vaseline* petroleum jelly.

*

Even if, by law, Africans couldn't grow cash crops or become members of the Kenya Farmers' Association (KFA) or other boards, most farmworkers never felt the impact. With their small plots, most rarely had enough food for their own families, let alone surplus to sell. Our family was one of those.

During Kamunge's time, a handful of women cut into their families' supplies and sold meager pinto beans, kidney beans, and peas, measured by the can, at the Bahati or Kabazi Sunday markets and later at Njeki's Shopping Center. But this was a roundabout barter system to raise money to buy other items.

But when Major Miller introduced chemical fertilizers, he also introduced a share-cropper system, which gave villagers access to the KFA. After harvest, farmworkers who grew extra maize sold it to Major Miller, who sold it to KFA alongside his own.

Lured by a chance to make more money, people who hadn't started using chemical fertilizers began using them in their small gardens and even on the forsaken land. Some parents—including some of my relatives—kept their children from school for days at a time during planting, weeding, and harvesting seasons. A handful of parents bragged about how many maize sacks they had sold. Meanwhile, their children's education suffered.

"I blame my mother for my lack of education," Wanjirũ, my adult half-niece, told Mami once.

"I can't equate maize with my children's education," Mami said if asked about selling maize.

She never got sucked in by money. My siblings and I had to be sick to miss school. I never missed a day during my eight years in elementary and middle school.

But my siblings and I never talked about it, nor did I think of the crucial role Mami played in our getting an education. With several of us in school, and Baba's wages barely covering the cost, I doubt he would have objected if any of us had dropped out and joined Mami in the fields.

*

To pack the maize, men ordered from Major Miller the number of gunnysacks their families needed for the KFA sale. The new sacks came branded with the farm's identification number in bold black ink.

On designated days, men carried half-sacks on their shoulders and women carried them on their backs to the main dirt road. They combined the half sacks and filled them to the brim with dry maize kernels. They sewed the tops tight with sisal strings, using humongous curved needles.

Major Miller's tractor-trailer hauled the sacks to the huge barn. With the help of his workers, he counted and recorded each person's sacks in his logbook and stored them with his harvest.

The villagers' work ended there. They then waited months for him to pay them after he received payment from KFA.

Before the shipment day, a lorry made multiple trips to deliver the heavy sacks to Solai Train Station, where workers loaded them on a cargo train for the last journey to KFA. KFA processed the kernels for export or into five-pound packets of maize flour for ugali or porridge for townspeople.

We didn't eat that kind of maize meal; we used unprocessed flour that we ground at the farm's flour mill.

# Chapter 11

# Inhumane Children

Despite all our farm work, we children enjoyed a social school life, especially during break time and on our way home.

From Tindaress Primary School, yards west of Nakuru/Solai Road, at least 20 of us chattered as we crossed the road to the eastern side to enter Kamunge's farm. Soon, a few pupils broke from the pack and hurried on.

Other times, we broke into smaller groups that could fit on the tractor trail or its banks without weaving around little islands of scrubby bushes, sparse clumps of grass, or random weeds in the swath of open savanna.

Occasionally, small animals like squirrels, rabbits, rats, and mice dashed away from us. Boys chased rabbits for sport, but the swift animals sprinted and won the race every time. No one bothered with the many colorful insects, such as grasshoppers, butterflies, and beetles, that harvested cow dung and rolled it into small balls to take back to their abodes. That was part of our landscape, which we observed, mostly ignored and took for granted.

Tortoises weren't as common, or perhaps because of their unhurried manner, they avoided *dangerous* footpaths.

One day, we spotted a couple of tortoises. The boys threw stones at them. The tortoises retreated into their shells, and the boys lost interest and sought amusement elsewhere.

But the boys weren't as forgiving when they encountered a loner tortoise; they became downright cruel.

One naughty boy detoured into the scrub. When the tortoise turned its long neck sideways, and its beady eyes sighted the tormentor, it retracted its neck and legs and cocooned itself. The boy sat on the tortoise and rocked it back and forth to nudge it out of its shell. The boy's cohorts cheered. But the tortoise stayed inside. Another boy joined in, and the two tried to roll it. Because of its convex shape, the tortoise couldn't roll. The boys gave up and left the poor animal flipped on its back.

Their actions bothered me, but I felt thankful they had left the tortoise alone. I didn't know that leaving the animal flipped over endangered it; for a tortoise, it was a major assault.

Years later, I would learn that a healthy tortoise left upside down takes a long time to turn upright. It twists and maneuvers its body inside its shell, trying to flip over. It's worse when it has to do this in the daytime, under the merciless tropical sun. If it's sick or weak, it would suffer and likely die within a day or two, or get attacked by a predator.

But besides two or three boys who harassed animals for sport, we never bothered with them. We saw snakes, too, but, individually, we children rarely dared to harass them, even small ones, because of the fear that our parents had instilled in us.

Every parent, especially mothers, told and retold a story of giant predatory snakes in the forest that preyed on unsuspecting people and animals. Even cobra stories sounded mythical and terrifying, especially their spitting abilities. But, except on rare occasions, the snakes we encountered measured only about one to six feet long. Those snakes didn't wait to assess whether we were friends or foes. They quickly slithered away unless somebody sneaked up on them or caught them in a compromised state.

That happened one Friday when our group came to a lush green spot by the trail, likely the site of a small spring. We spotted two snakes stuck together, one on top of the other.

A handful of boys rushed at the snakes, throwing small stones at the couple. The two struggled this way and that, trying to separate and get away. But they remained stuck together. Angry and frustrated, the snake on top raised its kingly head and spat, sending a spray of venom at least seven feet away. Its partner did the same, but the spit failed to reach the boys, who had quickly retreated when they recognized the cobras.

Aware of what type of snakes they were, and my mind already poisoned against cobras, I joined the rest of the children in the mob mentality. We made merry, hollering, flailing our arms, or flinging pebbles from a distance. The two cobras raised their torsos in unison whenever a boy ran toward them.

This routine went on for some rounds. Then, the top cobra raised its torso well above its partner, opened its mouth wide, and produced a creepy, guttural noise, ready to tear the attackers to pieces if it could. Apparently, it had run out of venom.

The image of us throwing rocks at two helpless cobras gave me a stab of guilt. I stopped at a safe distance and watched.

While fear kept us at bay, the two lovers struggled long enough to reach the taller grass. They slithered away to finish their business elsewhere.

# Chapter 12

# The Family Contrarian

When school let out at 3:30 or 4:00 p.m., we walked with the group of children from our village.

But on Fridays, when we reached halfway home, my three siblings and I, and a few other children, branched off on a footpath that led to the gardens, still in uniforms that we wore five days a week and washed on Saturdays

That was what we did every Friday during weeding season.

The first round of gardening started in April, during our school holidays. This, and the rainy season, made me hate April with a passion. I couldn't wait to return to school in early May, when we worked only on Fridays after school and on Saturdays. By mid-May, we finished the first round of weeding and started the second round back-to-back.

Unlike those mothers who kept their children from school to help catch up on weeding, to our relief, Mami used to say, "I won't be your excuse if you fail in school."

But, like many other parents, she extracted maximum labor from us on Saturdays and during school holidays. The only gardening we didn't mind was after school on Fridays. We supervised ourselves away from authoritarian teachers and demanding parents.

When we arrived at our garden, we retrieved the hoes Mami had hidden under the plants' canopies. Depending on our ages, we used any of the hoes—small, medium, or large. From age thirteen, I used the medium hoe; only strong, grown men used the big hoe.

We worked for an hour or longer, depending on how long we spent chatting with our friends or frolicking in the inland areas where vegetation turned robust. Sometimes, we gathered wild fruits on the wayside, closer to Tindaress River. Even in a small group of about ten, or just with my siblings, we never ran out of tales to tell or things to entice us.

Before we arrived at the gardens, we crossed my main attraction—Tindaress River with its clear sparkling water. I loved that crossing, water as clear as a bubbling spring. It merrily trickled down, flew over various-sized smooth pebbles, and waded around centuries-old jagged rocks.

To cross, most of the children stepped on the big rocks. I waded through the water instead, then skipped back on the rocks, and walked through again. If the group slowed, too involved in their chatter, I sat on a rock and splashed water with my feet. (Since childhood, trickling water around rocks and smooth pebbles has always enticed and soothed me.) Picking wild blackberries, raspberries, and gooseberries and crossing the river were our two highlights, until another came to our attention.

It was common knowledge that somewhere downstream, the river disappeared underground. One Friday, we flocked to our usual crossing when someone, likely my brother Joseph, enticed us to see the river's natural wonder. The story went that: In the middle of the river-less patch of thicket, the ground split into a bottomless trough that the bold could jump across.

I had heard that only agile adults, mainly younger men with no luggage, jumped. I had no interest in seeing the split.

But that Friday, Joseph, the oldest in the group and a confirmed know-it-all, claimed some of us could jump over. The rest got hyped, happy with the suggestion. A couple of boys hesitated and lagged, but no one objected. We retraced our steps and branched off to the narrower path that led downstream.

I didn't care about the jump but was curious to see the split.

The split turned out to be nothing like the tiny hole in the ground I expected. It measured about 4ft wide at the top and 8ft long, while the ground tapered off and narrowed to about 2ft wide at the bottom. Along the banks, small tufts of grass and small shrubs grew. The ground hardened in the spots where agile men stepped,

We walked up and down the bank to familiarize ourselves and strategize. The brave among us bent and looked down into the darkness, a perfect black hole. Some of us thought they heard a faint whoosh of water below, but we couldn't say for sure.

Joseph, two boys, and I jumped across without difficulty.

Tabitha, at eleven, hesitated, fidgeted, undecided.

"Are you afraid?" one child asked.

"She's afraid! She's afraid!" the others taunted in chorus.

I kept my eyes on my sister, waited, and mentally cheered her on. She ignored the taunts, set herself, focused, and jumped.

Nduati, an only child and the only one with a store-bought bag, unlike the homemade slim bags that we slung over our shoulders, and the same age as Tabitha, refused to jump.

"I'm not old enough to jump," he said. He shifted his shoulders, repositioned his schoolbag on his back, and headed upstream to the usual public crossing. The remaining three children followed, happy they were not the only cowards.

That left Gĩthũi, our nine-year-old brother, alone across the chasm.

"Follow the others upstream," Joseph called to him.

"Go before they leave you," I said.

He refused to budge.

"I can jump," Gĩthũi said. "Tabitha jumped."

No matter what we told him, he remained adamant.

Based on his young life, I knew it would take us great effort to convince him otherwise.

*

Gĩthũi, four years my junior, had proved himself the most stubborn child in our family. He did things his own way. A confirmed contrarian, he refused to do anything he didn't want or considered unnecessary. If he set his mind on something, nobody except Baba, not even Mami, could make him change course.

I recalled one Sunday, Mami filled a tin basin with water and placed it on a patch of grass by the granary. She summoned her three young children, one by one, starting with the youngest. She washed each one, standing by the basin, our homestead's Sunday routine—a full bath for women and young children. Grown males bathed in the river, sometimes at the crack of dawn. People alleged that the cold water toughened men's bodies. Years later, I heard it cooled and maintained the health of their seed.

After Mami washed Morry, the six-year-old Gĩthũi came next. He balked, gazed at her, and refused to budge from where he kept vigil. Tired of pleading with him, Mami went and pulled him by the hand while he trotted behind her, fussing. Instead of a whole-body wash, Mami left his clothes on and started washing his head. He upped his tantrums and screams. Tired of his fuss, Mami washed his arms next and let him loose.

Gĩthũi rushed to the side yard by the goats' cottage, breathing hard as if he prepped for an attack. He rolled in loose dirt, then scooped it with his cupped little hands and smeared it on his wet head, face, and arms. The dirt-wash made him resemble a perfect prehistoric cave dweller. Mami let him keep that image for the rest of the day. She knew to pick her battles.

Now, three years later, my siblings and I hoped Gĩthũi would heed our advice and join the other children at the usual river crossing. Joseph, six years older, could have forced Gĩthũi, even dragged him upstream. Or we could have all returned to the crossing. Instead, Joseph merely offered to go back with him.

"But I can jump," Gĩthũi insisted.

Joseph and I jumped back to keep him company while we pleaded with him.

"Why didn't you tell Tabitha to go upstream?" Gĩthũi asked, pouty.

"Because she's older than you!" I said. I didn't know better. Comparing him with Tabitha, a girl, made him even more determined. To him, the two years Tabitha had on him didn't count; if she could jump, he could do so, too.

"But I can jump," Gĩthũi said again, with a lower tone, lacking conviction.

He moved about the riverbank, stopped now and then, eyes fixed on the chasm.

He set himself, then changed his pose.

We begged him.

He went up and down the bank of the chasm, now with urgency.

We watched helplessly.

Frustrated, Joseph jumped back to the opposite bank while I remained on the same side with Gĩthũi.

The two boys who jumped with us stood a few feet behind Tabitha, impatient.

"Why don't you do what they're telling you?" one boy said. "You are delaying everybody."

Deaf to any pleas, Gĩthũi focused on his mission.

I gave up on trying to convince him. Instead, I wished he could jump already and get it over with. It never occurred to me what would happen if he didn't make the jump.

He had then taken several jumping stances and aborted them.

He assessed the split once more.

Finally, he focused, left leg in front, right leg behind, settled into his best stance, and took the jump.

# Chapter 13

# The Jump

Gĩthũi's jump was doomed from the start.

When he took the jump, he fell flat on the opposite incline, on the slanting side of the chasm's far bank. His feet dangled close to the edge of the opening at the bottom. He grabbed clumps of grass and pulled himself up. Each clump strained to support his weight before it slowly gave way, and he let go. He grabbed the cluster of anemic scrubs nearby with the same result. There was no nearby grass strong enough to hold his weight.

"Grab that one!" we said in unison, bent over, pointing to a stronger scrub a foot away. "That one! The bigger one!"

Gĩthũi heaved himself up. His efforts covered only inches. He needed to reach a foot to grab a scrub strong enough to hold him for a moment until the next heave up. Or two feet to reach firmer bushes and grass that could hold him long enough for a rescue.

Desperate, his hands flailed this way and that, clawing at whatever he could, as if he were drowning.

Joseph attempted a rescue; he bent and reached out to grab Gĩthũi's hand, a treacherous attempt. At least a foot remained between their outstretched fingers.

It was too late, anyway. Our mouths clamped shut, our eyes on Gĩthũi, as his outstretched form and the tiny scrubs he hung onto slid down and were swallowed by the chasm.

Tabitha and I froze where we stood, gawking at the chasm in horror. Now, our mouths were open, but no words came out. In seconds, we heard a thud, followed by an eerie silence.

Joseph recovered first. He fidgeted, crossed the chasm back and forth, confused.

We all ran amok. "Gĩthũi! Gĩthũi! Gĩthũi!" we called out, bent over, peering down the chasm.

No answer.

Our racket attracted the children further up the river. Already finished with their crossing, they rushed to join us.

"What happened? What happened?" they asked.

"Our Gĩthũi fell through the hole!" Tabitha and I said.

The two boys who had jumped with us and witnessed Gĩthũi 's fall slowly backed off, then turned and joined the others. I heard their exchanges, but I couldn't discern what they said.

Meanwhile, my siblings and I crisscrossed the trough and peered down into the dark hole for a sign, maybe a sound. Nothing happened. It was sheer luck that one of us didn't slip and follow Gĩthũi.

The group of six children inched backward, horror plastered on their faces. Their full reaction didn't register with us until much later.

Finally, Joseph became decisive and sprang into action. He tried to push through the bushes alongside the river, but their overgrowth proved too dense. He jumped back across, walked a few yards out, and plowed through a lesser thicket along the river. His busyness and take-charge manner calmed us. Tabitha and I focused on him. But I couldn't help thinking, Gĩthũi is dead.

I had no point of reference. I knew no one who had died, although Mami had evoked death on several occasions.

After the colonial government started forcing Gĩkũyũ people into secure villages for easier monitoring in 1953, we moved into two hovels—mud walls barely dry and the thatch still green.

Mami claimed the dampness would kill her young children, her youngest, Morry, barely six months old. And three years later, when we children caught measles, overwhelmed by the sheer responsibility of tending to five of us, Mami evoked death again,

But nobody died.

People came close. One time, Baba beat Joseph until he lost consciousness because goats in his care went astray. And Tabitha, our family's *wanja kahũ* (tomboy), at nine years old, fell and hit her head on a rock while bottom-skiing on a mudslide with the boys. The boys scattered. A man who happened by brought Tabitha's limp body and deposited it on Baba's thingira's floor just before dusk. With no transportation, my parents sent my brothers to fetch the medical assistant who operated the clinic at Njeki's Shopping Center. After examining her, he said she would be okay; she remained unconscious all night long. She came to in the morning.

Tabitha's limp body flashed through my mind as I braced myself for Gĩthũi 's death. This time, the real one, I believed.

My mind returned to the here and now "WoooooWoo! WoooooWoo!"

At least Gĩthũi is alive! I thought. But after the two screams, the eerie silence returned. We waited for another sign; none came. The screams were his last effort to hang onto life, I concluded. He's now dead.

For about ten minutes, now on the same bank, Tabitha and I anguished in our private thoughts while we waited for Gĩthũi to make another sound.

Then I realized the two of us stood by the chasm all alone. The other children had left, afraid we might finger them as witnesses to our family tragedy.

*

Joseph suddenly appeared about fifty feet behind us, Gĩthũi behind him, the two linking hands. As they came closer, Gĩthũi's khaki uniform looked drenched. He shivered, his pitiful face twisted, lips pouty, cheeks inflated.

When they reached us, I felt and looked all over Gĩthũi's body, as primates do while they search and pluck ticks off their babies. I found minor scrapes that my busy mother might not notice. Relief washed through me, glad the incident had shaken him more than hurt him, oblivious to the psychological effect.

Our group of four ambled to give Gĩthũi time to regain his composure. Meanwhile, Joseph filled us in on the details.

He entered the underground, where the river emerged. Previous floods had deposited gravel and debris on its banks. Now, with the river at its normal level, he walked alongside the canopied riverbank until he heard Gĩthũi's whimpers. He found him seated in mud, leaning his elbow against a big rock he had fallen inches from, dazed, while the river whooshed and flowed away. To wash off the mud, Joseph dipped him in water while fully clothed and helped him wash off. When he could walk, Joseph led him out of the underground, and the two walked to the regular crossing.

Gĩthũi's fall was at least twenty-five feet down. According to Joseph, he looked up from the river below but couldn't see any light from the chasm.

With the subdued late afternoon sun, by the time we arrived at our garden, about a mile away, Gĩthũi's uniform remained damp. As we busied ourselves looking for where Mami hid the hoes, we excused Gĩthũi from weeding that day. He said nothing as he shuffled a few feet away and sat on a sturdy clump of dirt. He cupped his cheeks with his hands, elbows planted on his folded knees.

Gĩthũi hadn't said a word since Joseph rescued him or responded to anything we said, even on our way home. Although he glanced at us now and then, I thought the fall had zapped his eardrums, and he couldn't hear us.

When we arrived home, he had the good sense to change from his rumpled khaki uniform into his home clothes before Mami saw him in that depressed state.

As Mami cooked that evening, I watched Gĩthũi nod off by the fire pit. I remained apprehensive all evening, especially when Mami said, "You are too quiet. Is there something the matter with you?"

Gĩthũi shook his head.

We didn't tell on him.

In adulthood, I mentioned the incident to him, but even then, we never went into details besides him saying, "Children!"

# Chapter 14

# Thieving Wild Pigs

The scarcity of food (and famine for some villagers) during the dry season, from January to mid-March, when the sun scorched the earth. It stopped in May, when short-cycle plants began to mature.

Along came plenty of green beans, peas, and potatoes to supplement our diet. But Mami kept using her signature *kauka* ("dry"—the greens she had dried and stored the previous year) by mixing it with fresh black-eyed pea leaves. Not a scoop of kauka went to waste.

The best playtime started in June and peaked in August when children had more leisure time. Boys made slingshots, hunted, or made toys. The extra enterprising ones made little "pickup vehicles" wired with a long shaft and a driving wheel. Others carved wood into tiny upside-down pyramids they called *mbirigûri* that boys competed to whip round and round until they vibrated and their shapes blurred or became invisible. The not-so-gifted boys used old bicycle tires to make rings, rolling them by hand or with a stick.

During my babysitting days in our first fenced village, we girls played house with children on our backs, or the toddlers tugged along. We also played hopscotch, jumped rope, and picked "coffee cherries," leaves from the skimpy shrubs between our homestead and the fence. We never made toys like the boys.

Now, in our second village and older, adults frowned at those childish activities. We girls had to help with chores besides gardening, like fetching and carrying firewood on our backs.

Our best season came in August when the school closed for a month. We enjoyed a mild climate—no weeding, no coffee cherries to pick yet—and plenty to eat. We fetched firewood two or three times a week, with only an hour of hauling the burden on our backs. Because we did it sporadically, the task didn't feel as oppressive as gardening.

Our maize started maturing in August, and by September, we relished the best steamed or roasted maize ears ever.

When maize kernels firmed enough to shell (our people shell with hands, not with a knife), Mami cooked mũkimo or mataha, a staple for the Kikuyus. It's cooked with dry or green maize kernels, potatoes, greens—*togotia, tharageti, kahũrũra,* or pumpkin leaves—and various beans, including kidney beans, pinto beans, and navy beans. One leaves out the greens when she cooks with green peas, black-eyed peas, white-eyed peas (njahĩ), or Kikuyu peas. Depending on the type of beans used, every mũkimo has a distinct taste.

I loved mũkimo cooked with green peas, potatoes, and green maize kernels, which I still make today, minus the potatoes.

Wild pigs seemed to wait for the maize, just like us. But they preferred to enjoy the bounty before it matured, before we could.

Baba, sometimes accompanied by Simon, spent at least three nights a week in the garden, protecting our maize from the animals that lived in the woods next to the slopes of Jumatatu Mountain.

He built a makeshift shack of sticks and grass where he spent those nights—returning home at daybreak, ready to leave for work after his morning tea—until our maize started drying; pigs didn't care for dry maize.

On the stake-out days, Baba arrived home from work and left after supper. He wore his greatcoat and a hat and carried a torch, a three-foot spear, a machete, some firewood, and a rolled sleeping mat.

Every few hours, Baba and Simon walked around the garden. Unlike a typical stakeout, where people stayed hidden, they made their presence known. Otherwise, in the animals' rush to escape, they could bulldoze and trample someone to death.

Occasionally, when the campfire died, Baba and Simon dozed off only to have the pigs' racket awaken them. They started hollering and making a racket to scare away the animals.

Baba also made several effigies or scarecrows and placed them at strategic spots along the periphery of our garden. Within a short period, though, the animals figured out the trick and resumed their raids. He had to change the dummies' shapes or vary them to confuse the pigs and stretch his trick.

Given time, pigs distinguished effigies from humans. But if they encountered a human in one garden, they didn't have enough sense to change course and visit an unattended garden. Instead, they trampled on each other, flattening people's plants, rushing back to the woods to try their luck another day.

The landowner never encountered that problem. His sprawling plantations thrived in the center of the farm, while villagers' gardens came farther out, closer to the periphery. The pigs had to cross the employees' maize gardens and walk across the open savanna to reach the employer's plantations. The employees' gardens, in essence, acted as buffers to the farm owner's plantations.

\*

Baba didn't plant or harvest beans, peas, and other short-season crops. Society deemed that work for women and children. But everybody—including him—harvested the maize when the time came. Before its stalks dried completely, Baba and Simon cut and arranged the maize stalks into sizeable pyramids. Within weeks, the maize dried for harvest.

All able-bodied family members stood around the pyramid, husked the ears, and, except for Baba, carried the dry maize cobs in sacks or half-sacks for the three miles home. We stored it in a pile in the granary.

From then on, the maize, or any other dry food, was up to Mami to get it to the plate, with limited help from Tabitha and me.

.

## Chapter 15

# In Care of Njoki

My brother David never gardened or harvested before he went to boarding school. But before he and Simon got old enough to ease into male privileges, besides goat-herding, they helped Mami with "women's chores." They helped with babysitting and carrying loads on their backs in a kiondo. But goat-herding took precedence, and David got off easy when he left for boarding school.

Mami sighed with relief when I came along, and in two years, Tabitha followed. With two daughters, she was no longer the only one to handle women's jobs.

Now, with her two budding pre-teen daughters, Mami didn't train her younger sons to do "female chores." She concentrated on us girls.

To train us, besides babysitting, carrying loads on our backs came next. She started with small bundles of firewood tied with short leather straps like the ones she used for the baskets she weaved. She increased the loads as we got older until we could tie the bundles ourselves.

When women were working, they sent their trainee daughters to fetch firewood under the watchful eye of other women, especially if the child could get her own firewood. Mami never entrusted my sister and me to anyone. But one day, she changed course. She sent me—a short, skinny, twelve-and-a-half-year-old girl—under the care of Njoki.

At the time, I had little concept of beauty besides thinking buck teeth or asymmetrical body parts were unpleasing.

But everything about Njoki looked pleasing. I admired her tall, flawless skin and white, well-lined teeth. She carried a well-proportioned body, from the head down to her well-formed legs, calves tapered off to feet that could have flattened anything she stepped on. She marched along as if nothing fazed her. Because of her childless state, however, at about twenty-eight years old, women pitied her behind her back.

"Poor Njoki," they said.

Having never accompanied another woman besides Mami, I felt lucky to have Njoki all to myself.

On the way to fetch wood, I trotted down the pathway behind her with ease, enjoying the open savanna. I said yes or no, or hmmm, or uh-huh to her questions and comments, buoyed by a chance to converse with a woman all by myself. She kept a normal pace, and I kept in step with her.

We ended up in the wild pigs' woods, three miles from home, my first time there. Besides the women, only boys ventured into the wooded area to set traps to snare wildfowl or rabbits. A handful of them used dogs to hunt.

The women went there to collect, break, or cut dry firewood from fallen dead trees or branches. They could also carry more firewood, and their families wouldn't have to wait for the wood to dry.

Njoki and I didn't go too deep into the woods. There was plenty of firewood a short distance in. Although I never thought about it, if we went too deep into the woods, we would likely have disturbed wild pigs or animals we had never encountered in the savanna.

Rumors had spread about a couple of lions roaming on the slopes of Jumatatu Mountain and even of a leopard sighting. (Tabitha claimed that one evening near our homestead, a leopard accosted her and bared its teeth. I suspect, in her case, it was a coyote)

Too young for such concerns, I collected old fallen branches and broke them down to the size of the firewood I needed without asking Njoki for help. My heap looked impressive. Mami will be proud of me, I thought.

When Njoki finished tying her load, she tied mine. I soon realized the load was twice as heavy as I had ever carried. My legs trembled when she placed it on my back. I steadied myself, clasped each hand around the leather strap across my head and over my ears, and waited for her.

With nobody to assist her in lifting her load, Njoki had tied hers on an incline near a shrub to grab onto and pull herself up. She sat in front of her load, put the strap across her head, bent forward, and held onto the shrub as she leaned from one side to the other, nudging the load into position on her back.

"Start walking," she said. "I'll catch up with you."

*

Njoki caught up with me and took the lead. After we cleared the woods, we branched east onto the gradually ascending footpath that led us home.

Slightly stooped, backs arched to steady our loads, we looked like two stages of human evolution. But soon the formation got messed up. Njoki's one stride covered two or three of mine. I struggled to keep up. When she looked behind and failed to see me, she waited.

When I caught up with her, she said, "Go on and rest. "I'll keep an eye on you," and resumed walking.

My entire body craved rest, but I rested for about ten seconds, afraid to lag too far behind and get swallowed by wiregrass and scrubs along the two-foot-wide path.

After several such stop-and-go rounds, my body protested; it didn't want to go on.

It started with tiny tremors in my arms.

I gripped the leather strap even harder.

Then the legs throbbed.

To get relief, I thought of jerking my head backward and letting the load roll off. It never occurred to me that the load could knock my legs and trap them underneath. And my action would hurt me instead of Njoki, the target of my wrath. But the thinking distracted me, and I rested a little longer.

When I caught up with Njoki, before she could take off and disappear, I tightened my grip and steadied my straps by my ears. I tilted my head up, my evil eyes fixed on her well-formed calves, whose muscles bunched whenever she stepped. I wished her calves would buckle, a thought inspired by a story Mami had told us about a stumpy old man, insecure about his height.

When the said old man mourned his first wife's death for a respectable period, he married a much younger, taller woman than he. Unknown to him, the woman wasn't shy about exploiting her advantages.

In time, she and her husband brought forth a couple of children. Now settled in, she talked back to her husband and even overruled him on important family matters, a role tradition gave to male heads of homesteads. The husband fumed inside but held his peace; a conceited wife was better than none. Except for the bad attitude, the wife fed him well, doted on their children, and ran the household smoothly, and the marriage thrived. Well, until word got around.

At a drinking party, a man asked the husband, "Why do you speak with authority among men and not a peep at your homestead?"

"Does your wife beat you?" another man chimed in, stirring chuckles.

After several such stings, the husband never invited men to his homestead for a man's drink, as they called alcohol. Even then, he couldn't join a group of men for a drink without getting anxious, expecting a zinger before the session ended.

At home, the man stewed, and his insecurities dominated his thoughts. He blamed his suffering on his wife's bossiness. To rile her, he began to complain about trivial matters. When the wife ignored him, he amplified his complaints, going so far as to order special food between meals. Fed up with the unreasonable demands, the wife pushed back.

"Who am I going to attend to?" she asked. "You or the children?"

"You better quit your ways," the man warned his wife, wiggling his finger at her.

"What ways?" she asked, arms akimbo, elbows winged.

"Behave like a wife," the man said

"You've been listening to your friends again?"

"I'm telling you! You'd better do it!" Otherwise, I'll sneak behind you when you are carrying a load and slash those fat calves of yours."

But no husband wanted a disabled wife crawling around his homestead, the brats she spoiled waiting to grow up and get back at him. And the wife lacked the guts to call her husband's bluff and test whether he was crazy enough to carry out his threat. So, the slashing never occurred.

I winced, and a jolt ran through my legs when Mami told us that story.

Njoki's calves looked full and smooth like the ones in the story, but I had no power to threaten her except to wish her harm. After all, she was doing Mami a favor by taking me along.

Preoccupied with calves, I had covered some ground, my fatigue forgotten momentarily, and Njoki had disappeared.

"Are you still coming?" she called out.

Defiance arose within me. My mouth remained closed. I was done. I had no spare energy to answer loud enough for her to hear.

The minute she saw me appear and satisfied herself that I was still on my feet, she walked on. I divorced my fatigue from her and instead concentrated on my steps. I rested for short periods whenever my body couldn't take the strain.

Njoki slowed as we got closer to home. At the entrance to our courtyard, between the granary and the chicken coop, I lagged only twenty-five feet behind her.

"Is anyone home?" she called out.

"You two have arrived?" Mami said as she appeared in the doorway.

I reached where Njoki stood.

"I'll go on now that your daughter is safely home," she said, heading toward the pedestrian gate on the side of our homestead.

I crossed the courtyard toward the side of Mami's house, where we heaped firewood in two piles. By then, my neck had anchored itself halfway to my left shoulder. Mami quickened her steps to help me unload. I arched my back as we did when resting or taking a load off, so it wouldn't roll down. Mami went behind me, held the load on both sides, and dropped it with a thud.

"Did you carry that all the way from *thiguota?*" (squatter's place? Homeless people had sneaked in and built shacks close to the woods, hence "squatter.")

"Mmm," I said, rubbing my achy neck.

"Does Njoki want to disable my child?" Mami asked. "That's how insensitive childless women are."

I never told Mami the effort it took to get that load home, but her reaction told me she got the message. She never entrusted me to another woman. But I continued with back-deforming work until I left home at eighteen. By then, one of my vertebrae had become knobby, with a prominent bump, and I had developed a permanent groove across my head.

On her part, Njoki left a lasting memory that resurfaces when I see grown people strut along, dragging their youngsters by the hand while the little tots sprint behind.

I have stopped several times, and once I pulled my car off the road to alert an adult who seemed unaware of the exertion she was subjecting her child to.

# Chapter 16

# Tailor Problem

During the exodus in early 1953, when the colonizers rounded up, moved, and corralled Agĩkũyũ into concentration and detention camps and secured villages, Baba's first family members had joined the exodus procession to Kikuyuland, the so-called *Native Reserve*.

By 1960, half of his grown children—Waigwa and his family, Wairimũ-big and her daughter, and Wanjirũ-big with her two daughters and young son—had trickled back to the farm, partly fragmented. A job at a cereal factory, deemed "essential," had kept Waigwa's family intact. But his two sisters and their children didn't fare too well. They returned husbandless and fatherless, their men turned rootless by the war turmoil, unable to provide or protect themselves or their families.

Njerũ-big, their oldest brother, who claimed he had enough of Baba's tyranny in 1945 and vowed never to return to Solai, stayed behind in Nyeri, on Aunt Julia's land, where he lived with his family. Their mother, Kaguyu, Baba's ex-wife, died in 1959. Njerũ-big buried her in a small plot that Baba had abandoned when he went west in search of work in the late 1920s.

Nobody counted Werũ, Baba's stepson, the bonus son. Although he had left with the rest during the exodus, his life started unraveling before he got on one of the caravan lorries. At the roadside, where he and Ruth, his bride of one year, waited with a group for the lorry, her father, Alan Kĩbuĩ, had marched right up to his daughter.

"Take your luggage and head home right now!" he ordered her, thrusting his index finger toward her and then homeward to the farm.

"I leave my husband?" Ruth asked softly, eyes wide, puzzled.

"You aren't going to that native reserve!"

Werũ remained by the roadside, stupefied and wifeless, the beginning of his woes.

In Kikuyuland, he marked time like the rest of the masses. Finally, the colonial officials threw him on death row for allegedly planning to feed the Mau Mau freedom fighters. He escaped the noose when Waigwa's white supervisor talked to Kamunge.

After Kamunge listened to the accusation, he deemed it bogus and intervened. Although exonerated, the experience had traumatized Werũ so much that in 1962, it had been almost seven years since his family had seen him.

*

The Waigwas were the first family to return to the farm when we lived in the old fenced village. Now, in our second village, they lived a block away from us, but it was farther because Baba had erected a fence behind his thingira that separated us from the main part of the village.

During the war, Waigwa had gained skills as an essential worker. After leaving his cereal factory job, he worked at a clothing factory where he trained as a tailor. He specialized in women's clothing and mending.

To help Waigwa reestablish himself, Baba bought a black treadle Singer sewing machine for 900 Shillings, fifteen months of his wages before taxes. He called the sewing machine a family investment, with Waigwa as trustee and tailor. I believed we had the same rights to the machine as him.

As the tailor and trustee, Waigwa kept what he earned. But Baba required him to tailor or mend our family's clothes at no charge. A man of mellow disposition, Waigwa didn't object or comment on it.

To our family, it seemed like an excellent investment. We would save on tailoring charges, Waigwa would earn extra income, and villagers would have the service at hand rather than walking the four miles to Njeki's Shopping Center.

But, with time, the plan didn't live up to its ideal, at least for us, Baba's second family.

# Chapter 17

# Daughters' Bad Behavior

Waigwa and his family lived in the same village with us. But his two sisters, Wanjirũ-big, her three children—Wambũi, Wamũyũ, and Mũrigũ —and Wairimũ-big with her little girl, Wanjirũ, lived in our previous fenced village across the Tindaress River.

After my half-siblings returned and I met them for the first time, our two camps didn't become one happy family. A negative undercurrent lingered in the family that no one spoke about. Baba's first family looked at our family as interlopers. I recall Gathoni, one of their sisters, implying that Baba and her mother divorced because of Mami.

For us, the second family, we believed Baba belonged to us, not them. It took many years before I acknowledged they were my full-fledged half-siblings.

Besides, Baba still harbored animosity toward his two daughters because they had treated him badly in their girlhood long before they married and left for the native reserve during the exodus.

Wanjiru-big's episode took place in 1939, three years after Baba became a polygamist when he married Mami. They lived at Kĩrĩma-inĩ, our first homestead, tucked away on the western corner of the farm, with untamed country all around.

Baba and Kaguyu, his first wife, usually held a party for a handful of friends or just the two of them on the Sunday he brewed beer.

On one such Sunday, Baba and Kaguyu entertained a handful of friends in her house. After their friends left, the two continued drinking. Mami hadn't joined the party. Much younger than her husband and co-wife, and not yet entrenched in the family, and nursing a baby, she didn't drink.

(When she picked up the habit for a short stint, she realized drunken husbands and wives were not conducive to happy homes and soon quit.)

Later in the afternoon, Mami winnowed beans in the court-yard with David swaddled on her back when she heard Baba's and Kaguyu's usual heated exchanges. Mami ignored their behavior when they drank. But this time, she heard a scuffle, grunts, and Kaguyu's threatening voice.

She went to check.

From the open doorway, right in the living area, Baba lay on his back, Kaguyu on top of him, her hands clutched around his neck. Wanjirū-big straddled her mother from behind, pressing her shoulders down.

"I'll choke you today!" Kaguyu said. "You'll never touch me again!"

Mami grabbed Wanjirū-big by her shoulders and threw her so hard she hit the wall. Mami then grabbed and tossed Kaguyu aside.

As soon as Baba got free, he steadied himself and scrambled out the door, his dignity in tatters. He flexed and rubbed his neck as he staggered toward his thingira.

Wanjirū-big's behavior horrified anyone who heard that story. Instead of separating her warring parents, she had preferred to become fatherless. Subsequently, she married and started a family. She, her husband Joel, and their three young children left during the exodus before she apologized to her father.

Five years after Wanjirŭ-big's incident, their lastborn, Wairimŭ-big, had intervened when her mother and Baba got into another of their drunken brawls. At sixteen, she didn't have the muscle to help beat him. Instead, she stayed outside, jeered and shouted to Baba, and capped it with several rounds of, "You are nothing but a cunt."

Wairimŭ-big matured, married Njoroge, and had a baby. The family of three also left during the exodus before she apologized to her father.

In Kikuyuland, the two sisters and their families suffered severe starvation, violence, and other atrocities they never spoke of, war-induced conditions so hostile that their marriages fell apart.

The two sisters couldn't wait to leave the turmoil behind, ready to return to Solai to face the father who had proved hard to love.

Baba could have petitioned the colonial government for the return of his daughters. But no matter what hell-hole the two floundered in, he remained quiet, still sore about their poor treatment of him. No other child of his had ever called him a name or assaulted him, and he wanted no reminders.

Mami was of a different mindset. She said the sisters should return to the farm like Waigwa.

"It is better to be controlled," she said, "than to live not knowing whether one'll live or die."

Baba ignored Mami's utterances. He had no interest in petitioning on behalf of his daughters.

Mami had her reasons. Despite her stepdaughters' disgraceful behavior, she never forgot a good deed. When Baba married her, Wairimŭ-big was a young girl. She and her sister Gathoni (the middle daughter who didn't join the exodus with her family) helped babysit my brothers, David and Simon, when they came along.

In those early years, because David went to school early, sometimes Baba told Wairimũ-big to join Simon in the pastures to herd the goats. The two half-siblings became close and experienced Baba's abuse together. In adulthood, Wairimũ-big would tell me, "Baba hated Simon and me the most."

Years later, the school aged out Simon at sixteen, and with David in boarding school, Simon had become the de facto oldest son in the family. He read letters for Baba and learned firsthand about the two sisters' dire situation. At about nineteen, he couldn't stay back and leave his half-sister to suffer.

without telling Baba, Simon petitioned for Wairimũ-big himself, which he could do because he had an ID, paid taxes, and worked on the farm.

To petition, Simon trekked twenty miles to Nakuru Town several times. If he had bus fare, he rode to town and walked back. He worked but had no money of his own. On payday, Kamunge handed his wages to Baba for safekeeping. He claimed at sixteen, Simon was too young to handle money, never mind the colonial government believed he was old enough to carry a passbook (travel permission papers), an ID, and pay taxes.

To process the petition, Simon dealt with Chief Joshua, a fellow Gĩkũyũ, in the District Commissioner's (DC's) office. The chief accused him of planning to "import a girlfriend" from Nyĩrĩ (Nyeri), Kikuyuland.

Although the country was experiencing its last war hiccups, it still took Simon a year to get the petition granted. And he only managed to do so when he found Chief Joshua absent for a day.

Two years after her return to the farm, at about age 30, Wairimũ-big married Mũriũki, a scrawny, quiet, older bachelor who seemed to have grown old before he fully developed. Our family should have frowned at such a mismatch, but they kept their judgments to themselves. Any husband had to do. Wairimũ-big had taken up heavy drinking to bury and soothe her eight-year war trauma.

To the family's relief, Mūriũki turned out to be the perfect husband for her. He never missed a day of work. During his downtime, he patiently stayed at home with their children while his wife took off at a moment's notice to sniff around for a sip of alcohol.

During Wairimũ-big's drinking years, she rarely came to our homestead sober. When she did, many times, she reeked of alcohol and wasn't fully in control of her words. My parents gave her side glances as they would a severely disabled person. Likely, it didn't occur to her to apologize for calling Baba names, or she thought Baba had forgotten. It took at least ten years before Wairimũ-big weaned herself off alcohol by joining Solai's version of *Alcoholics Anonymous*—Christianity.

As for Wanjirũ-big, the firstborn, no one petitioned for her or knew how she maneuvered herself back to Solai. According to Simon, it was sheer luck that she and her three children slipped through the colonial net. She even kept mum about what happened to her husband, Joel. Years later, he reappeared and sought a reunion with his son, who worked and lived in Nairobi. But he never returned to Solai to seek his daughters, who, without having gone to school, remained on the farm. Wanjirũ-big never remarried. She became the first in our family to raise her children on her own.

Unlike her younger sister, Wanjirũ-big was sober. She craved family connections besides her three children, the two girls already teenagers by then, and the boy in elementary school, a couple of years behind me. She dropped in at our homestead on weekends. Whenever she came and found Baba drunk, he would ask her, "Do you recall when you and your mother wanted to kill me?"

Wanjirũ-big would squirm and apologize softly, eyes downcast, head hung sideways like a timid child. Soon, she became tired of the constant apologies. After that, when Baba mentioned her shortcomings, her eyes fell to the ground, frozen in place, and she said nothing.

Mami became tired of the routine.

"Wanjirũ apologizes every time you remind her of her one failing," Mami said. "Is that not enough? How many times do you want her to apologize?"

"*Sawa! Sawa!*" (Okay! Okay!) Baba said, waving his drunken hand outward.

There ended any mention of the choking or name-calling incidents.

# Chapter 18

# David's Crimes

We, Baba's second family, had our own issues, starting with David, the oldest. He left for boarding school when I was seven years old.

Unlike our old raggedy clothes, David wore clean shorts, a white shirt, black shoes, and socks (sometimes knee-high stockings), and later trousers. Baba bought him all the school supplies he needed at the beginning of each three-month school term. Even if I couldn't relate to him, it buoyed my heart to have a special, "accomplished" brother who was above manual labor.

Later, when several of us attended school, Baba skimped or delayed our supplies and fees. It didn't occur to me that David had attended school as an only child—after the school-aged out Simon at sixteen. The rest of us started attending school in clusters of twos, threes, fours, or even fives at a time.

I cannot say what my siblings thought, but I felt Baba loved David more than he loved us. As David progressed in school, he grew into a young man, a young man every father would have wanted for a son. In the surrounding farms, only he and Alan's son had passed the national exams starting in the early 1950s to get admitted to a boarding school.

In those early years, before David grew too self-assured, outgrew the village, skipped coming home during the holidays, and became a stranger, he had been the darling of us all, family and the villagers. He could do no wrong. Well, except for the two he did when we lived in our first fenced village.

David's first "wrong" was during his school holiday. He skipped Sunday church service, a Sunday ritual that teachers and parents treated as part of the school curriculum. Instead, he joined Simon on the goat-herding trail. He paid dearly for it when my parents cornered him in the goats' cottage and flogged him with leather straps while he screamed like a snared animal. The villagers never learned of that "wrong."

But every villager learned about his second one because it involved *Gītharia,* a white man.

*

During the height of the war, British landowners forbade villagers from taking shortcuts across their farms. Some of them erected barbed wire fences. Because villagers had to take the main roads, they often walked an extra mile or two out of their way to reach nearby destinations.

Our school was a few yards off the Nakuru-Solai public road. Pupils walked from the farms where they lived to the road, then along it to school. But Kamunge's farm, where we belonged, was directly across the road from the school. After we hit the road, we walked for only 50 yards before we got to school.

When I was eleven, Mami sent me to the bus stop to carry David's luggage. He was on his way home from Kijabe Boys Boarding School, coming for his school holiday.

Before trespassing laws, people from our village used a shortcut through Gītharia's farm next door to get where David was getting off the bus. But because that wasn't our usual bus stop, I was unfamiliar with that shortcut. There were also trespass laws to consider. I now took the longer path across Kamunge's farm that we used to get to school. From the school, I walked another half mile to the bus stop.

As I pounded along the road, the bus passed me a short distance from where it dropped David off.

I found him by the roadside, next to his wooden suitcase. To carry it, I tied it with a leather strap on both ends, and David helped me load it on my back. With the strap across my head, I held it steady with each hand by my ears. With my load secure, I followed my brother.

After walking a few feet along the road, David stopped and strode this way and that between the road and the barbed wire fence that ran parallel to it about twenty feet inland, looking for a footpath for the shortcut across Gîtharia's farm. Because of disuse, the old path had disappeared under thick grass and scrubby weeds. When his efforts yielded no footpath, David started complaining about "these unreasonable restrictions." I expected him to turn back and lead me along the way I had come. But he walked toward the fence, determined to find a weak link.

"We are supposed to follow the road," I said from where I waited.

"To follow the road?" he asked. "That's a long way."

"We can use the path we take to school."

David continued his search, bent on finding the old shortcut.

"We can cross through here," he said. Whatever my big brother decided was fine with me. I walked on the grass toward him.

Before I reached the fence, David relieved me of the suitcase and rested it by the fence for easier retrieval from the other side. He separated two wires, bent down, raised his right leg through the opening, and stepped onto the other side. He pushed his body through; just before he cleared the wires, I heard, "Halt!" behind me.

I gasped. My entire body shook.

David turned his head, gawked, and froze.

# Chapter 19

# The Philanderer's Rules

When I heard "Halt!" I froze, too, as if the word linked David's body and mine.

Until then, I had heard no one speak English except for medics at Nakuru General Hospital two years earlier, when I was nine. A doctor had admitted me, along with my sick little brother, to help mind him. But I had heard enough war stories to know "Halt!" meant to stop and freeze.

My body tensed and stilled, terrified by the authority behind me. Soon, I heard heavy footsteps and rustling getting nearer and nearer. Khaki shorts and white legs appeared in my line of vision and strode toward David. I stayed in place, my eyes downcast, my eyebrows raised now and then to monitor the situation, a man's body in full view.

"How many times do I have to tell these bloody Africans not to trespass?" the man said in English.

I didn't know what he said besides the word "Africans," but he sounded furious.

He reached out, grabbed David by the shoulder, and yanked him out. As David straightened, I noticed his arm, leg, and shirt had been scraped by the barbed wire. He looked up at a much taller man in shorts, a desert green short-sleeved shirt, and a tan bucket hat. The man's other hand rested on a long-barreled gun with its strap slung over his shoulder.

David stammered his apologies amidst a barrage of verbal abuses reserved for "these bloody natives." It seemed each talked to himself—David in Kiswahili and the man in English.

David claimed that was the only path he knew to get home to Kamunge's farm.

"Bring your passbook!" the man said, now in Kiswahili.

David handed over his travel permission papers.

The man flipped through the passbook and returned it to David without comment.

I felt some relief. He might let us go, I thought. Instead, he pointed at the suitcase.

"Pick it up!" the man ordered David, pointing to the road. He then guarded him from behind.

Nobody paid attention that I, Wanjirũ, a scrawny, bare-foot, eleven-year-old girl, stood there scared out of my wits. I first turned my head, then my entire body, the farther they went. I inched toward the road, eager to observe the man's intentions. None of them looked behind.

They reached a Land Rover parked at a distance.

"Get in!" the man said.

David's unsteady hands dropped the suitcase.

"Pick it up!" the man said, about to kick David, but he restrained himself. David didn't look like the scruffy village teenagers.

Finally, David, suitcase in hand, clambered onto the canopied vehicle.

The man eased into the driver's seat and drove away.

*

Ordinarily, British farmers squeezed every ounce of labor they could from their workers and confined those workers and their families to villages. The landowners were indifferent to what happened inside the villages. They dismissed activities like child or wife assaults, female genital mutilation, or child labor as "That's their culture." Or they used terms like "bloody Africans, brutes, barbarians," and so forth.

I'm not sure how the landowners termed deaths, but to them, no African death made a ripple, not even that of an employee. Of the deaths that occurred while I lived in the village, families buried their dead, many times not knowing what killed them, and life went on. The only time these white landowners took action was if an employee broke a rule, like trespassing, brewing alcohol, or if an occasional child stole fruit from the orchards.

Absentee or elderly landowners who didn't have sons or whose sons opted for careers other than farming employed farm managers. They recruited those managers—usually bachelors—from recent arrivals from England, South Africa, or Zimbabwe [Rhodesia then] with whiteness and male gender as the main qualifications (sometimes the only qualifications).

Many of those managers were ruthless, soulless human beings. They took the law into their own hands while dealing with employees. They were quick to use physical violence toward younger African male workers deemed to have wronged the farms, especially if those workers became defiant and protested against verbal abuse or physical mistreatment.

The white man who drove David away was one of those managers. Rumors had it that he entertained different women, so the villagers nicknamed him Gĩtharia (philanderer), and the farm he managed became known as Gĩtharia 's farm.

*

When Gĩtharia drove David away, I recovered from the stupor, fearing he would harm my brother. My little heart trembled, but I needed to hurry home and tell my parents. I returned to the main dirt road. I quickened my steps to retrace the half a mile to the school and the short distance beyond the school and turned east on the tractor trail through Kamunge's farm.

Kamunge had the same trespass rules regarding that part of his sprawling land. But except for the scrubby land and the tractor trail we walked on, that part of the farm was an open savanna except for two five-acre pens in which he segregated cows and bulls. The bulls resembled buffalo and were even wilder when they were in heat. They grunted, spittle escaping from their mouths, ready to attack anyone close to the fence.

"He can't require young children to go all that way?" Mami said when Kamunge introduced the trespass rules. "What will he do? Arrest them?"

Gossip swirled through the village that if children trespassed, Kamunge would hold their parents responsible. I had never seen Kamunge on that sparse section of land. Most of his employees grumbled but still followed the rules. Some complained of the long distances, and others arrived late. Kamunge didn't respond, and nobody caught the rule breakers.

Before long, his workers and their children returned to their old ways. They resumed taking shortcuts. They had little to fear. Kamunge, unlike Gĩtharia, didn't trek around his farm like a hunter.

Because of David's incident, however, the thought of taking the tractor trail we used to take to and from school intensified my anxiety. What if Kamunge enforced his no-trespass rule? How would my parents handle two arrests? It didn't occur to me that it was late afternoon and the school was closed. It was unlikely for anyone to see me.

If I had followed Kamunge's rules to the letter, after reaching the school, I would have needed to continue on Nakuru-Solai Road for about three miles, branch off on Subukia Road, and walk for about two more miles before I reached the turn to Kamunge's mile-long private road. I didn't know that long roadway home. Even if I did, darkness would have come before I arrived home.

In a rush to get home to report the matter, I took a chance. After all, I belonged to the farm.

"Gītharia took David away," I told Mami before I calmed my breathing. It could have been any white man, but because I knew whose farm it was, I knew it had to be him.

"Oh! My child!" she said, dropped the firewood she was getting from the pile by her house, and beat the sides of her body with both arms. "They took my child before he arrived home?"

Mami's reaction alerted Baba, who was already home from work. He came outside to ensure he heard right. He and Mami didn't speculate what Gītharia did with David. They "knew." Soon, Baba left and headed to Solai Police Station, three miles away.

As Baba reported later, by the time he arrived, the police had already charged David with trespass, ordered him to take off his shoes and socks, and locked him in a cell.

It was David's lucky, unlucky day. Unlike what Gītharia often did to the young African men he caught, he had controlled his urges to slap and kick David around. He had come from boarding school in uniform, black shoes, hair parted on one side, clean-cut, unlike the barefoot, scruffy, overworked village teenagers who didn't qualify for such "civility." Instead, Gītharia settled for insults and an arrest only.

Baba returned to the police station the following day and bailed David out, along with his luggage, a first in our village. Most people had no savings to pay bail or fines, and no one borrowed money or held a fundraiser. But Baba had the money. He had worked for decades, in addition to running a hides-and-skins and tobacco business for about fifteen years. He was also an avid saver and a miser in his own right.

He and David went to court in Nakuru three times. After the second hearing, Baba asked Kamunge to persuade *Gītharia* to drop the charge or plead with the court. This would have taken

Kamunge one phone call to either Gĩtharia or the court; such were the colonizers' powers.

"My son is just a schoolboy," Baba pleaded.

"Let's leave the law to take its course," Kamunge said.

David wasted his month-long school holiday worrying about going to prison.

A public defender who represented him used an "exemplary pupil" defense. He outlined the deprived state of native boys and that David had overcome all that, passed his national tests, and attended a boarding school.

"The boy had only one foot on the farm," the lawyer said, "which he mistook for the farm where his father works."

The lawyer's claim was half a lie. A stranger might have confused the boundaries, but although the grass and weeds had overgrown and covered the path, David was no stranger. He knew whose farm it was.

After the prosecutor and the public defender made brief closing statements, the magistrate delivered his judgment at the same session.

In his ruling, the judge warned David not to become a criminal. He fined him seventy-five shillings, a huge amount in late 1957—about a month and a half of Baba's supervisory wages.

Baba paid the fine, and our family sighed with relief. My parents had feared David might end up in prison and wave his education goodbye.

Mami said no other man in the village could afford to pay such a large amount. At such times, I don't doubt she was thankful she married a much older man, even though she had sworn against it before her father insisted Warama was established and stable and the right man for her.

# Chapter 20

# David's Lofty Goal

David had come far since Aunt Julia visited our first homestead in Kĩrĩma-inĩ in the late 1940s. During her visit, she learned that David, at nine years old, hadn't started school. Baba blamed the five-mile distance to the one-room school over Jumatatu Mountain Range. Regardless of distance, Aunt Julia threw a fuss—David needed to be in school. She said she would take him with her. My parents caved in and let her take him to Nyeri, Kikuyuland.

In Nyeri, when he wasn't in a school uniform, she dressed him like a little colonial master in a jacket and a hat.

Single and a full-time nurse, she found it hard to mind David. She farmed him out to Njerũ-big, Baba's allegedly *lazy* oldest son from his first marriage, and his wife, Njoki. The couple lived on Aunt Julia's land at Ndũndũinĩ, Kĩamariga, Njeri.

The one year he lived there, attending Kanyota Primary School, David suffered terrible neglect. When my parents heard of it through a man who had visited Nyeri, Baba traveled to Nyeri and left with David the following day. On hearing this, Aunt Julia wrote to Baba, accusing him of preferring his children to remain illiterate.

"Now that you've withdrawn Njerũ (David) from school," she said. "Let's see whether you can afford to educate him."

No more words passed between the two siblings regarding David's education, but the dare was on.

In his quest to prove he could educate his own son, Baba considered neither the hazards a boy could encounter walking over five miles over Jumatatu Mountain Range to a one-room school nor the challenging national standardized tests. David had to get an education!

David hung in and paid his dues. He weathered the distance, loneliness, and bullies, aced his grade four national exam, and headed to boarding school—a big deal in that era.

"Julia can now see that her brother can educate his own children," Mami said.

Unlike the rest of us, David had to attend school, if only for Baba to prove to his sister that he could educate his own son.

Baba kept mum but looked at his "boy" with satisfaction. By Gĩtharia time, Baba's admiration of his son was complete.

As the only child from our family in school, David had led a "privileged" boarding school life; his passing every national exam reflected that. Baba gave him money for transportation back and forth, school fees, and supplies to cover the three-month term. (By contrast, when I reached grade four, my family had five children in school, and the cost had overburdened Baba. Whenever we asked him for school fees or supplies, he gave them to us with his jaws tightened to prevent his mouth from blaming us for his financial strain.)

David finished his four years at Kijabe Boarding School and continued for another four years at Kabete Technical School. By then, Baba and Aunt Julia had reconnected and had laid their dare to rest. Otherwise, Baba's gloating would have swelled David's head.

For the next ten years, David was the only one in our family to go that far in school. He behaved and walked with a buoyance the rest of Baba's children admired but lacked. It was in this state that he strutted into our homestead, self-assured as always, clean-cut like one going for an interview, tan trousers, white shirt sleeves folded halfway, hair neatly parted on the left, shiny black shoes, his face and eyes aglow with success; focused only on his mission.

The following day, David spent time in Baba's thingira. I thought nothing of it until I noticed his quiet demeanor and sensed a negative undercurrent between him and Baba.

As usual, Mami let us in on the family's latest quake.

David had gushed out to Baba what he believed would send our father and the rest of us into jubilation.

First, he had graduated from Kabete Technical School with high marks. Second, based on his qualifications, he had earned a full scholarship to study abroad. He wanted to go to Ũraya (England or Europe) and needed Baba to pay the airfare: 3,000 shillings.

Instead of jubilation, Baba suffered a mental spin, Mami said.

First off, Baba said it was a dangerous proposition. He wasn't going to send his son to white people's country! If they brutalized Africans in our country, how would they treat David in their own country?

Plus, it was a colossal amount of money. When we heard about it, my siblings and I couldn't imagine how much three thousand shillings was. The largest amount I had seen was a twenty-shilling bank note Baba gave me for my school fees.

Besides safety and money, Mami said, Baba worried David would disappear in "England" and never marry and raise a family. Baba didn't have to spell it out. "Going abroad," to him, meant David would remain single because he would never find a Gĩkũyũ woman to marry.

My siblings and I added our own spin. We speculated that Baba refused because the place was too far—maybe an entire day's travel. I couldn't even imagine how far David had gone to boarding school, let alone abroad. The farthest I had gone was Nakuru Town, twenty miles away.

I never learned what carried more weight with Baba—safety, marriage, or the astronomical price of the air ticket. (Years later,

I calculated that at the highest point of an overseer's job, 3,000 shillings amounted to five years of Baba's gross earnings before taxes.)

David had thought of none of this. He had no qualms about focusing only on what he wanted, having developed a me-me selfish streak that would become a part of his lifelong persona. He never paid attention to our family's size, Baba's financial load, or his aging. Neither did my dear brother appreciate that Baba had already met his goal; he had more than won his dare with Aunt Julia. I doubt it crossed David's mind to prepare Baba before he touted his alien, lofty goal.

Jolted by Baba's refusal, David wasted no time registering his displeasure. He hit the road on the fourth day of his visit, his worldly possessions stashed in the one suitcase he owned, without a word of where he was headed. Most of us returned home and found him gone.

Over the following months, my parents were worried about David's disappearance. For eight years in boarding school, no one had visited him. Schools had no provision for African parents' visits in those days. The first time David left for boarding school, he accompanied Simon Mburu, Alan's son and a former classmate at the one-room Kwa-Ndege's Primary School.

Except for Aunt Julia, my parents had never met anyone who knew David outside our village, or knew where to look for him.

# Chapter 21

# The Kennedy Airlift

Living in Solai, as you might have gathered, was equivalent to living in a cave, separated from the outside world, with only tidbits of authentic news seeping in now and then. Without newspapers, TV, or radio, we received news and gossip by word of mouth through school, an occasional visitor, or a letter.

Otherwise, the news that governed our lives came from the people who wielded the power and had the means to control all the caves. They decided which cave received which information, when, and how much.

By early 1960, through those authoritative sources, we learned that the colonial government had long hanged Dedan Kimathi [Dedan Kĩmaathi], the leader of the Mau Mau freedom fighters.

When the colonizers captured him on October 20, 1956, we lived in our old fenced village across Tindaress River. A plane dropped leaflets inside our village showing a topless handcuffed man in dreadlocks, his torso slightly propped on his back in a hospital bed. I picked up a stray flyer, but since I wasn't attending school yet, I couldn't read it. The image seemed scary. I tossed the flyer to get it off my mind.

In the following days, I learned through the village pipeline that the colonial government had captured "the biggest terrorist."

With curfew, restrictions, and illiteracy, the news didn't cause a ripple. I never even heard when they hanged him four months later, on February 18, 1957. Villagers were in total surrender mode.

The masses in towns and Kikuyuland, closer to the news or in the thick of war, who never knew what the next day would bring, had their hopes dashed. To them, Kĩmaathi's death had signaled that the British had overwhelmed the Mau Mau and minimized any possibility of a return of their alienated lands and independence.

But there is a Gĩkũyũ proverb that says: mũteng'erio na mũteng'erania gũtirĩ ũtahũmaga. (The chaser and the chased both get tired.)

As it turned out, the colonized weren't the only ones worn out by the war. By the end of 1960, to the colonizers, the natives had become tiresome and a nuisance; the Mau Mau freedom fighters had dug in, no matter how many of them died. Behind the scenes, the colonizers' representatives and those of the colonized engaged in discussions on how to phase out natives' servitude and possible future independence.

However, the parties faced a challenge. Colonization had held diverse Kenyan ethnic communities together. But with independence, would the current system of a central government hold? There was a likelihood that the natives would gravitate toward autonomy. That meant forty-plus former pre-colonial independent micronations (now tribes) with distinct languages and cultures. How would the country function?

The men privy to such discussions determined that for Kenya to operate as an independent nation without slipping into anarchy, it needed more educated Africans, not only to fill the political and administrative posts that the British would vacate but also to run and unify the country under a single African central government.

That monumental task wasn't lost to the Americans.

Through funding from the Joseph P. Kennedy Foundation, Senator J.F. Kennedy (later to become the 35th President of the

United States), Andrew Young (who later became mayor of Atlanta, Georgia), Harry Belafonte (Singer and human rights activist), other well-wishers, and the United States State Department organized scholarships with universities across the USA for promising students in newly or about-to-be-formed African nations. Besides helping the emerging African states, this gave the United States a say in Kenya's operations and policies, and access to a new emerging market.

Dr. Gĩkonyo Kĩano and Tom Mboya, who would later become Kenyan cabinet ministers (senators), had already attended universities in the United States. They then played a central role in coordinating with the Americans regarding scholarships for Kenyan students.

Records show that about 600 young Kenyan men and women (But according to Wanjirū Kamau, PhD, one of the scholarship recipients, the group comprised 900 young men and 100 young women) received scholarships and flew to the United States for further studies.

That group—dubbed the "Kennedy Airlift"—included the Harvard-educated economist Barack H. Obama Sr., PhD (whose son would decades later become the 44th President of the United States) and Wangari Maathai, PhD, who became a science professor at the University of Nairobi, a member of parliament, and later won the Nobel Peace Prize for spearheading the Green Belt Movement.

After their studies, the former students couldn't return home fast enough to help build Kenya. David Njeru Warama wasn't among them.

My dear parents had no way of knowing the details of such matters that David had won such a highly esteemed scholarship, the only one in the entire school. I doubt David had explained to them, besides asking for money.

When finalizing this book, I asked him why the 3,000 shillings. He stammered, fishing for an answer before he said he didn't know.

But back then, after he received the scholarship award, he said, the officials told him he only needed to pay 3,000 shillings for the scholarship expenses. But about 86, I suspected the details David remembered—if there were any—had become fuzzy.

The amount was likely for his air ticket. However, the scholarship provided travel, education, and a full board. Or it was David's entire pocket money for his three-year university stay.

Whatever the case, according to Mami, within one year of David's disappearance, Baba regretted his decision many times over and blamed himself for his son's desertion. Mami claimed Baba had enough money saved at the post office to afford the amount.

My parents endured the agony of their lost son for three years before we learned what happened to him.

# Chapter 22

# Big Family Lonely People

I can't say I missed David when he left. We had nothing in common. I had grown up without him. Even when he came home for school holidays, he never associated with us, his younger siblings, typical of adults in that era. From his late teens, he stopped coming home during school holidays. He likely went to Aunt Julia's or his classmates' homes.

That was the story of our family, a big family of lonely, independent individuals. Things were different with my parents in my early years, when Baba ran his own business dealing in hides and skins and tobacco. He processed and sold hides and skins himself. With tobacco, he grew, harvested, and dried it, and then Mami processed it into snuff.

Two Sundays a month, they interacted on their way to Kabazi or Bahati markets, where they sold their wares. Mami sold the snuff in scoops of tiny spoons, while Baba sold hides and skins. When they returned home, Mami counted the money and handed every penny to Baba as a depositor would do at a bank.

Things changed when I turned eight years old. Mami got an "Awakening" in the wee hours one night. In the morning, she claimed Jesus had visited her and said all her sins would be forgiven and cleansed if she repented. She went to church, repented her sins, became a Christian, and quit the "sinful" tobacco business.

With no one to process snuff, the tobacco business soon collapsed. Disillusioned, Baba abandoned the hides and skins business, although Mami hadn't played a part in it.

Her adopting a foreign religion and quitting the business traumatized Baba so much that he accused her of being an undisciplined wife who had taken over his homestead. He set out to punish her.

One Sunday afternoon, Mami returned from church. On her way to the granary to get supplies to cook our lunch, Baba, who had been drinking beer since mid-morning, something he had never done before, rushed toward Mami in the courtyard, calling her an undisciplined wife. He tried to slap her. Whenever he threw a slap, his drunken body went along. As he tried to recover his balance, he swayed this way and that. Realizing he might end up on the ground, he gave up on trying to hit her and instead hammered Mami's new tea mugs into wrecks.

In Baba's eyes, he and his wife were even. They made peace and reinvented themselves as a devout Christian wife and a traditional Gĩkũyũ husband. They managed their family through a symbiotic relationship, but went nowhere together again.

We children followed suit. Except for the family chores, the checker games we loved to play, and our evening banter around the fire pit with our mother, we did our activities independently and never knew each other's whereabouts. We didn't snitch on each other; we handled our personal issues. For instance, I heard an occasional girl tell a boy who was bullying her, "Wait until I tell my brother he'll pound you like your mother pounds maize."

Although no boy attacked me, I don't recall thinking I could issue such a threat.

Even later, as teenagers, after we changed schools, I couldn't keep up with Joseph when we walked home. Many times, I walked to or from school alone.

I saw many animals on the way, mostly birds, insects, and other small animals. Fortunately, the more dangerous animals that supposedly lived on Jumatatu Mountain never came close to human paths. And the snakes didn't like the cooler high altitude; they preferred the warmer climate, starting a mile out in the savanna.

At one time, on the slopes of the mountain range, right in the middle of the thicket of hundreds of tree wannabes and undergrowth, I spotted a beige/black/white owl. I watched in awe when it swiveled its head to the back. It was the most beautiful bird I have ever seen, despite my family and community believing its cries—like coyotes'—were a bad omen signaling imminent death.

On another day, near the same spot where a predator could have waylaid someone, a form appeared mysteriously smack in the middle of the pathway, about ten feet away. I faced one of Major Miller's wolf-like, fierce German shepherds. Besides fame and hearing their WOOFS from afar, I had never seen the duo. I stopped, unsure of what to do. We faced each other calmly, with no sign of hostility, likely telepathically sizing one another. I can't guess what went through the dog's mind, but my mind was empty, void of thought or panic. Finally, the dog kept its mean ego in check, yielded the right of way, and disappeared into the woods.

The highlight was a scrawny old two-legged animal seated on a jutting stone on the side of the rocky road before the turnoff to the footpath home. After I passed by and reached about fifteen feet ahead, the old man called out to me. When I turned, he flashed and fondled his long-retired private member and invited me to touch it. I stared at him, confused about what to say. Conditioned to treat old people with deference, I kept my lips sealed. I felt sorry for him and embarrassed for his family. I wrinkled my face, turned, and continued downhill.

I never mentioned the pervert to anyone, but not because I thought it was a secret. The incident was as if I had tripped and steadied myself.

# Chapter 23

# Sports & Leisure

Despite toiling on colonial plantations and enduring adults' tyranny, we children seized moments of quality when we could. We watched the lively "sinful" dances by the Tugen tribe, which the school and church forbade, played checkers and hopscotch, and visited the riverbank where we feasted on ngoe—a cherry-like fruit—from a gigantic tree and swung across the river hanging on its vines like acrobats.

One afternoon, my vine broke, I tumbled down, and my brain shut off on impact. When I came to, my friends had abandoned me, and the sun had gone below the horizon; I shivered with a bruised body but intact bones. That trauma ended my acrobatic feats, but my river drop-ins lived on.

Soon, I joined village girls at the river. We hand-washed our clothes, and while they dried spread on the riverbank, we skinny-dipped and created quite a racket, splashing water and shrieking with unbridled excitement. I also learned how to awaken my flat, dormant chest.

A girl in our group told us the bites of njereri—black, roach-like insects—nudged breasts to sprout faster. At every skinny dip, we hunted the slippery, hard-to-catch njereri. When I caught one and held it by its head, I couldn't get it to take a single bite, no matter how much I tried to force it. But one lucky day, I coaxed one to nibble on my left nipple.

On the day I searched for a candidate for my right nipple, determined to even out the magic, I focused on one of the biggest njereri yet; when I realized our boisterous chatter only came from a handful of girls, I sensed someone was watching us. I shut up and raised my head. A woman standing on the riverbank was observing us. We all fell quiet as we darted to the deeper end and squatted, submerged to our shoulders. We gawked at the woman and waited. Soon, we learned the woman had eavesdropped long enough to hear our self-help secret.

"Njereri will make your breasts grow," she said to my internal glee. "But wait until you become an adult; your breasts will get large and saggy and flap on your thighs while you walk."

I shuddered when I imagined a woman bent over from the weight of her gourd-size, flappy breasts.

I doubt the woman told our mothers because I never heard of it, nor did a single girl mention njereri again.

Three years later, when my body was ready to welcome the sprout, the woman's words arose to haunt me. The left bump that received njereri treatment swelled and was painful to the touch, but the right one stayed dormant.

I agonized about why the new bump hurt and its projected future flapping against my thigh. By then, my cohorts had dropped out of school, and I had changed schools. I had no close friend to whom I could discuss or entrust such intimate matters. I could only worry alone in silence. It took another month before the right side started its own journey. But it failed to catch up with its twin, doomed to remain the laggard.

*

In Tindaress Primary, my first school, we had forty minutes of physical education at mid-morning every school day. Besides PE and running, we started playing sports in grade three. The boys played soccer (football) while the girls played basketball (netball). All genders played volleyball and tennikoit.

On two occasions, teams from other schools came to compete with us. I competed in netball and tennikoit. I never became competent in volleyball. I feared getting hurt and avoided the ball when players at the net jumped and hit it with such ferocity that it could injure a weak player.

As a sore loser, I stressed so much about winning I never enjoyed playing in competitions; I even got angry. I preferred to join the spectators. When I did so, we got so involved in cheering our team that we acted out throws or kicks, hollering at the top of our voices.

At another time, Solai and Bahati area schools held a sports meet at Njeki's Shopping Center. My sister Tabitha competed in track and field and won second place. Although Baba attended the occasion, he never went to the crowded field to watch her run. Instead, he waited in a bar. When I came across him at the center, I sensed he had drunk some alcohol because he had a brief conversation with me about sports, and he told me about Tabitha's win. It was the one time I saw Baba glow with pride. "My daughter won!" He said to a man close by.

The boys who won received pens, ink, and exercise books, while the girls received dishes. Tabitha took home two pots, a pan, and two bowls. None of us considered it odd.

Although I never thought about it, I valued school sports, perhaps because, as I grew older, my home playtime got less and less. Adults expected girls my age to phase out of "childish" plays like hopscotch or jump rope. After my chores, I started playing checkers with my brothers, an acceptable activity because adult males played the game.

But I was a mere follower, Joseph the trendsetter. He had cut a cardboard square, drawn squares with charcoal, and used Coca-Cola bottle tops as chips. Any top was acceptable, but Coke tops were more available. He collected the "chips" one by one, from

Njeki's, from Patel's General Store when my parents sent him, or anywhere he found one.

Joseph became so skilled in checkers that he played with champion boys in our old fenced village across the river.

Mami always seemed to call us at the height of our game when so few slots remained, and one wrong move guaranteed a loss. Her voice rang through our courtyard, loud enough for our close neighbors to hear her. She even named the chore one of us hadn't completed. If I played away from home, I recoiled when I heard her shout my name. Embarrassed, I abandoned my teammates and rushed home so she would hush.

Other times, I played with two of my siblings, and because we expected Mami to interfere, we played behind her house, seated on the ground. When we heard her voice, we shut our mouths and moved chips until a winner emerged. Afterward, if it were me she had called, I skirted the homestead and entered the court-yard as if I had come from the outside.

Later, after Joseph and I changed schools and the country re-laxed its restrictions, more entertainment came our way, where Mami couldn't interfere.

# Chapter 24

# School Chores

Our rectangular thatch-and-dirt school building stood several yards from the Nakuru-Solai Road. It comprised three classrooms, with only one main door on the narrow front. From the threshold, one could see straight to the back wall of a tiny, narrow, elongated enclosure where teachers stored books.

The senior class occupied the classroom next to the door, and grade three occupied the middle. The corridor divided the two classrooms into front and back sections. Grades one and two used the corridor to get to the extra big classroom at the back, which they alternated—grade one in the afternoons and grade two in the mornings.

The large classroom doubled as a church on Sundays, and churchgoers filled only half the room.

Why such a large room, then? While writing this book, the reason occurred to me.

The classroom filled up in grade one. But by mid-grade two, the pupils started dropping out. By grade three, half of them had dropped out, mainly because—especially the girls—they started school too late and found it hard to fit in with much younger children. Others dropped out because parents could no longer afford school fees.

By grade four, the twenty-five to thirty pupils strutted with an air of superiority. They seemed unapproachable when I was in grades one and two. Not to disturb them, I tiptoed down the corridor.

In grade three, I couldn't get to grade four fast enough. When I got there, some of my classmates were practically young men, many from the previous year, after they failed the national standardized test. But there were no young women—they had already dropped out. The few girls who remained were about my age. I was thirteen, a small-sized thirteen.

Besides school fees, girls dropped out of school for lack of money to manage menstruation or sexual harassment from classmates or, perhaps, a predatory teacher. I went through such an experience myself during an incident in our agriculture "classroom."

*

On Fridays, each pupil in grades three and four brought an old metal one-gallon paint bucket—before plastics came to Solai— to draw water from a stream half a mile away. The water was for the school's general cleanup—sweeping the classrooms and the front yard.

Our feet had compacted the classrooms' floors so well that we only needed to sprinkle water sparingly with our hands before we swept.

But we swept without sprinkling water on our dust-ridden front yard, where we held our morning assembly. On windy days, the dust sailed wild and became riotous. None of us minded. We romped through the dust as we shrieked, giggled, and rushed this way and that with our twig brooms.

The head prefect, as rigid as the teachers, complained about the dust and scolded us, perhaps to curb our unbridled racket. Soon, the school made changes. It required us to sprinkle water on the front yard as well. It took the water-drawing team several trips to the stream a quarter of a mile away. None of us minded the chores, though. We enjoyed the social aspect of it and did the work with much excitement.

But garden work was a different story.

The school had an agriculture subject. We learned the art of cultivation, terracing land, and composting. Our "classroom" was a good-sized garden behind the teachers' cottages.

The school grew maize, beans, tomatoes, and other vegetables. Where the harvest went is anyone's guess. Most likely, the teachers consumed it and gave out the surplus.

I didn't care one bit about the class. Like my fellow pupils, by the time the school introduced the subject, I had done more than my fair share of cultivation in our own garden. As for the compost manure, it wasn't practical in our situation, and we had no use for terraces on flat land.

One afternoon during our agriculture lesson, Watakū, our timekeeper and a prefect, supervised for the day. When pupils finished their portions, he dismissed them. When I finished mine, he inspected it and said I had left weeds. He told two other pupils the same.

I rushed back and quickly yanked out the few stray weeds I saw. Whether he re-checked the other two pupils' patches, I don't know, but he dismissed them as I returned to where he stood. He then turned toward me. "Go finish your portion," he said.

He had not even rechecked it.

The area he directed me to had maize stalks taller than me.

"I did it. Go check," I said.

The young man tried to speak, but his lower lip trembled. He closed his mouth and stared.

I wondered about his behavior and looked at him some more. His eyes were red and dilated. I couldn't figure out what the matter was with him. But a wave of fear washed through me. I started backing off toward the shorter maize plants. When he didn't object or follow me, I turned, hurried away, and ran toward the school. Later, I made sure I stayed out of his way.

He never reported me for defying him.

# Chapter 25

# Grade Four

Mr. Kimani, the headmaster, taught most of our grade four subjects and conducted the school choir, an ensemble of grades three and four. By grade four, he had declared me a non-musician when he ejected me from the choir after I mangled too many notes, unaware that his tiptoeing around listening for a misstep was hostile to my vocal cords.

Except for two altercations with older males, Mr. Kimani rarely caned us pupils; he never caned me. About forty years old, he wore knee-length tan shorts, shirt sleeves folded, and an inch of hair parted on the left. He walked with confidence and purpose, upright like a soldier, a presence that stopped any racket when he passed by or deterred "bad" behavior.

He explained his lessons well with clear, elegant blackboard writing. Some pupils always needed extra clarification but felt embarrassed or afraid to ask. When Mr. Kimani found out during question or test time, sometimes it ended with him swinging a cane.

Whatever went on around me, however, especially in our last term, I never got distracted. I focused on the Common Entrance Examination (CEE) in November 1960 so I could pass and attend a boarding school. Because certain subjects still confused or challenged me, I nursed a nagging feeling I wouldn't do well on that make-or-break national test.

Close to the test date, I crammed and memorized the notes in my exercise books, as I had with the multiplication tables in grade two.

On test day, I breezed through arithmetic and Kiswahili sections. But, without multiple-choice questions and no grasp of civics, history, English language, or composition, I muddled through the rest of the test.

Afterward, I clung to the hope my correct answers outweighed the wrong ones.

*

The CEE results came out in January 1961. A negligible number of pupils passed, including Priscilla Wanjikũ Kĩai from Gĩtũra, one of the two villages of neighboring Major Stein's farm, who is my sister-in-law today. My brother Joseph and I were not among the "lucky" few.

It was Joseph's second time to fail, a precarious situation for him because he had turned sixteen, the same age the school had aged out our older brother Simon.

The failure rattled me. I might never step into grade five, I thought. It would doom me to the life of a peasant, a farmhand. I envied Wanjikũ. How could she pass? I asked myself. In my recollection, she didn't do better than me in class. It didn't matter—she was a special girl headed to boarding school while I remained a village girl. We never saw each other again until she married Simon in the mid-1970s.

Between the test results and the opening of schools, I remained in limbo, unsure whether Baba would allow me to repeat grade four. Perhaps he would tell me to join Mami in the fields. The thought alone made me shudder.

While Joseph and I stressed, neither Baba nor Mami mentioned our failures. Our only option for schooling was to repeat grade four, but Baba had the final say—and he wasn't talking.

Meanwhile, I learned that a handful of parents in the village were angry that their children had failed the exam. They claimed Tindaress Primary School offered substandard education and that the teachers taught their children poorly—hence the mass failure.

I doubt the teachers were to blame. They followed the required curriculum and were strict about it. I now wonder how the Ministry of Education expected us to understand subjects like civics—that we started in grade three—let alone pass them after only two years of instruction. Other than Kamunge and now Major Miller, ordering their workers or parents to manage their households, I had no concept of a government.

The test required us to read passages and paraphrase—rewrite them in our own words, they said—or answer questions in English after just two years of learning the language. But besides our forty-minute English lessons, we had never spoken English or heard anyone do it in the village.

Without books to read or practice at home other than the one book the teacher read to us in grades one and two, or the occasional easy, low-content books we had shared and he collected at the end of each lesson, from grade three, we relied entirely on whatever our teachers wrote on the blackboard.

Mr. Kimani didn't even bring a book to class. He taught math and English from memory. I never saw or read a book in grades three and four.

But parents didn't know those details. All they knew was that most pupils failed the standardized national tests year after year. I never learned what triggered the parents this time because failure was the norm. Perhaps they merely reached a tipping point, or we were a bigger class than the previous ones, and more of us had failed. Whatever the reason, more parents joined the activists, and our entire village became restless. Parents complained they paid school fees and a building fund, but their children kept on failing. They were done with improving Tindaress Primary School; they wanted their children out of that "poor school."

We learned the details from Mami. Baba left the activism to her, as he had always done for village relationships. I recall feeling vindicated and thankful for her involvement and that of all those parents who had raised the alarm, although it hadn't occurred to me that I attended a poor school.

I wondered what the activism would accomplish. What was Tindaress Primary supposed to do? Joseph and I had two school options on the other side of Jumatatu Mountain Range. One was Ol Donyo Mara Primary School at Major Stein's neighboring farm, three miles away, and the other Kabazi Primary School at Major Ward's farm, a mile farther.

Because of the shorter distance, we favored Ol Donyo Mara. We didn't care that it was a Catholic school and that we would change from an Anglican Church affiliation to another catechism study ritual, now in Latin.

For a headmaster to admit anyone, however, he required prospective pupils to take signed transfer forms and letters of recommendation from their previous school headmaster. But when Joseph asked Tindaress for our transfers, Mr. Kimani had already stopped issuing them because it gave the school a bad reputation.

We panicked. If we returned to Tindaress, he knew we didn't want to attend his school and might victimize us.

Meanwhile, schools opened. I spent the next two weeks in a state of pure panic. I resisted the thought that the failure had dashed my aspirations to quit the village. As much as I racked my brain, no alternatives came to mind. I was stuck with no way out.

# Chapter 26

# Better Prospects

"When one door closes, another opens," the proverb says. When Tindaress Primary closed its door, with trepidation, Joseph and I waited for our door to open. It turned out that it was closer than we thought, thanks to Simon Mbũrũ, Alan's son. He and my brother David had attended a one-room school together at Kwa-Ndege's farm. Although they had followed separate paths as adults, they had been close in their youth.

In 1953, only two pupils passed the Common Entrance Examination—Simon Mbũrũ and "Unknown." Mr. Jacob Rũrĩrĩ, the headmaster, "knew" who the unknown student was based on his pupils' performance.

As my parents later learned, Mr. Rũrĩrĩ had traveled to Nakuru Town to consult with the Ministry of Education and to verify.

When the officials gave Mr. Rũrĩrĩ the unknown student's exam papers, he confirmed from the handwriting that they were David's; he had merely forgotten to write his name. The headmaster petitioned the Ministry and even offered to take in David's exercise book so they could compare the handwriting. The officials turned down the petition. David repeated grade four while Simon Mbũrũ joined Kijabe Full Primary School.

The following year, David aced the common entrance exam again and, this time, remembered to insert his name. He joined Simon Mbũrũ at Kijabe, about a hundred miles from home.

David finished four years at Kijabe and entered Kabete Technical School for another four years. During that time, he preferred to hang out at Aunt Julia's, who was then working as a nurse in Nairobi, instead of coming home. To top it all, he had disappeared when Baba refused to give him 3,000 shillings. David knew little about us, his siblings. The villagers knew his name, but they couldn't relate to him. He wasn't of the village.

But Simon Mbūrū was of the village. He had taken a different route. After completing his four years at Kijabe, he went to a two-year teacher training college and trained to become a primary school teacher. By the time of Tindaress School's mass failure, Simon Mbūrū had been teaching at some school for several years.

When we moved to the low-security village where we then lived, the Alan family became our immediate neighbors. During school holidays, Simon Mbūrū had a rectangular cottage built on the western side of his father's homestead—a two-bedroom with a living room in the center. The cottage was built of wood and compacted mud, and whitewashed on the inside. On the rare occasion a family in the village had a guest, they sought free lodging from Simon Mbūrū—his house was the only one good enough to accommodate a visitor.

He was the only farm-born and raised pride of the village. Elders eyed him as an example of their hope for their sons. (David had enjoyed that status before he abdicated it when he stopped coming to the village.) Simon Mbūrū spent four nights at the school residence, returned home on Fridays, and left on Monday mornings. He was of the village.

Unknown to us, Simon Mbūrū had transferred to Kabazi Primary School the previous year to be closer to his parents. Mami learned of this through his mother, Elithi, whom she had told about our school dilemma. Whatever the two women concluded, Mami conferred with Baba and, afterward, paid a visit to Elithi (a mangled Alice).

I knew of Elithi in our previous fenced village because of her mother-in-law, Mama Alan, who offered free massages to sick children. But it was only in the last year and a half, when our families became neighbors, that I got to know Elithi. She and Mami had become close friends. Besides, they were mothers of the only progressive sons in the village—although Mami likely wished David were like Simon Mbūrū and had kept ties with home.

During the visit, Elithi agreed to talk to her son when he came home that weekend. She would ask him to recommend Joseph and me to the headmaster of Kabazi Primary School and to admit us without transfer forms.

*

There wasn't anything else for us to do except fret and wait. Fortunately, it wasn't planting or gardening season, although I had to carry firewood on my back and do other home chores instead of going to school. Because of my unstructured schedule, I already missed Tindaress Primary.

I hated that our teachers had caned us, forced us to attend Sunday school, or prohibited us from watching the native Tugen dances when we lived in our old fenced village. But those details seemed unimportant; I just wanted to go to school.

Much later, I learned our teachers were repeating what they had experienced themselves. They had attended missionary schools where teachers followed the British system of tyrannical masters who believed in not sparing the rod. I had never heard of any instance where the Gīkūyū community beat their children while they taught them.

Only two incidents stained my nostalgia for the school. The first happened in grade one, when solving horizontal addition in arithmetic mystified me. After two weeks in the doldrums, something clicked, and I solved the additions. The teacher accused me of copying from my neighbor and brushed aside my denial.

The second incident happened a year later, when Mũthee, my nine-year-old half-nephew, who was two years younger than me, failed to do his homework. The same teacher shaved a cross through my hair to punish me because, according to him, I should have reminded my half-nephew to do his homework. At the time, the Waigwas lived at our homestead after they returned from Kikuyuland.

Otherwise, the four years I spent at Tindaress Primary, especially in grades one and two, were the only time I could say I was happy in school without external pressures.

But that was mere history; I was now anxious, hoping and waiting for positive news from Elithi.

# Chapter 27

# Kabazi Primary School

Elithi came through. Or should I say Simon Mbŭrŭ came through? He spoke to his boss, Mr. Kamau, the headmaster, who gave Joseph and me a nod without the precious transfer papers.

Toward the end of January 1961, Joseph and I joined a few pupils who had joined Kabazi Primary School in the lower grades.

Behind our homestead, we took a footpath from the dirt road and progressively climbed and wove eastward through trees, thicket, and underbrush for about a mile. It then emptied into a rocky, murram road that traversed one of Jumatatu Mountain's valleys. The road was so rocky that vehicles and the farm tractor rarely used it. Once in a while, Major Stein drove on it in his Range Rover.

Even then, it was hazardous for drivers, and when a driver used it, he took extra care while the vehicle dipped and rose as he navigated around rough and smooth jutting rocks. When road workers blasted and chiseled the mountainside, they couldn't break many rocks into murram.

In one rare incident, Major Stein's tractor driver dodged a rock and over-corrected. He lost control. The tractor veered off the road and rolled downhill, ejecting him. He fell in front of the tractor, and it rolled over him.

With vehicle ownership limited to landowners who lived miles apart, accidents were so rare that it took another decade before I heard of another vehicle fatality.

When we came to that road on our first morning, we cursed our luck, especially when we accidentally stepped on sharp rocks that hurt our bare feet.

About two months later, when the rains came, we preferred that part of the road to the sludge we plowed through non-murram parts.

The road meandered along the mountain ridge and turned into a pure dirt road before it joined the Nakuru-Subukia Road. We then walked southeast for about a mile to Kabazi Primary School.

The entire walk stretched about four miles, but the morning walk felt like five because a third of it was uphill.

Kabazi Primary School was in a small strip center where people held an open-air market on Sundays. My parents had previously sold tobacco and hides and skins there before Mami became a Christian and quit the "sinful" business. I had never visited the Center before.

The school was a weathered, historic cathedral-like edifice built of masonry stone, situated yards from the Nakuru-Subukia Road. It looked like a monastery. I would learn later that there was no other building like it for miles, perhaps in town.

Over the years, I learned from Kabazi farm residents that Major Ward, the farm owner, with other European landowners in the area, built the relic as an Anglican Church in 1926.

In 1942, the congregation—the British landowners and their families—moved their church north to a farm we called Sidai Farm. In need of literate Africans to help with record-keeping or to run his shop, Major Ward converted the vacated cathedral building into an adult school and a Sunday church for his farm workers.

The men attended adult classes—reading and writing—after work, and those who converted to Christianity attended church on Sundays.

In early 1950s, about the time the colonial governor declared a state of emergency in the country and landowners corralled their workers into villages, Major Ward converted the building to a regular primary school, starting with grade one and finally reaching grade four, the level Joseph and I found it in 1961.

A two-foot-high concrete wall, set three feet from the foundation, surrounded the building like a moat. The area between the wall and the building was always damp, with patches of green moss.

A set of wide stairs led from the public road to the main double-door entrance. The doors stayed shut, likely because the parishioners became tired of climbing the steep stairs. We entered through one of the rusty, heavy double doors on the south side of the building, similar to the ones I later saw depicted in movies from old Roman dungeons.

The interior walls had no plaster, but the stones were well-chiseled. It also had pretty stained-glass windows. The concrete floor resembled cobblestones, and the roof was wood-shingled. Temporary foldable partitions of skinny reed sticks, about six feet high, divided the interior into four classrooms. We swept floors on Fridays, and the strong boys rolled and removed the partitions, ready for church service on Sundays

With minimal maintenance, the building looked aged. It looked nothing like it looked decades ago when it was a whites-only domain with staff to maintain it.

The overwhelming atmosphere of the "cathedral" made me dislike it the first time I entered. The ceiling was so high, perhaps twenty-five feet or higher. I wondered how builders climbed that high to install the wood roofing. Lighting came only from the big stained-glass windows, which remained shut tight. If the building had other lighting fixtures before, I couldn't tell.

On gloomy days (Kabazi area had a more temperate climate than Solai), the classrooms turned dreary, cold, and depressing.

The building seemed like a haunted house; the bright days couldn't lighten it enough.

But I liked the school because there was minimal maintenance required. The garden was smaller than that of Tindaress Primary School, and with no dirt floors or dusty front yard, we didn't have to fetch water to tame the dust while we swept. The only downside was that because Kabazi Primary had been a church, it lacked enough land. We had no PE or sports.

About fifty yards to the east stood teachers' quarters. They enjoyed views of the school, Kabazi Canners factory, a sprawl of orchards, and Jumatatu Mountain Ridge far to the west.

Mr. Kamau, the headmaster, and his family occupied a two-bedroom concrete row house. About 15 yards away, next to it, was a duplex that housed two teachers. The last unit was a house that Simon Mbũrũ shared with a fellow teacher. When I later entered the house, I realized it was a replica of his Solai house.

Except for Mr. Kamau, the other teachers were all bachelors.

I don't recall feeling like a new pupil, perhaps because Joseph and I joined the same class. Except for the stories I heard of the occasional boys' fight on their way home, pupils teased one another in jest but never bullied each other. Teachers did enough of that.

I planned to spend only one year at Kabazi, time enough to pass the national exam and attend a boarding school in grade five in 1962. I pledged to myself: *if three pupils in my class pass the Common Entrance Exam, I'll be one of them.* That plan stayed with me. It was the only purpose of transferring to Kabazi.

I failed to factor in teachers' power over us pupils, which sometimes interfered with our learning. This got settled within two months when Simon Mbũrũ named his desired payback for helping Joseph and me join the school.

# Chapter 28

# Cook and Delivery Boy

Like other landowners, Major Miller sold his milk and butter-cream to Kenya Creameries. He gave each of his permanent employees half a quart of skim milk, which people called mathache. Because it was too watery, people didn't feed that milk to their children. Instead, they used it for tea or porridge.

To help mothers leave their babies at home while they went to work, Major Miller offered to sell their husbands whole milk on credit and deduct the cost from their wages at the end of each month.

I didn't learn how much he charged for a bottle of milk, but people complained the monthly charge equaled casual employees' monthly wages. Besides our neighbor, I never heard of anyone else signing up.

Simon Mbũrũ, our benefactor, signed up for one bottle of whole milk through his father, Alan Kĩbui. It was then Elithi's task to figure out how her son would get the milk. She solicited Mami for a milk carrier. That was how families conducted many of their transactions in the village. Depending on the transactions, the women decided—they knew which transactions to consult their husbands about, or acted as their husbands' intermediaries. I'm not sure whether Elithi's request qualified for consultation, or if Mami merely mentioned it to Baba after she agreed. Most likely, she did. We, children, didn't qualify for consultation.

After our parents settled the matter, Joseph became a milk delivery boy, and I became the lunchtime cook for Simon Mbũrũ and his roommate. We didn't complain about the extra duties. After all, we owed Simon Mbũrũ for our school admission and were merely returning a favor. Each morning, five days a week, Joseph detoured to catch up with us later, passed by the dairy next to the cow-dip pen, picked up a bottle of milk from Mr. Warũgũ, the head milkman, and deposited it on Simon Mbũrũ's doorstep at school. I felt pity for Joseph.

My cooking job is special; I told myself before that those thoughts would turn out just the opposite. I felt honored to have a teacher who had attended the same boarding school as my brother—I considered them friends. And the teacher's parents were our neighbors!

Under the new arrangement, I mused, I would eat better food at the teacher's house. Just like Mami ladled our food into various portions if Simon Mbũrũ didn't object, which I believed he wouldn't, I planned to do the same—carve for myself a share of whatever I cooked for the two teachers. What an honor to eat at Simon Mbũrũ's house!

After teachers dismissed the classes for the one-hour lunch period, pupils rushed outdoors. Those who lived at Kabazi farm went home for lunch. The ones from farms farther out gravitated toward their lunch groups with whom they shared lunch, which they carried in small kĩondo bags. Instead of joining other pupils, I headed to Simon Mbũrũ's house for my culinary duties.

On my first day, Simon Mbũrũ gave me a quick orientation tour through a little circular kitchen shack beside his house. It contained a small wooden cupboard with two shelves against the wall. Inside were three pots, four white-coated aluminum plates, some mugs, spoons, and a flat spatula called mwiko. The other items were a paraffin Primus pressure stove at the center, a matchbox beside it, and a low bench. It surprised me how basic the kitchen looked.

When we finished the tour, Simon Mbūrū asked me to follow him to the big house. On entering, I noticed it resembled his own house at the farm, a two-bedroom with a sitting room in the middle. The sitting room contained a four-chair dining table at the center and a cupboard for bigger dishes next to the wall.

He supplied me with one bowl of maize flour and another one of stew ingredients—vegetables, oil, and salt. Rumors said Major Miller's wife did something similar: she weighed the ingredients on a scale daily before she gave them to the cook, who nonetheless ended up with a well-rounded body.

To cook, I lit the pressure stove and pumped it until it made a swooshing sound, so loud I could hardly hear anyone calling from outdoors.

I first cooked the stew, which I soon learned was the standard fare, sometimes with the barest ingredients of onions, tomatoes, oil, and salt. I saw meat only once or twice during my culinary career. I put the stew aside, then boiled water, and slowly poured in the maize meal as I stirred and cooked *ugali*.

Although I rarely cooked at home, by then, from watching Mami cook, I could whip ugali to the right consistency for our household if Mami were absent. So, cooking ugali for the two teachers wasn't a hard chore. I patted the ugali with the *mwiko* (wooden spatula). If it didn't stick to the mwiko, it was done. I flipped the ugali pot over onto a plate, ending up with a mound shaped like the pot.

By then, aware of the smells and impatient, my stomach growled. I chastised myself for forgetting my station in life, for thinking Simon Mbūrū would care about me like I believed my brother would. Well, what was I going to do? It was all on me. I decided it made no difference even if I carved off a little piece.

But the mound seemed too small for two men, I thought, attempting to talk myself out of tasting it.

Whatever!

While I patted the ugali with a mwiko like a cake for better presentation, I trimmed and ate a swallow or two. I never exceeded two swallows. Often, I settled for a single one. It was plain, packaged, store-bought refined maize flour and water, but it tasted delicious, "better" than our healthier ugali that we made at home from coarse, unrefined flour.

During my cooking stint, before Simon Mbũrũ and I reached a stage where we would have strangled each other if we could, I ate no lunch. I fumed the closer my last morning lesson neared the lunch hour.

Initially, I never disclosed this to my family. Neither did I tell the other pupils who, by the envious looks they gave me, oblivious to my ashen skin and sluggish body, believed I was lucky to eat at a teacher's house.

# Chapter 29

# The Hazards of Mavuno Day

In the second term, Mr. Kamau, the headmaster, taught us math during our last lesson before lunch. Instead of instructions on Fridays, he gave us a test. "You'll harvest what you saw during the week," he said at the beginning of each Friday lesson.

Pupils dubbed Fridays *Mavuno* Day (harvest day). Each day during our arithmetic lesson, our class counted days to Fridays, not because of the weekend as we had done previously, but because of Mavuno Day. The day became so noteworthy and terrifying that it overrode my concern about passing the national common entrance exam. Instead, my pledge became immediate—to pass the Friday test and escape Mr. Kamau's wrath.

The test comprised five long-division math problems. On one Friday, he included the classic one about calculating the speed and meeting point of two trains traveling from opposite directions.

After the test, Mr. Kamau had us exchange our papers with our neighbors behind us. Because we sat two at a desk, he didn't trust the neighbors we shared desks with. He then solved the problems on the blackboard.

Meanwhile, a pile of canes up to an inch in diameter, cut from young trees, lay in wait on his table in front.

After he finished solving the problems, and pupils tallied answers and returned the papers to their owners, Mr. Kamau said to prepare for the "harvest."

Each wrong answer counted for two lashes. But anyone who solved a problem correctly avoided punishment altogether. It never occurred to me, and I bet to my classmates, that we dealt with undemocratic and abusive system as we meekly resigned ourselves to the punishment. We had accepted insults and assaults from parents and teachers as normal.

The boys formed a line in front to receive their harvest, and the girls did the same. Mr. Kamau started with the boys. Each boy stretched out on his stomach on the floor, and Mr. Kamau dished out the harvest. It was the boy and the teacher, while the rest of us kept still, eyes in front, watching and ears listening to the cane swing and land.

When too many pupils failed the test, Mr. Kamau took abrupt breaks between the bouts of caning. He clenched and unclenched his fingers, rotated his shoulder, and complained about the suffering we were subjecting him to. Subsequently, he beat the last pupils with less intensity until he realized he could cane by proxy and give his right hand a rest.

Forthwith, he caned the first pupil to show what he expected. The caned pupil then caned the next, and so forth. If a pupil landed soft canes, Mr. Kamau showed him how he wanted it done. The soft lashes and the demonstration ones didn't count. Subsequently, pupils whipped each other so hard that some pupils sat tilted at their desks in the afternoon.

Fortunately, Mr. Kamau had outlawed buttock caning for girls. Rumors claimed that if girls received canes on their buttocks, it would interfere with their breeding later on. Girls received their harvest on their palms. But if a teacher went berserk, walking on the aisles and weaving around desks, wielding and landing his cane at random, as it sometimes happened, girls sometimes got caught up in the melee.

Mr. Kamau had to make another change for the girls. He learned that afterward, girls had problems holding their pens. He decreed that girls be caned only on their left palms. There were no lefties to worry about. By the end of grade one, teachers had weaned them from writing "with the wrong hand."

I usually solved two or three problems. One Friday, I solved four, and my heart welled; I never got a perfect score. But one day, when I got my paper back, I had only one correct answer, which separated me from mavuno. I squeezed my body tight and shut my eyes to savor my narrow escape. I hated anyone caning me. My parents didn't cane me except for the time Baba whipped me with a twig when I was four years old.

But I had suffered caning on my palm because I was minutes late to morning assembly or in class for reasons I can't recall. If the lashes strayed to my wrist, the pain numbed my hand. Even if I didn't get caned, I suffered an undercurrent of pain if I watched another person getting brutalized.

Now that I was older, I got so angry if a teacher caned me. To contain my venom, I "fought" back. I stretched my hand, palm up, eyes ahead, froze in place, and took my punishment stoically. Oh, teachers hated that. They wanted us to show remorse.

One pupil failed to solve a single problem, and another missed the cane only once. Mr. Kamau turned those two boys into his exclusive project. One time, I stared as he ordered one of the boys to lie still and receive his punishment while a stream of canes kept falling on him, one after another. The boy fidgeted, flailed one arm as he raised his torso off the floor, turned this way and that, and hollered. Mr. Kamau turned murderous and landed the cane on the boy's shoulders, back, arms, and in between.

The beating became so excessive that the boy defecated on himself.

"Enda ujioshe, kijana pumbavu!" (Go clean yourself, stupid boy!) Mr. Kamau said while the boys laughed and jeered.

After our December holidays, the two boys never returned to school. One boy lived at Major Holman's farm, miles from Kabazi farm. I never learned what happened to him.

The boy who defecated on himself and who, I now suspect, suffered from dyslexia lived in Kabazi village. Pupils from Kabazi said he was an only child of an older widow. I later heard that the boy had died. Some rumors said he committed suicide, and others said he died in his sleep.

Mr. Kamau was the only teacher who formalized student beatings. Each of the other teachers, however, used various other methods to assault pupils, including verbal abuse, jostling, slapping, or sporadic caning.

# Chapter 30

# Mr. Foolish

Teachers were our nurturers (only in grades one and two), educators, and tormentors. They could be mean, petty, and even vindictive. Mistreating pupils, inhibiting their learning, and expecting them to do well in their schoolwork were part of the school's culture. Ruler striking in grades one and two and cane beating for the bigger children were a part of our classroom's landscape, just like desks, chalk, and blackboards. And the worst part was that we pupils and our parents expected it.

Simon Mbũrũ didn't bother with a cane like the other teachers. His hands did the job well enough. He used a series of slaps—fronts and backhands—while he spewed out, "Foolish! Foolish!"

Pupils nicknamed him "Mr. Foolish."

Because of our two families' connection—as my brother's former classmate and schoolmate and my mother's friendship with his mother—I never expected him to be mean to me until he did on that fateful Friday when most pupils failed Mr. Kamau's Mavuno Day test. It was the day I got only one problem correct. But I had but a minute to savor my lucky escape.

The caning orgy gobbled up at least twenty minutes from our one-hour lunch break. It was the same day Mr. Kamau's boy project endured his worst assault. He rained lashes on the boy as one would to immobilize an enemy.

I cringed and shut my eyes every time a lash landed, afraid Mr. Kamau could permanently maim the boy. The image of that boy, half-seated on one side, howling, flailing his arms, and begging that he will do better next time is stuck in my memory.

Meanwhile, I grew restless, anxious about my cooking "duty."

The minute Mr. Kamau dismissed our class, I shot out the door as if someone called out "Fire!", my mind on Simon Mbŭrŭ. I have failed him, my mind admonished. But what could I have done? What will I tell him? I asked myself. I couldn't guess. I turned east and power-walked toward his house.

He stood smack in the middle of the sloping footpath, fifteen feet from his front yard, in gray trousers, a white shirt under a navy-blue jacket, and short hair parted on the left.

When I saw him, I wished I could turn around and mingle with the other pupils. I would later beg Mami to apologize for my failure. I hated to deal with him only hours before my weekend. But adults had indoctrinated me to kowtow to authority figures, even when they were doing me wrong.

I hurried toward him. About ten feet away, he asked, "Where have you been?" His voice had so much venom it quaked my insides. I wasn't used to such intense anger directed at me. I gave him a remorseful look and no answer.

He started his "Foolish!" regimen and spat out "Foolish!" at least three times, his face distorted, eyes turned into slits, and his hands restless.

I stopped, and my brain stalled, my eyes downcast. I thought of taking a different route to get to his kitchen. This meant walking about fifty feet back to school and taking the footpath that led to Mr. Kamau's residence, which emptied into the common footpath in front of all the teachers' residences. I did nothing of the sort. Instead, I inched forward, ready to detour on grass, sure Simon Mbŭrŭ would yield and let me pass. I needed to hurry to the kitchen to get the stove going.

Meanwhile, my mind dashed this way and that, scrambling for an acceptable reason. No one left, least of all on Mavuno Day, until a teacher dismissed a class. If the school caught on fire, we would have gawked at the teacher, waiting for him to dismiss us.

If I blamed my tardiness on Mr. Kamau, the headmaster, no less, I couldn't guess where that would lead; it would likely have compounded my problems.

My mouth remained shut. Simon Mbūrū remained planted on the path, blocking it. I stepped aside to pass on the grass.

A hand shot out so fast its speed startled me. The slap landed smack on my temple—my very first in all my fourteen and a half years. Lightheaded, my body swayed this and that while fake fireflies cascaded before my eyes. My elbow and forearm broke the fall.

"Foolish! Foolish! Foolish girl!" Mr. Foolish said. "Lie down right there," he pointed.

That year, it had rained in Solai and the surrounding areas day and night. The ground got so saturated that clear water gurgled from the ground like a spring. We sloshed through small tributaries on our way to school. Like my fellow pupils, I owned no umbrella, sweater, or jacket. My shield was my school uniform— a blue pinafore and a short-sleeved white blouse. Although I don't recall catching a cold, I was constantly wet, cold, and shivering. With no shoes, I suffered from occasional fungal infections.

Even sadistic Mr. Kamau knew to give us a break. One morning, I arrived late to the assembly with my uniform drenched, which wasn't unusual during the rainy season. As I reached the assembly, Mr. Kamau, the master on duty that morning, asked, "Why are you late?"

"I'm wet," I said. I could then make simple sentences in English.

He didn't punish me.

And now Mr. Foolish wants me to lie down on the wet ground? I asked myself. What is a pupil to do? I stretched down on my stomach on the dewy grass, focused on my predicament, oblivious to the residents around me. It was too cool for the insects to wander, or I would have squashed them under where they hid.

Mr. Foolish shook his head several times before he strode off and disappeared inside his house.

Under normal school life, I should have reported the incident to Mr. Kamau, especially since he was the one who delayed me. Besides, he didn't know about my lunchtime duty. But my going without lunch and failing to interact with my peers from other farms during our lunch hour meant nothing—teachers asked pupils to do all sorts of chores.

I couldn't dare claim my rights because we pupils believed, like our parents, that we learned at the pleasure of our teachers. And unless I planned to quit school, reporting Mr. Foolish would have made me a target of teachers' taunts. I had noticed how some teachers egged on older teenage pupils to provoke them and give an excuse to assault them.

When I compared the teachers I had had, I realized teachers at Tindaress Primary School didn't ask pupils to cook for them. I don't recall any other pupil cooking for a teacher at either school.

But, although no teacher beat pupils like runaway fugitives at Tindaress, teachers there wouldn't have earned medals, either. Our grade three teacher was fond of ordering pupils to kneel in the dusty, gritty front yard under the tropical sun and then forgetting about them while he continued teaching indoors.

Other times, he ordered us to crouch, hold our earlobes, and waddle like a duck—we called it frog-walking. Meanwhile, he supervised, cane in hand to cheer and whack the slow and the fallen.

Audible winces, outright moans, or scrunched faces with jaws clenched and tears streaming were typical.

After I compared Kabazi and Tindaress teachers, lying down on wet grass was among the new lows.

After a long while, I heard pupils romp and horse around, meaning they had finished lunch. It seemed Mr. Foolish had forgotten about me. What bothered me the most was lying on wet grass in full view of the school compound.

My mind raced.

What do pupils think of me now? Do they still think I'm a teacher's pet? Why didn't he punish me away from view? In private? I asked myself like a typical beaten-down victim. No! He wanted pupils to witness my downfall!

I'm so embarrassed. They will make fun of me and laugh. What would David say about his friend slapping me? He, or any of my other brothers, had never pushed me, let alone slapped me. What next? Why not quit cooking right now? Yes, I turn the slap and humiliation into my way out. Will Mr. Foolish count that as disobedience?

As I debated with myself, the prospect of making a unilateral decision caused a twinge of satisfaction to sail through me.

Because my head faced toward Mr. Foolish's house, I could only hear my schoolmates laugh and horse around. I turned and looked. My longing for that freedom got to me. In minutes, the noise trailed off. When I turned again, pupils were milling back into their classrooms. That was it. I made my decision.

I rose, brushed my dress several times to remove the wetness and creases, then hurried and joined the line of pupils.

That afternoon, I half-listened to the teacher, wondering how Mr. Foolish would react to my walking away before he came to dismiss me. I felt relieved I didn't have to see him for two days. Although he went home to Solai on weekends, our paths never crossed.

As for cooking, I was tired of it. But under the school's arbitrary rules, a slap and lying on wet grass weren't serious enough to allow me to break "our contract." But I could lobby for a family intervention. Perhaps Mami could talk with Elithi. I never considered how an intervention would help me. Mr. Foolish would likely apologize, but nothing would change. Afterward, any chance he got, he would taunt me for reporting him.

When I arrived home that Friday, I reported the incident to Mami. She snorted, stopped what she was doing, and got quiet. Then, instead of sending us to fetch the items she needed to cook supper, she fetched the items herself. She quickened her pace, the one she adopted whenever she fumed against a higher authority or had no solution to what bothered her and was figuring out what to do.

I wondered how my mother would have reacted if I told her Mr. Foolish had already felt my bony chest with his fingers, after which he had said, "Not yet ready."

# Chapter 31

# Big-Mouth Reporter

Why didn't I tell my mother about Simon Mbũrũ, aka Mr. Foolish, feeling my chest when it happened? I don't know. I may have worried that it was too shameful for her to learn he wasn't as upright as we all in the village believed. Or I ignored the incident to save her the anguish or to shield Mr. Foolish from the shame.

But I could handle a slap, I figured.

About an hour after I told Mami, Baba ambled home from work. He called one of my little brothers and handed him the empty kĩondo he had used to carry his lunch.

Meanwhile, Mami busied herself and brewed tea. But instead of sending one of us to take it to Baba in his thingira, his sanctuary, she took the tea herself. I then realized she intended to tell him, which I believed would take things too far.

When I told her about the slap, I expected her to tell Elithi and nothing more. The best outcome I hoped for was a promise from Mr. Foolish—through his mother!—that he would not slap me again. I realized that wouldn't solve my cooking problem, but I thought of no better solution.

"Did you tell Baba?" I asked Mami when she returned.

"Of course I did," she said. "This isn't something to brush aside."

"What did he say?"

"You know your father does things his own way."

That meant Baba listened without responding or with a mere "Okay."

After Mami told my father, I had expected him to call and ask me to recount the story. But because he didn't, I couldn't guess what he intended to do. He could blow the matter out of proportion and make my school life unbearable.

*

That Saturday morning, while my siblings and I waited for Mami's porridge, Baba entered the courtyard, coming from the outside, a blanket wrapped over his clothes like a shawl to shield himself from the morning chill, a style I hated that he had copied from Tugen men. Mami rushed to the porch as if she expected him to call on her.

"I didn't send Wanjirũ to school to cook for a man as if she were his wife," Baba said before he disappeared into his thingira.

Yes! That's my father.

The bravo was but a moment. I started agonizing over what Baba might have done.

In the evening, Mami headed to thingira. After she returned to the family house, she told my siblings and me what Baba did.

Before 7:00 a.m., my dear father knocked on the pride-of-the-village's door. Mr. Foolish, rubbing his eyes and still in his pajamas—the only one in the village to sleep thus instead of nude or in underwear—flung his door open, ready to spew venom on whoever had interfered with his Saturday sleep-in.

"Oh, it's you, Baba David," Mr. Foolish said meekly.

Baba remained mum on whose father he was. Instead, he spewed a barrage of soft, deliberate ultimatums, the details of which remained known only to the two men.

After Mami told us the story, I enjoyed a moment of euphoria. "Baba fears no one," I said.

My siblings chimed in, each trying to cite an incident where Baba showed his fearlessness. Joseph reminded us that men whipped off their hats as they approached the landowner. "But Baba has never removed his hat," he said.

"I knew he would do something," I said.

We then constructed scenarios depicting how Baba confronted Mr. Foolish and how Mr. Foolish responded. In the end, we had him saying, "Yes, yes," while he trembled with fear.

The satisfaction of Baba's action ebbed as Monday neared. That Sunday evening, fear crept in. I doubted Baba knew the power teachers wielded over us, pupils. Just because Mr. Foolish had behaved like a naughty boy didn't mean he would change his ways. Worry weighed down on me, unsure of what awaited me.

In the morning, I got ready for school, full of apprehension. I hated to miss school; I had never missed a single day. But I thought of missing school that day to avoid facing Mr. Foolish.

Then Baba appeared at his thingira's doorway.

"Wanjirũ," he called out.

"Yes." I rushed to the porch.

"Go to school," he said. "You'll not cook anymore. I didn't send you there to be a cook."

Relieved, I felt such gratitude for my father. He had delivered more than I expected. But I still had to deal with Mr. Foolish. He taught my class one lesson (a lesson I have since forgotten).

When I entered the schoolyard, my luck couldn't have been worse. Pupils had already lined up for assembly, the duty master in front. Even with his back to me, I could pick out Mr. Foolish anywhere in the school. He was taller than the other teachers and dressed like an executive; I never saw him without a jacket.

The assembly had already sung "God save the Queen" (the British national anthem). I didn't excuse myself for the few minutes' lateness. As I hurried, I passed parallel to Mr. Foolish, a few feet away, and he turned toward me. He ignored me and turned his attention back to the assembly. I joined the grade four line at the back.

Instead of checking our cleanliness, Mr. Foolish remained planted in front. "There is a big mouth reporter in our midst," he said. He then walked up and down the front line. "She had nothing better to do over the weekend than her reporting duties."

A restlessness ensued as pupils looked around, confused, unsure of what Mr. Foolish was talking about. Suspense hung as they waited for him to name the culprit.

I recoiled inside, hoping he didn't mention my name. Why that concerned me, I didn't know. We admired any pupil who took a stand and defied a teacher.

Mr. Foolish continued with his litany of the unnamed, undisciplined pupil until he exhausted himself. He then dismissed the assembly without making another announcement or conducting an inspection. I walked to class, relieved and feeling proud of my father again.

Unfortunately for Joseph, his path and that of Mr. Foolish had not crossed enough for him to rebel against delivery duties. He delivered milk for the entire year.

The following year, parents from Kabazi farm complained that Mr. Foolish was excessively caning and assaulting pupils. When complaints gathered momentum, parents called for a school strike if he continued teaching. (Mr. Kamau indulged in "excessive caning and assaults" as well, but parents didn't know who to complain to.)

"Excessive" was the operative term. The other teachers' abuse stayed under the radar because pupils and their parents expected occasional borderline assaults.

Kabazi Primary School couldn't weather the parents' pressure; Mr. Foolish moved on. He got a teaching job at the Kenya Youth Service—on the outskirts of Nairobi—teaching young men in a boot camp setting, where training came with assaults, verbal or otherwise, allegedly to toughen the recruits.

Sadly, although corporal punishment has diminished or been eliminated in towns, teacher assaults against pupils have withstood the test of time and continue in many schools in rural Kenya.

# Chapter 32

# The First Death

Beginning in the first quarter of the twentieth century, Kenya's colonial disruption had forced young and middle-aged men to leave their communities and flock to towns and European farms in search of work. Subsequently, women became heads of households, especially those women whose men worked in urban centers and returned home monthly or quarterly.

On the farms, however, British farmers needed stability and had enough land to accommodate families, so they preferred married men. After employees stabilized, they returned to their homelands and brought their wives and children to the farms.

After the emergency declaration in October 1952, the exodus that followed and the Mau Mau war with the British further disrupted families.

By the 1960s, hardly any child in Solai had grandparents, many having died after the exodus to the Native Reserve. (My maternal grandparents, who joined the exodus after Major Holman, their employer, included them in the list, died from harsh war conditions.)

Mr. Foolish's family was an exception. The family stretched to four generations, living west of our homestead at Major Miller's farm.

The family comprised Mama Alan and her husband, Mũgono, in brownish traditional replicas of Gĩkũyũ wear. Both were born in the mid-1800s before the British invaded Kenya. They both stooped over, but Mama Alan walked without props while Mũgono used his long walking cane, his head full of white fuzzy hair. Alan Kĩbuĩ—their only son—the patriarch, had two wives. He inherited Elithi, the older wife, and a young daughter when his brother died in the mid-1930s. Now, their three older children already had their own offspring.

Wanjikũ, Alan's younger wife's children were still minors.

Alan wore a hat that matched his gray trousers and shirt and walked in measured steps to avoid "hurting" the ground. His body slightly hunched, his stomach sunken like every older man in the village. Ordinarily, men, including my father, had sunken stomachs because they ate only one or two meager meals a day with no snacks. Baba drank a mug of tea for breakfast, carried his lunch, and ate supper in the evening; some men never carried lunch. According to Mami, Alan suffered from digestive problems, not a lack of calories.

A year after Mr. Foolish got ejected from Kabazi Primary School, tragedy struck his family. Wanjikũ, his stepmother, reported the incident to Mami.

One morning, while Alan sat on a stool in their house (Alan had no thingira), she said.

A rumble rang in his stomach, followed by gurgling noises like those from a burst water pipe.

In seconds, he slumped, slid, and hit the ground.

Wanjikũ rushed in.

"Ala! Alan! Alan! Wake up!" she called out, shaking his shoulder.

He grunted, but words failed him.

Wanjikũ walked about as she wailed, hands on her head.

Elithi rushed in from her house. She felt her husband's carotid artery. "Nĩatũtigire" (he has left us), she said.

The family sought help from Major Miller. He telephoned the Kenya Youth Service authorities. Mr. Foolish made it home on the last bus that day.

Nobody else in the village had died unless we considered the incident at our old fenced village. A newborn came out with the top half of its head missing. The traditional midwives—because of their experience, Mami among them—got spooked. The infant died after taking only a few breaths. In telling us the story, Mami implied it was a bad birth, not a death. So Alan's death was the first one in the village.

In my family, we became mute with sadness and fear, mainly fear. Children, perhaps adults too, feared death as if it would infect them.

The following day, which could have been a Saturday, around noon, a group of children and I peeked in from behind our granary on the side of Elithi's house. Mr. Foolish and Mr. Mbuthia, Alan's son-in-law and the pastor at Tindaress Primary, carried the body on a stretcher, wrapped in a brown shroud like a Muslim. They kept it by the gravesite, the spacious area between Mr. Foolish's and his grandparents' houses, close to the path we used to get to the larger part of the village. Three brothers—teenagers except for Mr. Foolish and Mr. Mbuthia—made up the rest of the funeral procession. They likely dug the grave at night with the help of others.

Grief-stricken, the rest of Alan's family watched from the courtyard. Wanjikũ didn't join them; she remained indoors, unable to contain her grief. Wachuka, Elithi's fifth and last daughter, missed the funeral. She was away at boarding school, and the family decided not to tell her because she was studying for her end-of-year test. She learned of her father's death when she returned home and wondered where he was. Wachuka got so distraught that she froze in place. Later, Elithi found her daughter huddled at the side of their house, palms hugging her temples, tears rolling down her cheeks without her making a single sound.

Today, children's and young people's sadness never gets the attention it deserves. People talk of shielding them from adversities their minds are not ready for. Communities are slowly coming to a better understanding and compassion, but not fast enough.

Back then, I thought Wachuka's behavior was a tad dramatic. I didn't understand the gravity of her burden until I had to deal with something similar.

After Alan's death, Wanjikũ, the younger wife, suffered the most. She stayed indoors for a time, then walked like a zombie. Although Elithi helped, Wanjikũ had to get a grip and tend to her minor children.

Despite his casual attitude about Alan's death, Major Miller made an honorable gesture. He let Alan's family continue gardening the plots he had assigned to Alan. Of course, the women continued to work as temporary employees. Because Wanjikũ didn't earn enough to replace her husband's lost income, Mr. Foolish stepped in and became the honorary patriarch of the family and paid the children's school expenses. But he could do nothing to ease the sadness that befell his family.

Besides Wanjikũ, Mama Alan and Mũgono suffered the most when their son died. Alan was already a grandfather, but after his death, weepy and distraught, his mother told Mami. "My only child has died; what's the point of my living?"

She even heaped blame on Ngai for taking her boy instead of her. She died of a broken heart within months.

After her death, her husband, Mũgono, left all alone in their small circular house, couldn't handle life on his own. I never saw him outdoors again. He reportedly often forgot to eat the food the family took to him. The family didn't think to get someone to spend nights with him. Soon, his mental state deteriorated.

Sometimes, he forgot his wife had died, and he called out to her. Two or three times, when I passed by, I heard him shoo away or reprimand nameless, strange beings he thought were about to attack or grab him.

"Get out of here! Go away!" he admonished, grunting and wielding his stick on the cottage walls.

When we wondered about the strangers, Mami said they were strangers that Mũgono alone could see. He ended up damaging his walls.

In months, Mũgono followed his wife to the land of ancestors.

Two generations wiped out within twelve months.

For a time, Alan's family's entire compound had an aura of death. Because we had to pass by their homestead to get to the village, the river, or our larger garden, I rushed by the gravesite, spooked. Fearful thoughts crowded my mind before they morphed into images that the dead neighbors—like Michael Jackson's *Thriller* characters—would rise from the grave and attack me. I forgot death does not rattle or wake the dead; it rattles the living.

In two more years, death rattled my family when it grabbed one of our own.

# Chapter 33

# The Lucky breaks

While I waded through tides of peasantry, others' actions led me to each critical step that changed my life.

If we pay attention, such incidents occur all around us. We dub them manifestations, answered prayers, focus and affirmations, lucky breaks, coincidences, fate, and so forth. Of course, I hadn't developed the capacity to think of such matters in my youth.

By the time I became Mr. Foolish's cook at fourteen years old, however, I had pinned down an arsenal of four "Musts," triggered by my place of birth, my parents' powerlessness, grueling farm work, and our squalid living conditions. I questioned none of the Musts as they latched onto my subconscious. In my naivete, I never burdened myself with the "how."

My first "Must" came about when I was nine years old, when my father failed to take me to school. He did so a year later when I implied he couldn't afford it. I thought he didn't want me to attend school or lacked the money to take me, hence my Musts:

1. As an adult, I'll make enough money and never have to kowtow to others begging for it.

2. I will own a house, so no one can order me to move or evict me on a whim.

3. I will not follow in my mother's footsteps. I refuse to settle for scratching a meager living through toil under the scorching equatorial sun, piling loads on my back like a beast of burden.

4. And the final Must, which I vowed to when I joined Kabazi Primary School—if three pupils pass an exam in my class, I would be one of them.

These Musts lived in my brain, glued there throughout my school life. With time, as I accomplished them, they propelled me to places beyond, places I had never known or dreamed of.

These Musts came to be because of the lucky breaks I caught along the way.

My first lucky break came because of the declaration of emergency in the country. Terrible as it was, it gave me an opportunity for schooling that might not have been available otherwise.

When the colonizers ordered or hauled Gĩkũyũ adults and families into concentration and detention camps, native reserves, and fenced villages for containment, it became necessary for the British landowners in our area to build a school in a central location—to contain the children while their parents toiled in the fields—with parents paying into a building fund.

My second lucky break came when my father failed to take me to school, my life's first major disappointment. I agonized. After a long wait, I offered to make a trade with him: if he registered me in school, I promised to give up eating the delicious chunks of roasted meat he served to our family when he slaughtered a goat. He relented. "You can eat meat and go to school as well," he said.

In the next school year, Baba registered me. When I entered school, I was ten years and three months old.

I was one of the few exceptions because few fathers educated their daughters. The fathers either lacked the money or didn't see the need; the daughters would marry and benefit their husbands' families.

The next lucky break came as a surprise to my fellow fourth-grade classmates and me because we were used to the only system we knew and were not expecting any change.

The colonial system had all community schools reach grade four, the maximum level of education the colonizers believed an African man needed to read the Christian Bible, log information in farm ledgers, or become a better servant. Pupils who wanted more education had to pass the national standardized exam, known as Common Entrance Exam (CEE), to get admitted to any of the few boarding schools in grade five that the colonial government had set aside for Africans. Passing that exam and getting such an admission was like winning a lottery.

Having failed the national exam at Tindaress Primary a year earlier, no matter what else happened at Kabazi, the vital exam never trailed far from my mind. Because I did well in my class tests, I believed I had a shot at passing the second time around. If I failed again, I doubted Baba would let me repeat grade four a third time. Like my classmates, I knew a lifetime of grueling farm work awaited me if I failed.

Then, one day during our morning assembly in our last term in 1961, Mr. Kamau came to the assembly in high spirits. He couldn't wait for us to finish singing the British national anthem, the one we had to sing every morning, praying for the queen of England to rule over us while our freedom fighters were still dying in the forest, trying to ensure she didn't do so.

"I have an announcement to make," Mr. Kamau said. "This will change all of your lives."

I couldn't think of a single thing that could change my life. Not a single one.

"The Ministry of Education has abolished the Common Entrance Exam!" he said.

From the back line, I doubted I heard correctly. I perked my ears as he continued.

"Pupils will advance to grade five based on year-end test results."

A rustle and uncertain murmurs coursed through the assembly. Is our class included? Our test was two months away. Is it too late for us? I wondered. I stood still, anxious and eager to hear everything Mr. Kamau had to say.

He paused, perhaps to let us take it all in.

"The national exam abolition starts this year!" Mr. Kamau said. "Our senior class will be the pioneers!"

I became so giddy, crossed my arms over my chest and clutched my shoulders tight to contain myself. Murmurs echoed. The lower classes turned to face us, the pioneers, as if we had suddenly become special.

After all that worry. And just like that. Poof! My class and the rest of the Kenyan grade four pupils would advance to grade five based only on our school's end-of-year tests—by our own teachers—not on some invisible authority in the Ministry of Education in Nairobi or some corner of London.

I couldn't wait for Mr. Kamau to finish his routine so I could talk to someone. As if he could read my mind, he dismissed the assembly without inspecting us for cleanliness or fussing about pupils who came in late. In the short distance to our classrooms, pupils' jubilation became the rowdiest after-assembly morning I remember.

At home, you would think the abolition of the exam would excite my parents, at least my mother. Perhaps they were happy in their own way, or they didn't appreciate the extent to which the burden had been lifted from their children's lives. When I told Mami, she smiled and said, "Oh, that's good news," and resumed what she was doing. End of celebration. When she told Baba, I didn't witness it, but I bet he merely said, "Oh, okay."

The school started building a three-room wooden bungalow north of our "Cathedral" Building. They set the foundation and corner posts before we broke off for our December holidays.

When the building started, I had mixed feelings, as if I still wanted to sit for a national exam to prove I could pass it. The building also confirmed I wouldn't go to a distant boarding school, away from the farm, as I craved. But the relief that coursed through my body when Mr. Kamau announced the exam abolition was so huge that it dwarfed my minor disappointment.

I spent my December school holiday in a relaxed state.

# Chapter 34

# Off to the Movies

Before I started school, our news trickled down from the land-owner or from occasional letters villagers received from relatives in the *native reserve,* Kikuyuland. After I started school, we got additional news from teachers, an occasional man who shared a Kiswahili newspaper, or a man who owned a radio.

At one time, a philanthropic organization offered to show us, the disadvantaged peasants, a free film. In my mid-teens then, I hungered for such an opportunity.

On the appointed evening, I joined Joseph and the other youngsters and walked to the venue at the Solai Police Station, three miles away, next to Patel's General Store.

At an open area between the station and the staff's white-washed one-room duplexes and bungalows stood a white van, its back double door ajar, with a crew of three men—one white and two Africans—crowded inside. The white man tinkered with a piece of equipment, and the Africans helped him. About two hundred expectant individuals, mostly young men and boys, crowded around. Subdued, people watched, talking in low tones as if waiting to witness a marvel. Having never seen a projector or a screen, I was impatient to see how the pictures would come and how so many of us could see whatever the men wanted to show us.

Oh! When the van men turned on whatever they had worked on, it produced crackling noises before a beam of light projected on a white sheet, like a volleyball net, a distance from the van. I gawked as images appeared on the sheet that magically became a screen.

It disappointed me that people in the film spoke only in English. I knew only a few basic English words. How will I follow the story? I agonized.

Like the rest of Solai's community, few people in the audience could read and write, let alone speak English. The ones who understood rudimentary English couldn't catch a single word from the fast-paced and strange accent. The men's voices sounded as if they were suffering from a cold or chewing potatoes. Tall and suited in well-worn clothes and hats, some of them with flowery, burgundy-colored kerchiefs around their necks, the men looked like the ones in our village, except they had pinkish-white skin and showed more confidence. I marveled at white people dressed in humble clothing, living in dusty places.

Their women wore pleated dresses or skirts down to the ground, unlike our African shin-length dresses. They talked in rapid, high-pitched voices as if they had no time to spare for a breath.

The film ended before I figured out what it was about. But I forever debunked my belief that all white people were rich, lived in elegant homes, had everything they wanted, and never did lowly work.

There was no moonlight on our way home, but because of the cloudless night, we could see our colleagues' silhouettes. Plus, we knew each other's voices. And because the footpath didn't allow two people to walk side-by-side, we walked in a single file. People, eager to keep up with the robust exchanges, rushed on grass, off the path, or around short scrubs.

We chattered about the quarrels, men carrying guns in their holsters, and the lack of gunfights. It was my first film and outing, and the moviegoers' excitement, especially the boys', infected me. We commented or told disjointed versions of the film, the episodic highlights, talking over each other.

At home, I don't recall how much of the film Joseph and I talked about; perhaps we had exhausted ourselves. And I don't remember whether Tabitha went along. We shared a bed until we were pre-teens, then a cottage, and I remember very little of our interactions. We didn't even share teenage secrets. Because Joseph was my classmate and was so outgoing, he overshadowed my relationship with my other siblings.

*

Our benefactors must have received glowing reviews. Within months, they offered another film, but this time at Njeki's Shopping Center because of its central location. Village gossip said it would be all about cowboys!

I had heard that cowboys, cow herders like our goatboys, rode on horses and fought with real guns. Our goatboys walked everywhere and fought with slaps, kicks, and fists. They reserved the deadly slingshots for leisure target shooting or birds.

I itched to see a gunfight with real guns. And now that I knew they spoke English, I wanted to test my progress in the language. The only challenge was the venue. It was four miles away, and I could get nobody to accompany me. Or perhaps, although my memory is fuzzy, the film came during the month Joseph and Tabitha languished at Nakuru General Hospital after they contracted typhoid, a disease no one else in the family caught.

I worked fast to finish my chores. Alone or not, I had to go. I expected to join others along the way. I crossed Tindaress River and snaked through our old fenced village. We didn't need to circumvent on the periphery anymore; the colonial rules were dead, loosened, or on their way out; the fence had deteriorated. I entered the dirt road and didn't see anyone else headed my way. I concluded filmgoers had already left; I regretted taking too long to finish my chores.

Besides joining a group in the first film, I had only walked alone a block through village pathways at night. However, anticipation for that film gripped me for an entire week. No thought crossed my mind about the perils of going alone. Nothing or nobody could have persuaded me to skip the film.

About half a mile away, I branched off into a well-beaten tractor trail that ran across a vast two-mile grassland through Gĩtharia 's farm. The grasslands had scanty scrubby bushes, the biggest about two feet high—a true African savanna perfect for wild animals to roam free. In 1962, I didn't concern myself with trespassing. With Kenya's independence talk in the air, the British farmers had mellowed and now had little concern about lone Africans trekking on trails through their vast farms.

When I reached Nakuru-Solai Road, about a mile from the shopping center, I met two people walking in the opposite direction, hurrying to get home before dark. Nonetheless, my heart bubbled with eagerness to arrive on time, so I quickened my steps.

At the open "theater," I found a bigger crowd than at the last film. The crew was adjusting images projected on the whitewashed back wall of the canteen. Wow! Who knew they could turn a wall into a screen? A bigger and permanent screen that the wind couldn't disturb! Another tidbit to share later, I thought.

I weaved around people, scouting for an ideal spot. To avoid missing anything, I skipped looking for people from my village. I will look around after the film ends, I told myself.

Soon, cowboys strutted or galloped on horses, wide-brim hats on and checkered maroon kerchiefs around their necks, guns dangling from their waists. One cowboy dangled a gun on each hip; I figured he had to be the toughest.

Men drank beer at counters or tables in saloons with swinging half-doors. Occasionally, if a man entered the saloon, the customers gave him suspicious or challenging looks. The newcomer treated the gawkers in kind. At one bar, three cowboys strutted in. They sat at a table, away from the others. After a drink or two, facial sparring, an occasional meeting at the counter while getting a drink, and a few words thrown in, a fight erupted. Everyone joined in. Fists, chairs, and bottles flew. With broken bottles and chairs and groaning bodies strewn about, the place turned into a wreck.

In another incident, two men quarreled inside a shop. The feisty woman shopkeeper fetched a long gun and aimed. The men eased out to fight elsewhere.

Such incidents and chases on horseback, as well as the shootouts, caused the crowd to break into raptures. Although I hated the destruction, the film gave me quite a thrill. I felt a camaraderie with my neighbors as we shared brief anecdotes. Although I enjoyed the action, just like in the last film, I couldn't follow the storyline or understand what the cowboys said to each other. Maybe cowboys didn't use the type of English teachers taught us in school, I concluded.

When the film ended, people chattered as they called their friends or rushed away in clusters across the poorly lit front of the canteen. They soon melted into darkness. It was too dark to recognize people's big and small silhouettes, so I followed the excited crowd toward the main road, sharing nothing. But I kept my ears perked, hoping to catch familiar voices. But all was in vain.

On the Nakuru-Solai Road, people dispersed in different directions. Some disappeared across the road into foot pathways, others went south, and others walked north in my direction. I stayed close to the group, hoping some individuals would branch off to the tractor trail and walk with me, at least up to Gĩtharia's farm, before they branched off to their village. None of them did; the group walked on.

After I branched off a distance ahead, among scattered trees and bushes, I noticed three silhouettes, likely boys, who walked fast. They soon disappeared. I blamed myself for waiting until the end; people from our two villages had probably left earlier. Or they never went, unwilling to walk the four miles at night. I now felt afraid of tackling that distance alone. With no other choice, I kept on while my mind reached back to the past.

Years before, in our old fenced village, Mami and Njeri, my half-brother Waigwa's wife, had told us stories about ogres. Henceforth, I had always feared that a horrible, formless creature lurked behind every shrub or structure at night to spook or grab me if I got close.

There were snakes, too—big and small. They concerned me because they were everywhere, and one came by them abruptly, with no time to prepare. But they only attacked someone who bothered or accidentally stepped on them. Besides, snakes slept at night, away from footpaths. I was never aware of any nocturnal snakes in the savanna.

By the time I reached Gītharia's farm in the open savanna, the moon was in full bloom, a welcome consolation. But by then, thoughts of imaginary predators lurking behind bushes had set in. Never mind, the scrubby bushes were too tiny to hide any self-respecting predator. But with the moonlight, I stuck out like an emasculated ogre or Bigfoot. To ensure all was clear, I scanned the savanna every few feet.

Just as well.

Way, way behind me, about 25 feet inland, I noticed a dark form that wasn't there when I passed by. I stopped and did a double-take. Yes, my sight hadn't failed me. Panicky, my heart picked up pace. I ran my eyes all around the savanna. No one else was in sight besides me, a teenage girl and a wild beast.

What shall I do? I stood. To think. But I couldn't just stand there. I resumed my walk. This time, I sidled along half the time to monitor the beast. To my horror, its shape had become clearer. To confirm my suspicion, I stopped. It stopped, too.

When I walked, it walked; if I stopped, it stopped.

By then, my insides quaked, my heart galloped, yearning to break loose. I begged my mind to focus.

I thought of running. But if I ran, the beast would run too and even outrun me.

My assessment turned right. The beast's image became bigger and bigger. Yes! It walked faster than I did.

It was on all fours. And it limped.

I had heard enough stories to recognize a scavenger, a coward that never attacked its victim unless it was fallen, infirm, or dead. The only time the coward became emboldened and a menace was among its gang.

I enjoyed a flicker of gratitude; thankful the predator was alone. But it could be hungry and desperate.

While the two of us paced and assessed each other, my heart began to race; it concerned me. If I fell, it would be the end of me. I coaxed it to slow down as I looked around in case the beast's companions lurked nearby. After all, every creature came from somewhere.

But it seemed we were just the two of us, in lockstep, each focused on coming out ahead. The hunter waited for the prey to fall. It would then dash in for a quick feast. The prey bet on the hunter's companions staying away.

Fifty feet apart, our dance continued until we got closer to human habitation, the dirt road that led to our first fenced village.

After about twenty-five feet on the road, I looked behind one last time. Like magic, my hyena companion had gone—poof!

Then I ran and ran and ran.

# Chapter 35

# Grade Five

In January 1962, we found a new classroom—one in a row of three rooms—built of wood and roofed with iron sheets, desks arranged, and a blackboard set up. My emotions went in all directions when I entered and sat at a desk in front, a desk in grade five! I experienced a sense of superiority and apprehension that we were the pioneer class, the ones to chart the course for the rest of the school, a historic event.

For the first time, we had to learn our subjects in *English*. Subjects included arithmetic, English, geography, and European history, including how Dr. Livingston and other Europeans "discovered" Kenya and its remarkable landmarks. (It was a decade later when the Ministry of Education had history books updated to show, "The first white man to discover. . .," which I still believe is a misnomer because after a person or a group of people discovers a place, which Kenyans had done centuries or thousands of years prior, "discover" becomes inapplicable as far as that place is concerned.)

Our learning started as a crawl—a slow, arduous mental process. Having previously learned all our subjects in Kiswahili, with English lessons introduced in grade three, we understood only a little English. We often didn't ask questions; we let our blank faces, eyes fixed on the teacher, speak for us. Except during lessons, we pupils spoke in Gĩkũyũ the rest of the time. There were no non-Gĩkũyũ pupils in Kabazi Primary.

"I know you understood nothing of what I said," a teacher would quip, then give us hints. If we failed to get it, he translated the word or phrase into Kiswahili (never into Gĩkũyũ, our native language). If we still didn't understand the Kiswahili version, the teacher gave examples until we got the idea.

In grade three, I had enthusiastically looked forward to learning English. But after it became the only mode of instruction, and its glamor wore off, I didn't care about the language anymore. I had expected to learn the language as easily as I had learned Kiswahili—without awareness or effort—from age six when we moved to the fenced village.

But English had become hard to learn, which had slowed my learning of other subjects. My only consolation was that we were all in the struggle together.

To speed up our English learning, teachers outlawed speaking Gĩkũyũ on school grounds; we were only allowed to speak English, which we knew little. The prefect carried a one-by-two-inch wooden block that we called a "monitor." He gave it to any pupil he heard speak in Gĩkũyũ. When the school let out, the English teacher punished whoever remained with the monitor. The pupil either did a project for a teacher or stayed in an empty classroom for an hour after school.

Because we spoke in simple, short, declarative sentences—I am going to class, I am going to eat lunch, I am going out—we couldn't hold a meaningful conversation with our fellow pupils. We suspected anyone who came close concealed the monitor, waiting to pass it along. We avoided each other during lunchtime and recess or conversed in undertones in Gĩkũyũ among one or two trusted friends. If another pupil came near us, we dashed away, giggling to imply we knew the person's intentions—to unload the monitor. If one in our circle of friends received the monitor, that day's social whispers or friendship went by the wayside.

This English learning style had a double-edged outcome. Distrust festered among pupils across the school (and, I learned later, on other Kenyan campuses that used the same system). Teachers unknowingly added to and strengthened the dismissal or trivialization of our native languages by our colonizers.

Even after the colonizers "left," Kenyans unconsciously continued to dismiss their languages.

Today, the belief that native languages are inferior is an indisputable conclusion among the middle class and upper echelons of Kenyan society, most of whom teach their children English only, while children of the working class speak a pidgin-type Kiswahili. Most townspeople don't teach their children their primary languages. The practice, sadly, has spread to rural areas.

According to one high school principal, besides students being poor in languages, they mix two or three languages when they speak or write. Beyond watering down children's learning, the practice has created a social divide between older and younger generations, especially between grandparents and grandchildren, and even between parents and their children. Communications between generations are now conducted in a shallow pidgin-type Kiswahili, suitable only for basic transactions. Stories about our community's way of life and history, similar to the ones our parents told us as children, have been lost to most youngsters.

I have already noticed a similar divide between my younger relatives and me. Because I have been away from Kenya for decades, my Kiswahili has become rusty, and I don't speak the pidgin Kiswahili that my young relatives speak. I communicate with family and friends in Gĩkũyũ (which I have kept up) or in English. Because my young relatives speak rudimentary English at best, we get by with basic hellos and no chance of stories about my American experience. Or I communicate only with their parents, which, sadly, the parents don't seem to mind. It's a sad, collective ignorance that many parents and grandparents embrace without thought.

For the English-only younger generations, exchanges with older generations that don't understand English are nonexistent. I sense a community's pathetic attitude of "what does it matter?" It's likely that the affliction of "hating" one's native language and dabbing down a people's way of life, or interpreting them through their former colonizers' culture, has also inflicted many other Kenyan communities, not just the Gĩkũyũ, who, having been born into it, I'm most familiar with.

Somalis seem to be an exception. (I'm talking about Kenyan Somalis only.) Arbitrary colonial boundaries separated a small part of their population from Somalia, and that part became part of Kenya by default. Unlike the other Kenyan micronations (tribes), who spoke different languages, worshipped differently, and were mixed like jelly beans during colonization, Somalis remained intact with a common language and religion and are said to have come from a common ancestor. Their culture withstood colonialism intact, which came in handy after independence as they multiplied—while others were reducing the size of their families—educated their young through the constraints of Islam, and, with time, built mosques and spread their religion to every corner of Kenya.

# Chapter 36

# Pests and Hair

Grade five came with other benefits. In our second term, the school required us girls to braid our hair in cornrows or singles.

I snorted. Braiding hair didn't seem a worthwhile perk anymore. A year earlier, my classmates and I had asked—no, begged—for the school to allow us to braid our hair. The teachers turned us down, saying we couldn't manage our hair properly. And now, they dare to make braiding mandatory for girls in grade five!

Unlike Tabitha, my younger sister, I never learned to braid hair well. How she learned remained a mystery to me because Mami, like other mothers, wore a headscarf and didn't braid her hair. And I couldn't rely on Tabitha; we seemed to live in parallel worlds.

I went along with the new requirement. Because I had been cutting my hair often to keep it manageable, it was about two inches long. When I braided it, I ended up with ugly scrubby balls like anthills—a hairdo worn by men who didn't comb their hair in mental institutions or jails. (Today, though, the style could pass as fashionable among certain groups.)

During morning assembly, the duty master called me out twice for untidy, oily hair. This turned my efforts into an unpleasant chore. In addition, the braids caused a tightness in my scalp that hurt.

(Today, braiding hair has reached its zenith. It's not only for adults and teenagers. I see braids on children and even on babies, while the two major soft spots on their heads [fontanels] are still pulsing before the skull's bones complete their formation.)

Well, before long, I got fed up with the ugly style, my scalp discomfort, and the pressure of the morning inspection.

One Saturday, I asked my mother to shave my head.

That Monday, during the assembly inspection, the on-duty master called me a "stubborn girl" several times for not following school guidelines. I didn't know what "stubborn" meant, but I knew it was something negative about my shaved hair. I pouted in reply, glad there wasn't anything the teacher could do. From then on, I kept my hair an inch or two long until I left Kabazi Primary School.

We pupils lived in dirt houses, in squalor, sharing courtyards with goats, chickens, and cats—only two households had dogs. I now wonder how teachers expected boys to keep their hair squeaky clean and girls to wear stylish hair.

Besides, we had to put up with fleas, lice, and even bed bugs. For bed bugs, Mami doused the beds and bedding with boiling water. Sometimes that didn't work, and some bugs survived and revived their community.

In our old fenced village, Gĩthũi and Morry—my younger brothers—shared a bed set by the wall in Baba's thingira's living room. Since they were out of Mami's sight, she forgot to inspect their bed. During David's school holiday, he snooped around thingira and became astounded by how his young siblings slept. Their bed was so infested with bedbugs that he didn't bother to tell Mami to eradicate the pests. Instead, he broke the bed into pieces and discarded them. After that, Baba didn't make them a bed. My two brothers slept on the floor until we moved to our second village.

But now, in grade five, which I thought was a remarkable transition, I expected to be free of pests when I stepped into the class. But the little parasites stuck with me.

Fleas didn't bother me much. If a bite startled me, I slapped the spot, and the flea jumped a few feet away to sneak back to me or someone else later. A flea rarely escaped my lethal finger, though. If I felt a sharp prick, I kept still so I wouldn't scare the attacker while my forefinger moved like a hunter, pounced on the spot, and trapped the little bugger. I then rolled it over the spot with my finger twice to disorient it. If the flea had not had its fill, its body felt like rolling a teensy skin, and it took twice or three times longer to disable it. If this were the case, I rolled the little creature several more times. With the flea disabled and now between my finger and thumb, another roll or two, and it joined its ancestors. But if it had fed, a couple of rolls burst the poor pest's bloody-puffed body.

Fortunately, unlike lice, fleas never followed me to school; the occasional one that bit me could have come from other pupils.

Most fleas waited at home, where animals and humans congregated and had learned to coexist. People considered fleas clean because, unlike lice, which left poop all over their colonies, fleas were feed-and-go without leaving their clutter behind or bringing shame to a family. We all blamed our animals.

"If a home has animals," Mami said, "you can't get rid of fleas."

Besides, fleas were not needy or clingy like lice unless, of course, they liked the host so much that they burrowed under the skin and established a jigger habitat. But for whatever reason, my family members hosted a few jiggers here and there, but they never became ideal hosts.

But lice were another matter. They colonized the creases of my uniform—a blue pinafore with a white blouse with sleeves and collar exposed—which, like everyone else, I washed on Saturdays.

The lice didn't care for the lower body; they loved the upper torso and the clothes that covered it—the crevices of sleeves' seams at the shoulder and underarm. When the sun shone, lice came out to bask. A nomadic louse would stroll along its host's neck to visit its neighbors in the hair colony.

Any lice that migrated to the hair loved it so much, or like people, they assimilated. In this case, they changed from white lice to black ones and blended into their environment. They never strolled down the neck or returned to their home around the torso or sleeve creases.

To us, having lice meant poor hygiene, a dirty person. Having a louse spotted on one's body was a great shame. Fortunately, the lice mostly stayed undercover, closer to their meal. Although we pupils looked down on our infested colleagues, we understood that each of us had suffered a lice infestation, a fact we kept to ourselves or spoke of only in the presence of our family members.

Although we blamed lice infestation on poor hygiene, I wondered why men never complained of lice. My father suffered no infestation; otherwise, Mami would have mentioned it when she washed his clothes. And somehow, lice mysteriously disappeared when I became an adult.

# Chapter 37

# Too Many Mouths to Feed

It never occurred to us that our crowded households—the norm in half of the village—and the dire shortages of necessities contributed to the pest infestations besides the animals. Without birth control, women controlled the size of their families by breastfeeding their babies for an extended period. I heard women say it reduced a woman's fertility.

Mothers took their large families in stride. Mami and the other women said, "Ngai doesn't give you more than you can handle." Or "Every child comes with its own share." Mami had another favorite I have caught myself repeating occasionally—"An elephant is never defeated by its own tusks."

But no matter what my mother said, we were too many "tusks" for her to handle, although I doubt that concerned me at a conscious level until later.

Mami was the ultimate multitasker. Between her farm job, our garden, fetching firewood, and a myriad of chores, she had ten children alive—three girls and seven boys.

A year into the nineteen-sixties, David was on his own, somewhere safe, we hoped. What a breather! Simon, who the school had aged out five years earlier, floated around or came and went, doing temporary farm jobs he picked up at Major Miller's or the surrounding farms. Five of us children were in primary school, and the youngest three remained at home, babysitting themselves. Without a grandmother, the practice of a young child watching smaller children had gone on since we moved to our first fenced village. So far, it had enabled Mami to concentrate on her job and, later, enabled Tabitha and me to go to school. We didn't yet know there could be any danger to young children watching over their younger siblings.

For the school crowd, our morning commotion was legendary. We never seemed to locate soap or a comb. I suppose Mami couldn't afford multiple combs, or it never occurred to her that morning would have been smoother if, over the years, she had bought each of us our own comb. Mũrĩithi, our youngest brother, about two years old, added to the commotion. He fussed or cried, expecting Mami to drop everything and attend to his needs.

Mami woke at least an hour before her "herd" stirred. She cooked porridge for us to eat and prepared something for us to carry for lunch. Our household had all sorts of food aromas in the mornings.

When Joseph and I started working for Mr. Foolish, Mami cooked ugali and greens for us to eat for breakfast before we left for school. After that, we ate or drank nothing else until we ate supper about seven or eight in the evening. The school had no water except for the nearby river, which we never visited.

Baba drank a mug of tea and left for work before we left for school, carrying his lunch in a small kĩondo unless he and Mami worked at the same plantation, and she carried it for him. After Major Miller learned his way around the farm, he realized Baba was up to his job. Instead of going to job sites each morning, he left it to Baba. He gave him a watch and taught him how to tell the start and end of work hours. With the watch, we now left home before Baba.

My siblings and I continued using our sun vs. our shadows to tell time as we had always done. But when the morning sun turned too bright, especially because our courtyard wasn't level, and we doubted the size of our shadow estimate, we asked Baba for time. Although he could tell his work hours, he never got ours right. He always rounded the minutes. If it were between 7:00 and 7:25 a.m., he said, "It's about seven." He progressed to the next hour after the half-hour mark.

*

Baba paid for our school expenses, which included school fees, a building fund (Tindaress Primary School only. The money may have been to buy supplies because I never saw a repair job take place in my four years there.), uniforms, and other supplies like pencils, fountain pens, rulers, and whatever else the school asked us to buy.

It wasn't hard to ask Baba for the items we needed when we lived in our old fenced village. He lived in a one-bedroom thingira with a big enough living room for us to fit in. Mami cooked there half the time to save on firewood. Because we were little and few in number in school, she asked Baba—in a roundabout way—across the fire pit for whatever we needed.

"Wanjiru, did you tell your father you need ink?" she asked.

"Ink?" Baba would ask, looking at me, and I would nod.

"Yes, they have started writing in ink," Mami said.

Sometimes she got tired of asking. If she could spare the money, she bought the items herself. Or, occasionally, she said we needed to ask Baba ourselves. When that happened, we strategized and waited for the right time.

The opportunity presented itself soon enough because, unlike the stories we heard about the ills of alcohol-drinking fathers, ours was usually a happy drunk; the more he drank, the better. Alcohol mellowed and helped Baba open up, tell jokes, or share bits of his life. When he got into the mellow state, we sneaked in our requests. It intrigued me that he never forgot what he promised after he got sober. He gave Mami the money to buy us whatever he agreed to without fuss or further discussion.

But David never needed to wait for an ideal time to ask. When he attended school, he enjoyed an "only child" status, and Baba treated his school expenses as a family project.

Things changed as we grew older, and more of us entered school. The situation worsened when we moved to our second village; the size of Baba's thingira became unsuitable for father-children's interactions.

He was partly to blame for the homestead layout and structures we had ended up with.

Kamunge, the previous owner of the farm, allocated him a pear-shaped plot of land. I presume Baba and his colleagues, who helped him plan the configuration, mangled it when they built the structures too close together. We ended up with a narrow, elongated courtyard. This left a sizeable vegetable garden behind Mami's house—the "pear" part. Baba ended up with a much smaller thingira, a studio-type structure, the size of the living room in his former thingira.

Mami stopped cooking in thingira because we couldn't all fit in there. We never shared a fire pit with our father again, nor did we hear any of his stories. And Mami refused to make the multiple trips to thingira to act as our intermediary—too many "tusks" to handle.

"I'm not acting as a go-between anymore," she said. "I'm not the one getting an education."

We started asking for supplies ourselves. But we waited until the last minute, after we became desperate. We approached thingira after Baba drank his mug of tea, relaxed, and settled. Mami was adamant that we not bombard him with complaints or requests when he was about to leave for work or upon his return home—a consideration she and Baba overlooked to extend to us.

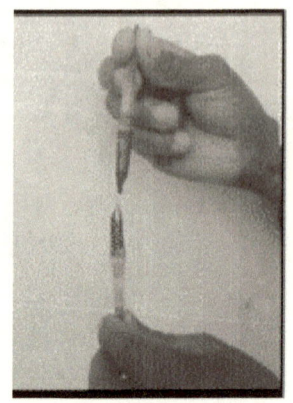

We hated how we agonized before we mustered the courage to approach Baba and ask for money. Meanwhile, we borrowed ink, pencils, erasers, and pens from pupils in our friends' circle, a practice that bothered and embarrassed me. Some pupils shared their last drops of ink (See image).

We never promised to reciprocate, at least I didn't, but we planned to do so when we bought ours. But often, we never did because generous pupils rarely ran out of supplies. Few seemed to mind; they understood the challenges of dealing with unapproachable fathers.

A handful of pupils from smaller families with amiable fathers refused to indulge in what they mumbled, "always begging, begging."

Sometimes, I postponed asking Baba for too long. When I couldn't stand to borrow a second time, or the pupils had little to spare, I braced myself and faced him.

Having to walk from Mami's house to thingira and enter Baba's range of vision ten feet from his doorway made me extra nervous. It also made me feel exposed. The second I landed one foot over the threshold, my mouth rattled. "The teacher said not to go to school tomorrow if I haven't paid school fees," or I blurted out whatever I needed.

Then I waited only seconds for his retort before I turned around.

"Uh! These children! They wait until the last minute?" Baba said in frustration. Or "Do you think I pick money off trees? That I can pluck it the minute you ask?"

Or he said, "Umm," which I knew was a form of "Okay."

It didn't matter what Baba said. By the time he opened his mouth, one of my legs was out the door, relieved I had transferred the load to him. He could complain, but the burden was then on him to ensure I wasn't sent home.

He came through every time, sometimes only minutes before we left for school.

# Chapter 38

# Another Mouth to Feed

Mother worked all the time but still spared time for her church service, socials, and weaving her baskets. We, the children, helped them on Saturdays and school holidays; she and Baba dished out punishments and complaints, and their marriage remained steady and predictable. We all knew who did what and when.

Unexpectedly, amid all that, Njomo, my parents' last baby, was born in late 1961.

Two years earlier, a seventeen-year-old girl had explained in graphic detail to two girls and me how men and women brought forth children. Like the other girls, I had scoffed, unwilling to associate such a disgusting act with my parents, hence my surprise when Mami gave birth.

I had noticed pregnant, ballooned stomachs. Sometimes, the women unzipped their side zippers for extra room. Except for thinking they were sloppy, I never dwelled on it. Mami never did that, and I never noticed her pregnancy. I now realize she must have been pregnant when she looked plumper than usual.

Besides the surprise, my mother's having a baby embarrassed me so much that I hoped no one in school learned of it. When Mr. Foolish came home to visit his family that December, he couldn't shut his mouth.

"I thought Mũriĩthi's mother is too old to have a baby," he told his mother, Elithi. Instead of keeping the remark to herself or telling her son it was okay because Mami was younger than she was, Elithi repeated the statement to Mami in my hearing right there at our house. I felt so disappointed that I didn't bother to memorize Njomo's birthdate, as I had done with my previous two siblings.

Mother loved Njomo. I had never heard her comment on any of our looks. But by the time Njomo crawled, Mami had called him cute several times. Other times, she would say, "He's as cute as David was." Because David was still missing, perhaps the last-born came to compensate my parents for their lost firstborn.

Whatever the case, Njomo's looks didn't change my negative reaction and possibly that of my siblings. I doubt it mattered because our household had reached its critical mass, a tipping point where one extra mouth made little difference.

*

Before Njomo turned one year old, at the end of 1962, Aunt Julia wrote to say she would visit us. We were beside ourselves with expectation; we couldn't wait to meet our special and only aunt. (Mami had one brother we hadn't met and no sisters.) She was also my father's only remaining sibling.

His two other siblings were dead. The British colonial military conscripted Mwai, his only brother, in World War I, and the family never heard of him again. His sister Wairimũ, whom my sister is named after, married and bore four sons. But when she fell terminally ill in the mid-1940s, her husband, Ndoogo, an alleged witchcraft peddler, traveled with her from their home in Nyeri and abandoned her at our first homestead in Kĩrĩma-inĩ. He promised he would return. She died within a month, and nobody in Solai saw him again.

Mami met Aunt Julia when they were both young women, over twenty-four years earlier, in 1937. After my parents married,

Baba took Mami to Nairobi to visit his sister. Aunt Julia took them to the Ngong Race Course and a dance in Kaloleni Hall. She gave Mami a set of china cups and plates, which proved impractical because we never used breakables.

Aunt Julia came along with Gĩthũi-big, the last son from Baba's first marriage. Gĩthũi-big now worked at Nairobi Hospital, where Aunt Julia got him a job before she retired. He brought his bride and a baby son named after Baba.

David, Gĩthũi-big, Aunt Julia

Like many city dwellers of that era, Gĩthũi-big lived alone in the city in a small studio provided by the hospital. His young family lived next to Aunt Julia in Nyeri, where he visited and took money at the end of each month.

I had never seen Gĩthũi-big, either. Aunt Julia left with him in the late 1940s. When she found it hard as an unmarried woman to raise him, she farmed him out to her married boyfriend's homestead in Mũrang'a County. The wife didn't mind her husband dating an educated woman or even marrying her. If he asked, I bet Aunt Julia turned him down. She was against plural marriages. She divorced her husband in the early 1930s after he married a second wife, following her failure to have children.

Before the visitors arrived, Baba made a plank bed for Aunt Julia opposite his bed in his studio-size thingira. Gĩthũi-big and his family stayed with his brother Waigwa's family.

I had never imagined what my aunt looked like. When I saw her, I noticed the uncovered salt-and-pepper hair. She seemed quite old to me. Baba was about thirteen years older than she but had no gray hair, a state he would enjoy well into his late seventies.

My aunt displayed townspeople's mannerisms. She was clean and dressed in a belted dress that reached her shins. She didn't tie her headscarf like the village women, who tied and placed their knots behind their necks, leaving the ends to droop down. Aunt Julia knotted hers above one ear and tucked in the ends; it looked like she was wearing a hat.

In my young mind, she looked more impressive than the photo I later saw of her.

Aunt Julia brought gifts to the entire family, including dress material for Tabitha, Wairimũ, and me; mine was turquoise. The gift delighted me, although I would have preferred a ready-to-wear dress so I didn't have to deal with Waigwa and his tailor shenanigans. But it was my chance to wear that circular dress I had craved for years. I don't recall what she gave Baba.

She spent most of her one-week stay with Baba in his thingira, or the two of them strolled along the dirt road that led to the wooded areas. Except for when Gĩthũi-big's wife sat with her baby in Mami's house, I don't recall Aunt Julia in Mami's house at all.

My sister Tabitha and I accompanied Aunt Julia for a walk on the dirt road behind our homestead. We met a herd of cows returning from grazing. She asked the Tugen herdsman in Kiswahili whether the cows would attack us. Aunt Julia pronounced the few words she spoke with a city accent. Even her Gĩkũyũ sounded different. Besides her Nyeri accent, she spoke in full sentences, unlike the village women who spoke fast, clipped their sentences, or ran them together.

Because of the joy I felt during that brief interaction with my aunt, I recapture or create such memorable incidents for the young relatives I associate with. This may come as a funny quip, clowning, or impromptu dancing. Or I speak kindly to young children I come across.

I have always indulged children and young people, even before I understood the positive effects of such gestures. This isn't something unusual. But sometimes, we adults get too busy and fail or forget to acknowledge children as we do our fellow adults.

*

When drafting this book, I learned of an incident I had no memory of. The uplifting feedback came from a much younger cousin, a highly placed government official, whom I rarely saw or had been with alone.

In October 2022, I joined him and another family friend for tea at The United Kenya Club in Nairobi. When the friend left, my cousin and I found ourselves together, alone. We spent about half an hour talking on a variety of subjects. Before we parted, he said he had something he always wanted to tell me. I wondered what that could be.

When he was in high school, he said, he visited my bungalow in Buru Buru Estate, Nairobi, once or twice. He said my place smelled so fresh that he admired me for living that well. "When I was doing my high school national exam," he said, "you sent me a 'best-of-luck card.'"

He said he couldn't believe someone out of his "league" who lived "so well" would remember him. He still treasured that card, he said.

*

After Aunt Julia left, I took the material she gave me to Waigwa, my half-brother, to make me a circular skirt dress.

It had been two years since Baba bought Waigwa a treadle Singer sewing machine, which Baba had called a family investment. But the plan of Waigwa keeping the money from his labor and making our dresses for free hadn't lived up to its ideal, at least for us, Baba's second family.

Waigwa took months to sew our clothes. Bad feelings simmered as we repeatedly dropped by his house to check on them.

We complained to Mami about the delay. In turn, she complained to no one in particular about how badly Waigwa treated her children. Waigwa and his family had stayed at our house for months after they returned from Kikuyuland, and now he denied her children minor generosity. Mami made her comments loud enough for Baba to hear in his thingira. He never acknowledged or acted on her indirect tantrums.

"You need to say something," Mami finally told Baba. "I don't understand how you remain quiet while Waigwa treats my children as if their rights don't matter."

To appease my mother or just shut her up, Baba talked to Waigwa. According to Mami, Waigwa blamed the delay on the sewing backlog. But I knew better, although I hadn't told Mami. From his body language, I could tell I irritated him whenever I checked on my dress.

When I appeared at his concrete circular cottage's doorstep and knocked on his open door, Waigwa stopped pedaling. And still holding the material in place, he would say, "Yes?" and look up. When he saw it was me, he tightened his jaws, bent back, and resumed pedaling.

"I want to check on my dress," I said.

Without pausing his peddle, he jerked his head sideways and said, "Look in the carton."

I rummaged through a carton filled with little rolled bundles of cloth material tied with sisal strings. I found my bundle at the bottom. When Waigwa took my measurements, he had written them in what looked like scrawls in an exercise book. How can he tell what scrawls match which material? I wondered.

"I'll come to check again," I would say, returning the bundle, this time on top.

Waigwa ignored me.

I failed to understand his behavior. My two sisters—Tabitha and Wairimũ—and I got only one new dress each in a year, an entire year of Waigwa's aggravation. Mami didn't take her clothes to him. I wondered why. But later, it dawned on me that, as a stepmother, she couldn't have him touching her while taking measurements. She bought our Christmas dresses and the boys' clothes off the store rack. And the tailor at Njeki's Shopping Center made our once-a-year uniforms.

It took us two years to realize that complaints through Mami were useless, including three months of aggravation while Waigwa botched the design of my turquoise dress. I ended up with a droopy, uneven, circular dress. My potential going-out dress turned into a work dress, which depressed me whenever I slipped it down my body.

Joseph, our family's comedian, who came up with creative insulting nicknames based on what someone wore, mannerisms, or looks, took advantage of my pain. He nicknamed me *k ĩhuruto* (circular). He never lost a chance to needle me whenever he could.

My botched dress became the tipping point for my sisters and me to walk away from free tailor services.

# Chapter 39

# Madam

One Monday during assembly, Mr. Kamau came with a woman in tow. Short like him, the woman wore a stylish green skirt and a white blouse, sleeves rolled up, and a salon-like hairdo. What a glamorous woman! What is she doing around our school? Is she a school inspector? I wondered. I had heard there were such people. There were no answers besides patience.

Mrs. Kamau didn't measure up. The few times I had seen her, she walked by on their small veranda in a regular home dress, sometimes with an apron. I had heard she lacked much education. Besides, she mainly stayed indoors or on the porch, never stepping on campus.

When Mr. Kamau introduced the woman as a teacher, my fellow schoolmates and I gawked at her. None of us expected a female teacher, let alone one so fine. Maybe she'll teach home economics, I ventured.

Back in Tindaress Primary, our grade three teacher had once said, "It's unfortunate there is no female to teach these girls home economics."

After that, I have a blurred memory of a teacher's wife teaching us various stitches in the schoolyard. She also showed us how to weave sisal and knit yarn mats, which she said people used to prevent teapots and other dishes from staining their varnished tables. Our parents owned no tables, let alone varnished ones. The mats were useless to us.

The thinking of what to prepare girls for was inevitable because, since birth, society had mapped out the girls' peasant futures. No adult questioned such bias. As proponents, I doubt they were aware of it, and we girls didn't recognize it, either. Instead, we went along, unbothered. By grade three, teachers had cemented the gender bias our parents had already conditioned us into.

At one time in grade four, a teacher told our class that we girls lacked the aptitude for arithmetic that boys had. Teachers would repeat this mantra for years to come.

But finally, here we had an educated, non-peasant woman-teacher before us.

When she came to our class, she said her name, but on the blackboard, she wrote "Madam," the only name I would later remember.

"This is how you address me," she said.

To this day, in Kenya, pupils still use "Madam" to address female teachers or women they respect.

Because my desk was in front of the class, I smelled whiffs of Madam's pleasant perfume. I observed her flawless, smooth skin, not ravaged by farm work. She wore bright, solid-colored dresses and skirts that were as good as new, with clean shoes as if she had never walked on dirt. I listened to her non-Gĩkũyũ accent more than I listened to whatever subject she taught us.

Madam kept to herself and never hung around in school. After her lesson ended, if she didn't have another one right away, she stuck her books in the crook of her left arm and returned to her duplex unit.

Not long after she came, I learned she owned an electric scooter but never used it for transportation, as men used bicycles. Pupils said she used the scooter on short, leisurely, and exploratory weekend rides along the Nakuru-Subukia Road or around the farms. That was a waste, they said—using the scooter to loaf around instead of using it to run errands.

I saw Madam once push her scooter into position, and another time I heard its engine firing as I walked home from school. I never saw her ride it. I wished she would ride it during school days instead of hearing about it secondhand.

Her owning a scooter was crucial for me. I had seen only a handful of progressive men ride on bicycles. The European farmers' wives never drove vehicles or rode on bicycles, either. They rode only as passengers. Madam owning a scooter was, therefore, a big deal. And to ride for leisure? Now, that was something!

The few boys who ran errands for their fathers, sometimes on borrowed bicycles, indulged in such "waste" as well. In transit, the boys invited their cronies and sneaked in joyrides. If an adult male caught them in the act, he scolded them for using the bicycle for thrills other than essential work. Girls never got such chances. They or their fathers never expected them to ride.

Because of Madam's detachment—nobody accused male teachers of such—and because of the scooter, pupils said she was proud. They liked "humble" teachers, like our teacher in grades one and two at Tindaress Primary. He laughed, told stories, and clowned like us and never even rapped us with a ruler. He once came to class in flip-flops and, one day, barefoot.

"What a humble teacher," we cooed.

"Proud" meant people who behaved as if they were better than us. I didn't care for "proud" people, either. But, engrossed in Madam's persona, I overlooked that part of her. Whatever she wore—she once wore flip-flops in class, too—I was okay with it, and I never labeled her humble or proud. Her owning and riding a scooter surpassed all that. Her lifestyle was inspirational.

Because of her, I promised myself that one day I would own my very own motorized scooter, exactly like her red one, which was the only one I had ever seen.

My scooter dream wasn't a silly, childish desire. Except for the two drivers who drove Solai and Kabazi buses, I had never seen an African who owned, rode, or drove anything faster than a bicycle.

Mr. Mbuthia, the pastor, and Mr. Foolish's brother-in-law didn't count. He had once bought a junky car for 500 shillings, just for show and bragging rights in the future. He drove the car home (with no license) from where it never moved again. To preserve it, he propped it up on stone blocks. During the day, the car provided chickens with much-needed shelter from the sun.

At least Mr. Mbuthia had the right to brag to anyone who would listen in the future that he once owned a car.

# Chapter 40

# A Mere Hiccup

One Monday morning, during Madam's lesson, a different teacher came to teach us. He never said why Madam was absent or when she would return. He acted familiar, as if he had always taught us.

During break time, rumors swirled and churned. I learned Madam was a mere hiccup—here today, gone tomorrow. Pupils said her pride couldn't let her stay in such a poor, depressed, boring community.

I felt the loss, my first time missing a teacher. It wasn't because of what she had taught me. But she had inspired me and showed me the type of life I could have if I stuck with school.

From her first day and throughout her few months' stay, Madam had seemed too polished for our school. She looked like a blooming flower in a desert of nutrient-deprived scrubs—too polished for the likes of us. She should teach in town, I had thought, where they had better amenities suitable for her kind.

Instead, she was stuck on a colonial farm, surrounded by bachelor teachers who ogled her and exhausted locals, men hunched in tired clothes, trudging home from work, and women with their backs laden with loads, hoping their children would escape the drudgery that kept every villager captive.

Yes, Kabazi Center was unsuitable for her, I had concluded.

It comprised the school, teachers' quarters, and a small white-washed concrete shop that Major Ward had sold to an employee on installment when its maintenance outweighed its benefits. There was also a Sunday open-air market and a mud-and-thatch canteen at the edge of the Center, open seven days a week.

That comprised the total of Kabazi Center. It wasn't much, but it looked better than Tindaress Primary School with its one mud-and-thatch building and three teacher cottages next to a dirt road in the middle of nowhere.

In the canteen, male customers sat at four-chair wooden tables, drinking or nursing black coffee loaded with sugar in white enamel mugs. (Farmworkers had no milk; it was for the landowners.) Most ate plain white bread slices. For an extra charge, a customer received a two-slice sandwich loaded with margarine called Blue Band, served on similar plates. The men socialized and discussed the latest politics or village news.

Teachers didn't patronize the canteen; they avoided mixing with the locals. Although people didn't talk about it, their general belief was that teachers were above such establishments or mingling with villagers. If teachers wanted a change of scenery, they rode on the bus to Nakuru Town.

Pupils blamed Madam's departure on the humble place. Nobody mentioned loneliness and the lousy treatment she had endured from the four bachelor teachers.

Before she left, teachers bad-mouthed her even to us pupils. Once in class, my English teacher—Silas, who had replaced Mr. Foolish—referred to Madam as "That fat pig."

But the main whisper, which those male teachers didn't expect would reach us pupils, was that they disliked her because she had scoffed at their sexual advances.

# Chapter 41

# Sex Education

One mid-morning in grade five, I gasped when our teacher announced he would teach sex education. It was so unexpected. Do they teach such in school? I asked myself.

Since the British invaded and conquered Kenya, indigenous practices by which young people learned such matters were eroded, diluted, and gradually degraded to a mere skeleton, or they became extinct. At best, what remained was body mutilation in the name of circumcision that did nothing more than curb or diminish sexual sensitivity and urges.

Young people, especially girls, had no opportunity to learn about sexuality. After the old system broke down, their busy and uninformed parents failed to step in.

The earliest brush with sexuality I encountered was back at Tindaress Primary School when our grade two teacher sent us to our break. A tall girl in her late teens, who towered over all of us except for the teacher, rose from her seat and froze as if unable to move. The teacher noticed her dilemma and approached. That drew our attention to her uniform that stuck to her rear, drenched, and to a blotch of blood on the bench where she had sat.

"*Njẹ! Haraka! Haraka!*" (Out! Quickly! Quickly!) The teacher said, flicking his backhand toward us pupils.

A few of us who sat close to her lagged, curious about how the teacher would reprimand the girl.

"Go home," he said softly, "and return tomorrow."

Confused, he wasn't cross with the girl. I hurried outside so my colleagues could enlighten or help me unravel the mystery. When we reached outside, we hung close to the door so we could see the tall girl leave.

When she appeared, she tilted her head to one side, her lips clamped over her buck teeth, while boys taunted and made fun of her. She continued without moving a muscle beside her legs, her eyes downcast until she reached the nearby Solai/Nakuru Road and disappeared, never to return.

Pupils now debated the cause of the tall girl's "malady." One girl said, "Perhaps her cruel parents beat her."

A chorus of laughter erupted among some pupils. Others threw in their suggestions. None seemed acceptable. I remained quiet and confused. Finally, a couple of boys settled the matter. The girl had blood because she did bad things with big boys. What were the "bad things"? I asked myself. The girls next to me didn't know either. My ignorance stuck with me for three years.

I had learned too much about sex at fourteen. A man I didn't know, possibly a visitor from another village, who I now guess was in his late teens or early twenties, attacked me. The experience terrified me so much, and I considered it so loathsome and embarrassing that I told no one.

About a year and a half after the attack, it was a big deal when our grade five teacher announced he would teach us sex education. I waited, ready to learn about things that had confused me about men, women, and sex. But I felt nervous about learning such an intimate subject among boys. Soon, I realized my concern was for naught when the teacher addressed the class. While we all gawked at him, eager, he said, "All the girls stand up!"

I suppose he will start with female stuff, I thought. Too embarrassing.

The girls and I rose.

"Girls," he said, "I need to teach the sensitive subject with no women around. You go wait outside." He pointed us to the door.

The girls and I left the classroom, covering our mouths to muffle our giggles. In my mind, though, I was disappointed to miss that opportunity. When will I ever learn about sex?

While we girls waited outside for forty minutes, we heard grunts and subdued chuckles.

Afterward, no boy, not even my own brother Joseph, divulged *the great secret*. Such discussion was taboo among siblings, anyway.

The community expected us girls to learn basic activities like cooking and rearing children from our mothers or by instinct. And our busy mothers seemed to expect us to learn through observation. But it seemed nobody wanted to teach us about sexuality. Well into my teen years, and I didn't know girls had menstrual periods! I didn't even ask myself how my mother brought forth a new baby every two years.

At sixteen, as I walked home from school, I squatted behind a shrub to pee and noticed blood. Horrified, I wept, fearing my previous violent attack had marked me for life. I didn't connect it to a natural process. As I matured, I understood the critical part the process played in life, but at a deeper level, I still took the monthly occurrences as a nuisance.

Over five decades later, I reconnected with Edward Chege, one of my classmates. As he and I reminisced about our years at Kabazi Primary, he told me tidbits about what they learned in the sex education lesson. The teacher told them how to choose an ideal mate, among other scraps of advice that I suppose Chege couldn't share with me.

"The ideal woman to marry," the teacher had advised them, "is the one with wide hips. You want to avoid complications during childbirth."

Even after all those years, Chege interrupted our phone call with chuckles.

Perhaps that is why some people claim men of African descent prefer hippy or plump women, I thought.

During those crucial teenage years, Mami had tried to impart her sex advice to my sister Tabitha and me. She told us how, back in her day, although an occasional pregnancy happened and a woman was quickly married off, Agĩkũyũ didn't condone sex before marriage. In Gĩkũyũ tradition, young men and women attended weekend dances and afterward indulged in *ngwĩko* (partner masturbation).

A young man courted a woman he liked; if she liked him back, the two indulged in ngwĩko. They would caress, and finally, the man strategically placed his penis on the woman's oiled thighs and gyrated his midriff until he ejaculated. Ngwĩko was supposed to teach the couple the pleasure of sex and the importance of boundaries because they couldn't indulge in the actual sex act before marriage.

In other words, the man couldn't go beyond the woman's *mwengũ* (pubic apron). If he did, which rarely happened, the partner told on him. As punishment, the community ostracized the hot pants for a period, and his reputation remained tainted.

After Mami finished, I wondered how that would help me. I considered her knowledge obsolete, based on time gone by. We lived in a new day when predatory grown men lurked all around us. The older we girls got, the more determined the predators became.

# Chapter 42

# A Rose Among Us

After Madam left, the adage "When one door closes, another opens" proved true. Our "other door" at Kabazi Primary soon opened, and Rose breezed in.

In her mid-twenties, Rose had skin as smooth as a baby's over a slim body, covered by a tailored skirt and blouse, as she walked elegantly into our classroom, a place where she looked out of place. In one word, she looked classy, with a distinct little black mole on the side of her nose.

Where do these women grow up? I doubt she will stay, I thought.

"Good morning, pupils," she said when she came to our class.

"Good morning, Madam," we chimed.

"My name is Rose 'Wahome'," she said and wrote "Rose" on the blackboard. "This is how I want you to address me."

I gawked at her. It had never occurred to me that we could address a teacher by name to their face. Just like that, Madam became a distant memory, as I, like my classmates, became smitten with Rose. " Beautiful and not proud," we said during break time.

Within no time, Rose had settled into one unit of the duplex and started exploring the school and the neighboring farms. Our other teachers left the school grounds only when they went to Nakuru Town or sneaked around incognito to dab in mischief.

"I know your cousin," she told me one day in the schoolyard.

"Oh!" I said, surprised. I knew of him, but he and I had never met.

"Your cousin said hello," she said to me occasionally. She also started sending me on quick errands—to fetch something or deliver books to her apartment.

Soon after, rumors circulated that she was dating my cousin Jaypee, whom I wouldn't meet until two years later. Pupils said Rose spent weekends at his house. Jaypee taught at Ol Donyo Mara Primary School at Major Stein's farm, a mile and a half northwest of Kabazi. On our way home, we pupils from Major Miller's farm branched west about half a mile before the school.

Schools were usually farther apart, but any landowner could choose to have a school on their farm, depending on their religious affiliation.

I'm unaware whether Major Stein was a Catholic, but he had admitted Catholics into his farm. His employees helped build Ol Donyo Mara Primary School, where pupils learned the Bible through Catholic doctrine, and farmworkers used it as a church on Sundays. My relatives on my mother's side and others at Stein's farm ended up Catholics, while we and peasants in the surrounding farms became Anglicans by default.

My friendship with Rose grew as she extended small favors to me. These included speaking to me in Gĩkũyũ or sending me to her apartment. (Before then, I heard no teacher utter a single word in Gĩkũyũ.) Did she like me because of Jaypee? Perhaps. It made me feel grateful for Jaypee's connection.

By and by, our relationship took a turn I never expected. One Friday after school, Rose told me she planned to visit Solai Center (Njeki's Shopping Center) that Sunday.

"Because you live on the way," she said. "I'll stop by on my way home."

Our home wasn't on Rose's way. From Njeki's, she had to walk farther north for two miles. I enjoyed her "friendship," but a visit to our home crossed the line; it unsettled me. Yes, the visit would be a great honor for my brother and me, but her finding out how we lived wiped out its benefits. Recognition and her friendship were what I wanted as long as our humble lifestyle remained in the background.

Teachers never visited pupils' homes. If a teacher had an issue with a pupil, a cane settled it. Only on very rare occasions did teachers invite pupils' fathers to the school. I had heard of only one teacher's visit during David's time at school in the early 1950s. According to family lore, he spent his day in the woods, exploring and terrorizing birds he targeted with small pebbles, scavenging for berries, and even squeezing in a nap after he ate the lunch he had carried.

He enjoyed the freedom so much he thought of taking an occasional Friday off—convinced our parents would never know. He returned home late afternoon, complaining of how tired and hungry he was.

Mr. Jacob Rũrĩrĩ, the only teacher at the one-room school at Kwa-Ndege's, trekked the five or six miles to our first homestead at Kĩrĩma-inĩ to check on what was the matter with his promising pupil. He put an end to David's truancy plans.

But Rose's visit would be purely social, something unheard of.

# Chapter 43

# Rose's Visit

I told Joseph about Rose's visit the minute we cleared Kabazi Center. "She has to be joking!" he said. "Whoever heard of a teacher visiting a pupil? What were you talking about?"

I sensed he wanted to blame the visit on me. "She isn't visiting me!" I said. "She said, 'Stop by.'" Joseph let it go. But the visit gnawed on me. I wished Rose would get delayed at Njeki's and run out of time.

The following day, we prepared for her visit the best we could. We spruced up the girls' quarters—the miserable, dirt-and-thatch shack where Tabitha and I slept, about thirty feet from Mami's nyũmba. The shack contained two homemade plank beds that hugged the walls on opposite sides, one for Tabitha and the other for me. Besides old threadbare blankets, the beds had no mattresses, but we never missed them.

The only other fixture was a sisal string strung across from the rafters, where we hung our clothes. We each kept our one Sunday dress in Mami's trunk in her house. The cottage was a cold, lifeless place where we never spent time except to sleep.

After our home chores, Joseph and I had the rest of Saturday and half of Sunday to spruce up the shack. Because of how far we walked to school, Mr. Kamau exempted us from Sunday school or adult service. He said we needed a break from the strenuous walk over the weekend. Sometimes, we attended church out of habit or because we had nowhere else to go. But we now had an important visitor to entertain.

On Saturday, Joseph and his two friends went to the field to cut grass using scythes. Because of sunny days, the grass was semi-dry. They spread the heaps of grass to ensure every bit of moisture dried out. Joseph went to turn it over twice. They then hauled the dry grass home in sisal sacks to prevent the dew from dampening it overnight.

That Sunday morning, my anxiety raged on. I thought of taking off and returning late in the afternoon, when I figured Rose would be gone. But I did no such thing. Instead, even before other family members dispersed to their Sunday activities, Joseph and I buried ourselves in getting ready for Rose.

We overstuffed two sisal "mattresses," Joseph's orders. In his wisdom, they would turn out okay when the grass settled in. After we filled a sack, I strained to hold its opening's sides together while Joseph sewed it shut with the gigantic needle and sisal strings that Mami used to mend sacks for the family's grains.

Our mattresses ended up so overstuffed that when we placed them on the beds, they looked like cylindrical anthills. Even our raggedy blankets had trouble covering them completely. To tame them, Joseph bounced on one and I on the other. They popped back up when we got off. Even worse, tiny pricks pierced through the sacks and the bedding and pricked us. I quit bouncing. Joseph kept at it, claiming the grass would flatten and settle before Rose arrived that afternoon. I didn't believe him, but I kept mum.

After we cleared the strewn leftover grass, I sprinkled water inside the cottage to tame any loose dust before I swept. That was the extent of our preparation—nothing about food or drink. I didn't even think I could cook anything. Mami always decided what to cook, and on Sundays, she cooked a late lunch when she returned from church.

Joseph and I hung around the courtyard, anxious, while we waited for our honored guest. It never occurred to us how Rose would find our homestead. She hadn't asked where my family lived. Perhaps I mentioned it in one of our interactions. Or Jaypee had told her. If she knew the name of the farm, all she needed was to ask for Warama's homestead twice—we all knew who lived where—first, at our old fenced village across the river, and second, when she arrived at our current one.

Rose appeared at the entrance in the afternoon. Her brow and cheeks shone with sweat shimmers while tiny beads of sweat dripped down her temples. More outgoing than I, Joseph rushed to meet her while I inched toward the cottage so she knew where to enter.

When she entered, Joseph directed her to sit on the firmer, better-looking bed.

Rose flopped her tired body on the bed as if it were a firm couch.

"Ah!" she said as she bounced and sank into the spongy mattress. Her feet went off the ground, her legs and arms splayed. Joseph spread his hands and stood slightly bent, ready to lunge and rescue her. She recovered before she tipped over and before Joseph gathered the courage to touch her. She steadied herself, shifted this way and that, and settled down.

She then slowly ran her eyes around the cottage, a human panoramic camera. She even looked up at the rafters.

Well, this is it, I thought. Her first impression of the conditions we lived under likely horrified her.

My brother and I stood by like wait staff, wringing our hands. Poor us! Her reaction had sent tremors through my insides as shame engulfed me. But I didn't hold Rose's curiosity against her. I admired her so much that I placed her above reproach.

"This is how far you walk every morning?" Rose asked. This was incorrect because she hadn't trekked on our route yet.

"Yes," Joseph and I said in unison.

It was my first time to get embarrassed by someone coming to our home. The other villagers didn't count. We all scrambled for crumbs in the same pit. Besides, my family and other villagers wore poverty as a badge of honor. Wallowing in it for decades without an exit in sight, it had become a mental state as well. We proclaimed our malady—our poverty—to God and humans without embarrassment.

Aunt Julia's visit should have embarrassed me, but it didn't. She grew up in similar conditions. Besides, she was family. Rose was different. We wanted to impress her from afar, without her peeking at our lives, the reason I never wanted her to come to our homestead.

Much later, I understood why we had embraced poverty in the village. In the colonial system, it paid to display one's poverty. Even if most Africans were desperately poor, the authorities helped only the poorest of the poor with school fee subsidies after parents had scraped together enough to get a bright son into high school. Handouts for the first eight years of education were nonexistent; pupils dropped out, no matter how gifted.

Employers also used poverty, especially in non-skilled jobs. As people had done in school when they looked for jobs in towns, they noted in their applications that their parents were poor. When called for an interview, the likelihood of getting employed increased if they wore the worst clothes they owned, walked with their shoulders hunched, and claimed poverty.

Although dressing poorly during interviews became extinct, I doubt Kenyan society ever outgrew that dehumanizing, engraved colonial mentality of poverty. They expect or rely too much on family members, even strangers, believing them—sometimes erroneously—to be financially better off than they are.

Much later in adulthood, when my life improved, I still claimed poverty when I realized the mantra helped keep needy relatives at bay. But even when I didn't have money, my relatives never believed me, which stressed me to no end.

But poverty repelled us during Rose's visit. Although it was obvious our family lived in squalor, a bare minimum existence, we recoiled to realize she noticed it.

She recounted her day's trek: To get to Njeki's, she had walked down the more ragged and steeper part of Jumatatu Mountain Range to our south. That was the usual gateway to Njeki's for people at Kabazi. On her way home, she walked two miles from Njeki's, bypassed the way to the steeper pathway, and continued for another two miles north to our village—a slog I knew only one other enterprising teacher from Kabazi to accomplish.

She would walk another three-plus miles back to Kabazi. Two-thirds of the way back, I guessed, she would pass by Jaypee's house. Under normal circumstances, as a man and a local, he would have accompanied Rose to Njeki's. But having walked everywhere in his youth and outgrown it, I doubt he would have agreed to take on such a strenuous adventure again.

Rose patted her sweaty face and neck with a handkerchief twice. Joseph remembered to offer her a drink of water. She turned it down.

Teachers boiled their water and, to keep it cool, stored it in potty-bellied reddish clay pots, closed tight with similar lids bought in town. They instructed pupils to do the same to avoid bilharzia infection and other water-borne diseases. But they should have told our mothers because we children didn't run households. Besides, the instruction was out of our minds by the time we left the schoolyard.

Otherwise, our families and we drank our water straight from the tap, water tinged brown that Kamunge pumped untreated from the Tindaress River.

We longed to entertain Rose, but we didn't know how. Besides, there was no food to offer her. Without refrigeration, mothers cooked every mealtime from scratch unless they cooked *mataha* or *mũkimo* (cooked with maize, a variety of beans, greens, and potatoes) that lasted for several days. Even if there was food, I doubted Rose would have eaten anything we offered on our sorry enamel plates, nicked and chipped thanks to my younger siblings, who dropped dishes anywhere and everywhere.

Joseph and I stood, stressed but deferential, without enough sense to sit on the opposite bed. We settled on answering Rose's questions. Unlike our other teachers, who never uttered a word of Gĩkũyũ, Rose spoke to us in Gĩkũyũ just like she did in school when we were outside the classroom. She asked us how we were doing in our other classes and about our families. When she ran out of things to ask us, she excused herself.

We escorted Rose through the pedestrian gate onto the dirt road behind our homestead. After we crossed the dirt road a few yards to the scrubby area, we showed her the path to follow, feeling relieved to bid her goodbye.

# Chapter 44

# Kikuyuland Safari

After our last class on a Friday, Rose waved from her porch to get my attention. She beckoned me and returned indoors. When I entered, she gave me a rag to wipe my feet.

"Try these and see whether they fit you," she said, handing me a pair of brown leather flat shoes similar to this old, cherished pair I own today.

Wow! What a gesture! I had never tried on shoes! The shoes fit perfectly. (Size 5 or 7.5 in the USA, a size I have worn to this day.) My very own pair of shoes! What a pleasant surprise! To preserve my dignity, I controlled myself. I felt special while my love for Rose blossomed. No other pupil wore shoes in or outside school.

I removed the shoes so I could carry them. Rose insisted I wear them. I was so self-conscious, almost embarrassed to be seen wearing shoes. I removed them the minute I cleared the schoolyard. Afterward, I wore them during my occasional visits to Njeki's Shopping Center. I also wore them when Baba and I went to Nakuru General Hospital to visit Joseph and Tabitha, who had caught typhoid fever and stayed in the hospital for a month.

That August, during the school holidays, Rose invited me to accompany her to her parents' home in Nyeri, about eighty miles away. That was my first time traveling to Kikuyuland and covering such a long distance.

I couldn't wait!

My heart welled up at the thought of a person like Rose associating with me and taking me on such a long safari—trip, journey, tour. I felt special. And to top it, she had given me the brown pair of shoes; I didn't have to walk barefoot and embarrass her. In hindsight, it's likely the reason she gave me the shoes.

I believed Rose liked me because of my cousin. But another faint voice within me wondered whether she had seen something special in me and wanted to nurture it and show me a different lifestyle, better possibilities than what she had seen at my home.

When Rose and I arrived at her parents' home, the disparity between our two worlds unsettled me. Unlike us, Rose's parents lived on their own land, where they grew all kinds of plants and fruit trees, such as bananas, oranges, and other perennials that the law didn't allow farmworkers to grow (although they, like us, couldn't yet grow cash crops like coffee or tea).

They lived in a masonry-stone house with red cement floors. Even their outside kitchen had a cement floor.

We slept in beds with headboards, real mattresses, pillows, and bedsheets. When I woke in the morning, all sorts of pleasant smells greeted me. Rose's mother served us plenty of tasty, delicious food I had never eaten before. It included eggs and bread with tea made with fresh milk from their own cows. After breakfast, her father showed me around their compound. I watched calves graze in a pen. Two other adjacent pens were closed off to let the grass grow.

Before then, it had never occurred to me that Africans could rear cows.

When my father turned down the twenty-five-acre land three years prior, I had only thought of the basics—school supplies, clothes, shoes, and a "good" house. With no point of reference, a wholesome, comfortable lifestyle like Rose's family hadn't crossed my mind. I wondered how people got to live such splendid lives. It was a basic three-bedroom concrete house, but in my eyes, it seemed like a mansion.

I don't know whether Rose's father had been a colonial government official, but their land had remained intact through the ravages of the Mau Mau and the British war.

I couldn't imagine that kind of life for my family. I doubted that we could attain it. Our lives comprised ragged clothes, shoeless feet, dirt floors, and a constant scarcity of basics that left permanent scars.

Unknown to me, however, my brief encounters with Madam and Rose had fertilized my mental ecosystem. The two women had textured and strengthened my belief in the need to escape the peasant lifestyle.

# Chapter 45

# Silas Gachiĩ

Meanwhile, after the Ministry of Education abolished the fourth-grade national exam, except for two pupils Mr. Kamau held back, the entire class, even the older ones that the school would have previously aged out, advanced to grade five based on our end-of-year tests.

But it was uncomfortable for the oldest boys. It bothered them when their younger classmates did better than them, and especially when a teacher pointed it out.

Although I fit right in, it seemed different for the other girls. They acted distant as if they didn't belong. By our third term in grade five, they kept to themselves, both in and outside class. I started joining grade four girls for lunch. When we rattled in class before our teacher arrived, the young women never joined the conversation. They sat at the back of the class and never raised their hands or answered questions unless the teacher called on them. Their performance trailed everyone else. Although I never thought of it, I was in my mid-teens, and those girls were older than me.

Some teachers shamed the older girls both in and outside the class. I recall one teacher who verbally terrorized one girl about her big bust every chance he got. Her bust measured about a C-cup, but without a bra, it seemed much bigger.

"Even you, five-pounder?" the teacher would say. "You couldn't solve that?"

After such a zinger, boys eyed the girl while they dipped their heads, muffling giggles.

Girls had dropped out of school, one by one, since we were in grade four; two had already dropped out in grade five. At the end of 1962, except for me, only four other girls remained in class when we did our end-of-year tests.

When we reported to grade six in January 1963, halfway through the first lesson, to my dismay, no other girl had appeared. The teacher partnered me with Gerald Wangunyũ Thaiya to share a front desk.

The other girls must be late, I told myself. As the morning crept on, I felt self-conscious and wondered about their "lateness." Perhaps they are waiting for their parents to get money for school fees, uniforms, or supplies; anything to explain their absence.

When we broke for lunch, I forgot about the absent classmates when I mixed and shared lunch with grade five girls. But, back in class that afternoon, my thoughts trailed back. Maybe the four girls fell sick during the December holiday. I doubted it. I didn't want to believe what seemed so obvious to others.

By Friday, I had accepted it was the boys and me.

For the next two years, in grades six and seven, I remained the lone girl in a class of about 32 pupils. Not once did I suffer a mean word or look from my classmates; I could as well have been a boy. Besides, I held my own and equaled or matched the brightest pupils' marks.

\*

Like every pupil, I had an inherent deference or fear of teachers. They were tyrants or displayed an aura of tyranny. I believed they could turn against me in a flash. Madam, Rose, and my teacher in grades one and two at Tindaress Primary were exceptions; they never used corporal punishment.

Then I came across another mellow, pot-bellied, fatherly-type teacher (whom I'll call Mr. Mwega) to teach us English. I expected nothing different from him. But I soon realized Mr. Mwega didn't use sticks or reprimands when we made mistakes. He patiently repeated the instruction until one understood.

At our village one Sunday, when I rushed through the small pedestrian gate that led to the dirt road behind our homestead, I stopped, surprised when I saw Mr. Mwega trudging on, face all sweaty. He came from Njeki's Shopping Center, he said.

"It's my first time to come to Solai," he said in English.

"Oh."

"Where do you live?"

"This is my village," I said. He didn't have to know I lived only yards from where we stood.

He spoke in English throughout our brief interaction, and I was surprised that I spoke that many English words for the first time.

Months after we advanced to grade six, he, too, left Kabazi.

Although I didn't think about the disruption to our learning, no teacher besides Mr. Kamau stuck around long enough for my class to finish a year's worth of the syllabus.

Whenever new teachers came, they never started teaching where the last one left off. I remained with gaps or blind spots in every subject.

But the best was yet to come. Or was it? Life isn't always that clear-cut.

When Mr. Mwega left, Mr. Silas Gachiĩ took over the English lesson.

In his late twenties, Mr. Silas Gachiĩ referred to himself by his first name. Unlike Rose, he didn't mention his last name when he introduced himself. He wrote "Silas" on the blackboard.

"Silas is what you call me," he said.

We never called him Silas to his face. It sounded "wrong" and disrespectful. We addressed him as "Sir," as we did with other teachers.

He displayed a no-nonsense, wholesome, clean-cut appearance. About five-foot-ten, medium build, gray, tan, or gray trousers, short-sleeved shirt, hair parted on the left, and never wore a jacket.

Unlike most men who hunched their shoulders, Silas walked with purpose, erect and confident in his steps. Unlike other teachers, Silas had no use for sticks. He had an aura of authority, with a persona that dared pupils not to stray. From the respectful demeanor the teachers adopted when they approached him, word spread that he intimidated them, including Mr. Kamau, the headmaster.

I revered Silas; in my eyes, no other teacher could measure up.

Before he came to teach my class, English grammar seemed like an assortment of rules with no cohesive logic. On his first Monday morning, it took him only one lesson for my heart to glow. I couldn't believe my luck. He cleared my confusion and laid my lifelong English foundation—at least, the spelling rules and the crucial tenses vis-à-vis the first, second, and third persons.

Silas taught English grammar as if he had constructed it, like steps on a ladder. He was a storyteller who ensured each scene led to the next. Unless a pupil started off unlucky and got stuck with an extra-slow brain, she could follow each lesson without any follow-up questions.

Not long after he came, he listed, defined, and summarized the eight parts of speech—nouns, verbs, adjectives, adverbs, pronouns, conjunctions, prepositions, and interjections—in one lesson. My classmates and I gawked at him. I doubted I had a slow brain, but I wondered how he expected us to remember all that heavy stuff.

"You seem confused," he said. "Don't worry. That's called an overview. I'll teach you those parts one by one."

I didn't know what "overview" was, but I understood "one by one." I sat back and thanked my stars for bringing such a teacher my way.

In the next lesson, he started from the beginning—the nouns, the verbs, and so forth. He didn't ask whether any other teacher had covered the material. I was grateful for it—until the cost became too high.

# Chapter 46

# Dubious Sleep Over

The teachers' duplex where Madam and now Rose lived stood between Mr. Kamau's house and the house formerly occupied by Mr. Foolish and his colleague. Rose occupied the unit on Mr. Kamau's side while Silas lived in the next unit.

Rose's small apartment was clean, furnished with basics—two easy chairs with wooden arms, a coffee table, a table chair by the wall, a side table where she kept a radio, and a "kitchenette" (small cupboard and a pressure stove) in one corner. As I learned later, her bedroom held a single bed, a good-sized suitcase on a low table, a small chest of drawers, and a side table.

Since we visited Rose's parents, she continued to greet me, ask about my family, send me to her apartment, and twice invited me for tea.

One Friday, she asked me to spend the night.

Spend the night at her place? I found it hard to believe. The specialness of that so filled me that it didn't even occur to me to wonder where I would sleep in her one-bedroom apartment.

It seems odd now, but back then, we pupils felt honored if a teacher asked us to help with personal chores. Although we had little choice, we agreed without hesitation. Like me, I doubt it crossed any other pupils' minds that they needed to ask their parents before accepting such requests. However, society held teachers in such high esteem that any parent would have approved and would have been even more thankful that their child was associating with a teacher of the same gender.

"I won't be going home," I told Joseph at the end of our last class. "I'm going to Rose's."

"Okay," Joseph said. No questions asked.

How long did Rose need me? I didn't know. She didn't say, and it didn't matter.

Early evening, she cooked a mixture of potatoes, beef, and vegetables. After our supper, she freshened herself. And just before dusk, she said, "I'm going to Jaypee's."

"Okay," I said with some hesitation, blind-sided.

"Take my bed when you get ready to sleep; I'll see you in the morning." Just like that, she was gone.

Disappointed, I felt cheated. I agreed to stay because of the specialness of a sleepover. Now, spending a night alone in her apartment terrified me. I had never spent an evening alone, let alone an entire night. It felt lonely and unnatural. The turn of events angered and confused me. I thought of leaving, but it was already too late to walk home.

Although I wondered why Rose asked me to sleep over, I still didn't harbor unkind thoughts toward her—a generosity I wouldn't extend to her a day later.

I had nothing to occupy me; Rose had no books in her apartment for me to read besides the instructional teachers' manuals. I thought of my family and their evening banter, seated around the fire. It surprised me how much I liked and missed the rowdy bunch and how I longed to be among them! Do they miss me? I asked myself. What is Mami cooking? Have they eaten? I craved everything about our household's evening—the warmth of the fire, the complaints, the commotion, the chatter, Joseph's jokes, embellished stories, and all of us eating together.

My family never owned a radio, but Rose's radio failed to interest me. Whatever it spewed never overrode my longing for my family.

I used cold water in a basin to wash my face, hands, and legs as Mami did—although she warmed her water—before she went to bed. At about 8:00 p.m., I shed my uniform and got into bed in my full slip and underpants.

I spent the next hour thinking, envying the human noises coming from Mr. Kamau's house next door. My ears became alert to any little noise—crickets and other insects' noises or fussing feral cats.

But my thoughts trailed back to my family, now close to our bedtime. I zeroed in on my bed, with a sisal sack-filled-grass mattress opposite my sister in our dirt-and-thatch cottage. The grass in the mattress had settled, and the bed felt comfortable. When my body got into that bed, I became oblivious to the world within minutes and remained under its spell for the next nine hours. I missed my no-sheets precious bed. I would have traded Rose's clean bed with white sheets for mine in a flash.

Meanwhile, the homey noises of an occasional person's heavy step or a clang of a dish or a voice or murmur died down. Tired of being lonesome and plowing through thoughts, my mind calmed down, ready to welcome sleep.

# Chapter 47

# Predatory Chameleon

Every time my head hit a bed, my brain wasted not a minute before it sank into dreamland. When that happened, no commotion could wake me, not even the house caving in. I slept the same way when Rose and I visited her parents. But at her apartment, besides the general fear of being alone, my mind wandered, thinking of all sorts of scary scenarios, as if the walls had become hollow and wouldn't shield me from an attack by any semblance of irimũ rĩa nyakondo (bogeyman). Finally, fatigue overtook me, and I dozed off.

I heard light scratches on the door, scratches I wouldn't have heard if I'd been truly asleep. The scratches rattled me. I raised my head, perked my ears, and listened. Rose didn't have a cat; perhaps one of the feral ones scratched the door as it passed by. Or my aloneness made me imagine hearing things.

But the "scratches" came again. Now fully alert, I realized they weren't scratches. They were soft taps. Three spaced taps. Fear grabbed me. I'm being dramatic, I chastised myself. No reports had ever come of house intruders in Kabazi or Solai. Maybe Rose had returned? But I doubted it. If she did, she would call my name or knock on the bedroom window to avoid disturbing her neighbors.

I needed to say something—do something. My brain wrangled—no one knocks on doors after people go to bed.

Unsure how to respond, I got off the bed, tiptoed to the half-open door between the bedroom and the sitting room, and sidled through so as not to touch it and cause a creak. In the sitting room, I stood still and waited. The wooden window let in slits of moonlight. I could see the furniture silhouettes.

I thought of lighting the pressure lamp to scare the intruder away. No, it would make too much noise and announce my presence.

Another three taps came.

"Who is it?" I asked, in haste, too fearful but too stupid to shut my mouth, ignore the knocks, return to bed, worry, and finally fall asleep and dream about attacks by ogres.

"Nĩ Silas" (It's Silas), the voice came in Gĩkũyũ, softly, almost in a whisper. "Hingũra mũrango" (Open the door).

Wow! I never knew the man spoke in Kiswahili or Gĩkũyũ.

"Sir, Rose is not in," I said in English, my voice shaky.

"I know."

I hesitated, confused. Why would Silas knock on Rose's door if he knew she wasn't home? What does he want? I asked myself.

A series of soft, insistent knocks came again.

"What's going on?" he asked in an urgent, authoritative tone. "It's me. Open the door."

Oh goodness, I fretted. He's angry. He'll accuse me of insubordination and disrespect.

I rounded the coffee table and proceeded to the main door.

*

How I opened that door and how Silas' silhouette entered is buried in my memory. I have fuzzy recollections of me offering him a seat and asking whether he wanted me to light the pressure lamp. He said no. Perhaps because he didn't ask where Rose went, I expected him to sit and wait for her and leave if she didn't return. Or I planned to leave him in the sitting room and return to bed. But I don't recall what happened next or the state of my thought process under such confusion and pressure.

What remains clear is how Silas and I wrestled in bed.

I whimpered, balled my body, flailed my arms, and kicked this and that as if my body had turned into that of an octopus. Silas tried to restrain my arms, grab my thigh, and get his knee in place to control my legs.

"Sir, leave me alone," I repeated over and over.

Except for an occasional frustrated grunt and forced breathing, the man never uttered a word. Afterward, I realized he never wanted to talk or cause too much noise; otherwise, my flailing limbs were no match for him.

But there was no quiet way to what he wanted. The creaking bed, a thump on the wall, and my pleas escalated high enough that somebody in Mr. Kamau's house could have heard and come to check on Rose. But I still needed a more lethal weapon that my brain couldn't figure out yet.

Sensing he was close to his goal, he ripped off my underwear.

A spontaneous squeal escaped my mouth. It worked like magic.

Silas shot out of that apartment as if a lion were chasing him.

I never shed a tear as I worried myself to sleep. I dreamed of being in the middle of a cacophony of attackers.

\*

After I dressed and made the bed in the morning, I waited for Rose in the sitting room. Meanwhile, I heard human noises coming from Mr. Kamau's house. At one time, I became awash in animosity toward Silas when I heard the clang of dishes in his adjacent unit. I thought of leaving before Rose returned, but failed to gather enough courage. I stayed put, and I wallowed in misery, replaying the sordid experience. I blamed myself for my weakness, for being overwhelmed by Silas's presence at the door.

Even then, I believed I couldn't have maintained my silence because, somehow, he would have known I wasn't asleep.

I lamented the loss of trust in my best English teacher. What a loss. I couldn't imagine facing him in class. But nothing happened; I tried to talk myself out of that line of thinking. But I couldn't control how violated my body felt and the heaviness of the loss of my "dream" teacher.

Rose returned mid-morning. "Did you sleep well?" she asked, all cheery.

I told her what Silas did.

"I'm glad you fought him off," she said. "Silas is bitter because I chose your cousin over him."

My mind is in turmoil; what do I care about such information? I asked myself. Between the two men, I didn't care who she dated. I expected her to tell me something to calm my erratic thoughts.

Failing that, and hopeful, I waited to hear what she intended to do. Perhaps she would report the incident to Mr. Kamau. I doubted that. But at the very least, I expected her to reprimand Silas.

"How come you didn't make breakfast?" Rose asked instead.

"I wasn't hungry," I said. "I'll eat when I get home."

"I'll make some lunch."

"It's okay. I want to leave now."

Rose had no objection. She wished me to go in peace and closed the subject. I was on my own. I don't recall further association with her before she hit Kabazi's revolving door.

As I walked home, Rose's invitation, the attack, and what led to it replayed in my mind over and over.

Except for the European landowners, Africans had no phones, which meant Rose arranged her visit with Jaypee a day or days before she asked me to spend the night.

Why did she ask me then?

What was the point of her having me spend the night?

Did she tell Silas about her plans? Was I the sacrificial lamb? My mind avoided thinking of such a possibility.

I ceased thinking of Rose as a friend. I concluded that the attention she gave me and the niceties were all because she dated my cousin.

I felt out of sorts. Meanwhile, I kicked myself for opening that door. I wished I knew of someone I could talk to.

How would I face Silas in class on Monday? I agonized.

# Chapter 48

# African Council vs. European Court

On Saturdays, everyone except a handful of the very old and the very young worked—digging, weeding, harvesting, chopping wood, working at the plantations, or performing a myriad of farm odds and ends. My family lacked the very old. So far in our village, only two had met that criterion—Mama Alan and her husband Mũgono. But they were dead by then.

Baba should have qualified as old based on his haggard face, leathery skin, and the slow pace he kept. He should have retired from an eight-to-five regimen. But he had strapped himself with an old man's burden—side effects of a younger wife. He had minor children to raise.

That Saturday, I felt relieved I wouldn't find the very old or retired at home. They tended to "see" through people. They would have known there was something amiss just by looking at me.

I then dealt with confusion—how to avoid setting my eyes on Silas again. Above all, I craved to talk to someone. But I had no one to entrust such a weighty issue to. I had debated whether to keep it to myself and suffer alone or tell Mami. But how would I tell her? It embarrassed me to think about it. And if I told her, I knew she would tell my father. And I knew he would never keep quiet about such a matter.

The thought of involving them in another conflict with a teacher saddened me. At least there had been mitigating factors in Mr. Foolish's case. Besides our families being neighbors, he had gone to school with my brother, and our mothers were friends. The reason my parents and I expected better of him was that he would protect me instead of harming me.

With no such connections to Silas, I expected no allegiance from him. My father had never heard of him. I doubt that Baba had met any other teacher besides Mr. Foolish and David's teacher over a decade prior. When Tindaress Primary called a parents' meeting to discuss changes like increases in the building fund, Baba never went; Mami went instead.

But my case with Silas was a man's issue. How would Baba deal with him? I wondered. But I had faith in his ability to deal with matters that didn't involve the colonizers. He would make Silas uncomfortable somehow.

When Mami arrived home, I ignored her standing mantra—not to bombard her and Baba with complaints or requests before they settled in and caught their breath. The minute she took a seat, I blurted out the story about the attempted rape. She took the news calmly without reacting and didn't seem to mind the bombardment.

When Baba returned from work, she took him tea in his thing-ira. By then, delivering tea instead of sending one of us had become her routine when she wanted to consult with him.

Back at her house, where my siblings and I sat around the fire, she resumed her chores. I understood she couldn't discuss such matters in my siblings' hearing. I wanted to ask how Baba reacted later before I went to bed, but I didn't want to revisit the matter.

Both Mami and Baba said nothing to me that Sunday while I reeled in anxiety and misery at the prospect of having to spend five days a week seated feet from my attacker. I thought of transferring to Ol Donyo Mara, the only other school in our area. But that involved a transfer letter from the headmaster and space availability. Perhaps I needed to talk to Rose to convince my cousin Jaypee to help me circumvent the rules. But I didn't want to spread my woes that wide or risk her further downplaying the attack's effects. And who could blame her? She had attended an all-girls boarding school where there was no chance of a teacher attacking her.

With no ready solution, I headed to Kabazi on Monday morning.

Despite the uneasiness, skipping school never crossed my mind. Closer to school, I wondered how I would face Silas. I sat only a few feet from the blackboard. Many times, he explained English terms only four feet from my desk. I wished I could skip the English lesson. But where could I go? Perhaps I could ask one of the big boys at the back to exchange desks with me. But as the only girl in class, whom one of my classmates had depicted as "a single bean in a heap of maize kernels," I already stuck out. Any change would have been obvious and made my classmates curious.

When Silas came that mid-morning—as composed and up-right-looking as ever—I fixed my eyes on my open exercise book. I looked up only when he turned to write on the blackboard. When he neared my desk, his fresh smell reminded me of how respectable I had thought of him before. But now, it revolted me.

When he stood in front of the row of desks to my right, near the entrance, I looked at him sideways. The man looked so respectable. No one would believe my story that he lowered himself to do such an awful thing. A flicker of doubt flashed through my mind. Maybe I shouldn't have told Mami. Did Silas really attack me? Could it have been a bad dream?

In answer, my eyes welled.

From that day until Silas left Kabazi, I never raised my hand during his English lesson.

After school that Monday, Mami told me, "Thoguo nĩagũthi-tanga mwaarimũ ũchio," (Your father will sue that teacher).

I said nothing. But I doubted Baba had come up with the idea of a lawsuit. I suspected Major Miller suggested it. I wondered how it would work and how the lawsuit would complicate my school life.

"What does Baba want to do?" my little brother Mũrĩithi asked.

"We'll have to wait and see," Mami said.

None of the others asked about it, then or ever.

Meanwhile, thoughts continued to swirl in my head. I never heard of a peasant suing anybody, let alone a man like Silas. Under Gĩkũyũ tradition, Baba needed to assemble a council of three or four trusted men, including himself, and take his complaint to Silas's doorstep, who had a right to bring his own witnesses. I would attend the council as a witness and take my mother for support. That was what wronged villagers did, from settling a children's dispute that got out of hand to an occasional out-of-wedlock pregnancy.

I had already participated in such a council at our old fenced village when I was nine. As I tell the story in *The British vs Kenya's Mau Mau*, ten-year-old Nyokabi Wainaina, a known bully, and her seven-year-old sister forced their way into our courtyard. When I told them to leave because Mami forbade them to come, Nyokabi snarled and rushed to attack me while I carried my little brother on my back. I bent down, scrabbled for a rock, and hurled it at her. The rock missed her and instead hit her seven-year-old sister on the side of her forehead.

The same evening, Mr. Wainaina, his two daughters, and two other men dropped in at Baba's thingira. Baba called Mami and asked her to take me along. As head of the homestead, he chaired the meeting and questioned the parties involved. The council debated, passed the judgment, and resolved the matter in one sitting.

Now, after Mami told me about the prospect of a lawsuit, European-style, a process alien to me, where they took a long time to decide and confined people in jail, I felt conflicted. Things had gotten out of hand. All I wanted was to attend school in peace. I wished Baba could use something similar to a traditional Committee of Elders, like an ad hoc Gĩkũyũ village council. It was swift, with minimal bureaucracy and expense on the parties involved. I still think the same today.

Because of our similar backgrounds, I'm sure the prospect of an elders' council forum would have been a big shame for Silas. He would likely have quickly left Kabazi Primary School without waiting for the council to meet, saving us time and stress.

# Chapter 49

# Peasant Girl's Justice

Despite preferring a Gĩkũyũ Council over the British court, I hadn't become bold enough to tell this to my father.

After an agonizing week, the following Saturday, the eighth day since Silas attacked me, Baba and I walked the three miles to Solai Police Station. I clutched my torn underwear in a khaki paper bag.

When we arrived, no one else was in sight except for two tall, wiry constables in khaki shorts and short-sleeved gray shirt uniforms. One constable asked how he could help Baba.

"Mimi nataka kushitaka mwalimu" (I want to sue a teacher).

"Kwa nini" (Why), the constable asked.

"Amefanya kitu mbaya kwa mtoto yangu" (He has done a bad thing to my child).

"Kitu gani?" (What thing?)

"Anataka kufanya msichana yangu kama bibi yake." (He wants to treat my daughter like his wife.)

The constable attempted to keep a serious face with little success. He asked follow-up questions in Kalenjin-accented Kiswahili. His colleague nearby stole glances at us while he strained to muffle his chuckles.

Just what I feared, I thought.

"Young girl," the constable said, "where were you when the teacher grabbed you?"

"In Rose's house."

"Who is Rose?"

"My teacher."

"Where was this?"

"In Rose's house, where she left me to sleep."

"Where do you go to school?"

"Kabazi Primary School."

"That's too far," the constable said. "Are you sure you don't go to Tindaress Primary School?"

"Yes."

"Ndio, anaenda Kaambathi" (Yes, she goes to Kabazi), Baba said.

"Ah! Mzee!" (Ah! Old man!) the constable said. "This is the wrong station. You need to report at Bahati Police Station. Do you know where that is?"

"Ndio, Afande." (Yes, Sir.)

That wasted Baba's entire day's work. The one Solai bus we could take left for Nakuru Town early in the morning and returned late afternoon. We couldn't trek the ten miles to Bahati.

*

The following Saturday, two weeks after the incident, Baba and I boarded the bus at our usual bus stop on Nakuru-Solai Road. We alighted at *Mailikumi*, Ten Miles, which is so named because it's ten miles from Nakuru Town. We then walked northeast for about two miles along the shoulder of Nakuru-Subukia road to reach the Bahati Police Station.

We looked a sorry sight—my elderly father plodding along, wearing an old hat, black sandals made from tires, and his signature gray coat, which he removed and draped over his shoulder since we got off the bus. I followed. I wore a simple short-sleeved dress, carrying my evidence in the now dirty, crumpled khaki paper bag.

I never asked myself or wondered what would happen beyond that day. I truly lived in the moment, or my mind went blank save for an occasional rogue thought. Now, one jumped to my mind as I looked at my father. I wondered why he wore the same type of trousers.

So far, I never cared what he wore, but I noticed it. When I was little, he wore shorts that reached down to his knees, like the safari shorts with functional pockets. Since we moved to the fenced village, he started wearing trousers. He always wore high-water trousers, nothing that reached to his ankles, and if it did, he folded them.

At Bahati Police Station, a constable behind the counter interviewed us and took cursory notes. Behind him, seated at a table, another constable grinned as the two commented on how best to address our complaint.

"Are you sure you want to press charges?" the constable asked Baba.

"Ndio, Afande."

"It's been two weeks. Why didn't you report when the incident happened?"

Baba told the constable about our trip to the wrong police station, my need to attend school, and that Saturday was the best day for him to get time off work.

The constable seemed distracted. As Baba talked, the man said something unrelated to our case to his colleague.

"You need to see the inspector," he finally said. "He's the one to decide, but he's out. You can wait for him outside."

We waited at a strategic spot under a sparsely leafed small tree. We could see the entrance and the inspector when he returned. At 1:00 pm, the constables walked out, rounded the small building, and disappeared into a cluster of white-washed square cottages behind the station. The smell of food alerted me to my hunger.

Except for what we drank in the morning—Baba, a mug of tea, and I, one of porridge—we had not eaten or drunk anything else. Although I didn't dwell on it, I recall how tired and listless I felt and how we both looked so lethargic.

After about an hour, the constables returned from lunch. Since we arrived, only one other man had entered the station, and he was out within five minutes.

Baba and I continued to wait. In about two hours, he looked at his watch. "It's close to 4:30 p.m.," he said. "We need to leave to catch the last bus from Nakuru."

I followed him to the office to report our departure.

"Okay, old man," the constable said. "Try another day."

*

We bounced on our next Saturday; we found the inspector either gone or he hadn't shown up.

On the afternoon of our final Saturday, an entire month since the incident, a constable approached us where Baba and I waited, seated on the grass by the same small tree.

"Mzee," the constable said, "let's talk privately."

"Okay," Baba said.

The two moved about twenty-five feet from me. I strained to hear what they were saying, but I heard only murmurs. Baba said nothing to me when he returned.

About half an hour later, a constable approached us. "The inspector will see you now," he said.

I must have dozed off and missed the inspector coming in, or perhaps there was another door.

We found him seated at a table behind the counter, dressed in a khaki uniform with brass star medals on the shoulder.

"Mzee," the inspector said.

"*Ndio, Afande,*" Baba said.

"Sit down. . .I'm going to tell you the truth," the inspector said, pen in hand, tapping a single sheet of paper where the constable had scrawled Baba's report. "You don't seem to have a case against the teacher." The inspector paused, waiting for Baba to respond. He didn't.

"And if you remain stubborn and insist on these charges," the inspector continued, "the teacher might sue you for defamation. This could bring a lot of hardship to your family."

When the inspector ended his lecture, I heard a muted "Uh!" escape from Baba's lips, a sign of disgust.

I angled my eyes toward him, awaiting his reply. He looked sullen, his jaw clenched, his dry lips tightened, deep in thought. The suspense tortured me. I fully turned my head to look at him. Isn't he going to answer the inspector? I asked myself.

No. Instead, he made a series of slow, knowing head nods.

He then stood and hitched his greatcoat over his shoulder.

"Ni sawa." (It's okay). He then turned to me. "Wanjirũ, let's go home." He waved me toward the door.

I bent and retrieved my paper bag from the floor beside me, hustled from the chair, and followed my father.

*

Today, I wonder how Silas could have collected money from someone who owned so little. Perhaps he could have sold Baba's goats, the only marketable property my family owned. But villagers didn't have the money to buy goats. In the decades my family lived on that Colonial Farm, I never heard anyone buy a goat. They either reared them or had none.

And I doubt Silas would have bothered to sue a peasant worker, not because he would have jeopardized his career, but because of the shame involved. He likely would have arranged a quick transfer and sneaked out on a weekend.

For Baba, however, the gravity of a lawsuit and a potential win for Silas must have sounded so profound.

Although I couldn't be sure, I doubt Silas ever learned that my father attempted to sue him. He maintained his serious persona and continued to teach us as I endured his presence, hoping Ngai's hand would punish him on my behalf.

\*

I endured Silas for about six months before I learned I wasn't his only victim. Rumors came to the fore one Monday when teacher Jimnah came to teach us the English lesson that Silas had taught us before. Poor Jimnah had a serious case of stammer. He stammered through half of the hodge-podge English grammar lesson. I couldn't wait for lunch break to learn what happened to Silas.

Rumors circulated that he and Mrs. Kamau had an affair. Others claimed he had forced himself on Mrs. Kamau's teenage sister. As a result, he hit Kabazi's revolving door.

I became conflicted when Silas left. I felt relieved that I didn't have to see him again, but I also believed his leaving had doomed my English grammar lesson; he hadn't covered parts of speech halfway.

A year after I left Kabazi Primary, Silas and the teenage girl eloped. Much later, I heard he had left teaching and worked at Kenya Airways. His workmate, a former classmate, said Silas and his wife brought forth three children and later lost one of them. That may have caused him to turn to alcohol. I never learned what came next, but he fell in his bathroom, hit his head, and also lost his job.

I saw Silas thirteen years later, a few years before he died. As I walked on one of Umoja Estate Market's walkways in Nairobi, I happened by a typical old man in blue overalls. The man crouched in front of an ironworks stall, pliers in hand, fixing a black security door frame. A slightly chubby woman leaned on the stall's door jamb.

I thought the man looked familiar. I did a double-take. He turned toward me, and our eyes met. It was Silas. I figured the woman was his wife, although she looked nothing like the slightly chubby teenager who stayed at Mr. Kamau's residence.

Silas and I exchanged pleasantries without dragging in our current lives or mentioning our pasts. In a minute, I left without his wife and me acknowledging each other.

# Chapter 50

# The Nanny

It had been ten years since the colonial government declared a state of emergency and rounded up the Gĩkũyũ population and moved them to the so-called Native Reserve, detention camps, and "secure" villages, town neighborhoods, and the Mau Mau freedom fighters hunkered down in the forest.

Five years in, the British had a clear upper hand in the Mau Mau revolt, but unknown to us villagers, they were also tired of the war. As the Gĩkũyũ adage goes, the chaser and the chased both get tired.

The colonizers had started slowly by admitting some hand-picked African activists to the Legislative Council (Legco) who had campaigned for inclusion under the British constitution. So, amid the Mau Mau agitation and criticism by the English press, civil society, and others, the colonizers started negotiations with the colonized to devise the best ways to dismantle the deplorable colonial system in Kenya.

We, school children, had already benefited when the Ministry of Education abolished the grade four standardized national exam in 1961.

The African inspector Baba and I met, when we went to report Silas, was also part of the progress. Before, no African reached a managerial level in the police or the armed forces. The dusk-to-dawn curfew and the hated travel permission (pass-books) had been lifted; adults could now travel during their free time without written permission from their employers, like small children.

Otherwise, our lives changed little. Years crawled by, the same as before. Incidents like Silas's attack and Alan and his parents' death remained each family's private matter.

Besides church, social activities were nonexistent. And marriages were few, very few. The handful of couples who married did so through the traditional style. Under the constraints of the village, there were no elaborate traditional parties; villagers rarely learned about the negotiations until the couple married.

So, when rumors started swirling about a marriage possibility for Mr. Foolish's younger sister Njoki, many villagers perked their ears not to miss morsels of gossip updates.

Njoki didn't grow up like a typical dusty and scruffy village girl like all the other girls, including my sister and me. She had left school in grade four after failing the standardized national exam, which the government later abolished. But, unlike other young boys and girls, she didn't join her mother in the fields. Even as an adult, I never saw her weed, pick coffee cherries, or haul firewood. She did housework and kept herself clean while her mother, Elithi, toiled in the fields.

Villagers referred to Njoki Alan as a spinster and claimed she lacked the skills to become a wife. Njoki was about twenty-five years old.

When her father, Alan, was alive, a man from afar had come with his entourage to ask Alan for his daughter's hand in marriage. It was the talk of the village until nothing else happened.

Later, I heard conflicting rumors that the admirer and his men would return to start marriage negotiations. Another rumor followed, claiming Alan had rejected the man because of his sinful ways; he drank beer, smoked cigarettes, and played guitar.

"The man is a rogue," Mami said. "That's exactly what I heard."

Rogue or no rogue was of no concern to me. I just wanted to attend my first wedding.

The village waited and waited. We gave up when we heard nothing further about the "rogue." To make matters worse, no other suitor came along or could reach Njoki in her home-bound lifestyle. Instead of claiming to pray for Njoki, women turned on Alan. They blamed him for Njoki's spinsterhood. None of them called the vanished suitor a "rogue" again. Instead, women claimed the man was more educated than Njoki, and he had been doing her a favor.

"Alan ran the man away," women's chatter claimed. "What's he going to do with his daughter now?"

But the Alans were a close-knit bunch. They kept to themselves and never associated or aligned with the village people.

*

During the rogue period, Major Miller had gotten the hang of running his farm. Next, we heard that his wife, Memsahib, had given birth to a baby girl. The couple now had two children: the big boy in boarding school in England and the new baby.

The happy couple started scouting for a trained nanny.

I didn't know women trained to look after babies.

"Wonders will never cease," women said.

Memsahib stayed home unless she accompanied her husband to Nakuru or wherever else they went. Her husband employed a cook, an assistant cook, a house cleaner, and several gardeners, yet she couldn't raise her own baby.

"Maybe she won't even breastfeed the baby," some women quipped.

Meanwhile, the Millers continued their nanny search, looking far and wide for a trained nanny—only the best for their little girl. Their search proved fruitless. They curtailed their aspirations after they realized that trained nannies followed the bright lights, not kerosene lanterns, in mud-and-thatch villages. They started snooping around the farms and learned of Njoki, the spinster.

Major Miller told Alan that Memsahib wanted to interview his daughter for a professional nanny job, not babysitting; after one interview, Memsahib offered Njoki a nod.

"Aaaah," women sighed with relief. "At least Njoki will have work instead of staying idle," they said.

Memsahib fitted Njoki with a blue dress with white sleeve cuffs and collar, a white belt and headscarf like other European nannies, and white orthopedic shoes. For her dawn-to-dusk duties, Njoki made a whopping sixty shillings per month.

A collective gasp coursed through the village when word of the astronomical figure spread. People dropped their spinster gossip and elevated Njoki to the "pride of the village" right behind her brother, Mr. Foolish.

To the villagers, the nanny job proved that women, like teachers, could get well-paying jobs and enjoy modern life on the farm.

To put it into perspective, Baba, the overseer, earned the same amount after thirty-eight years of service.

I can only guess how my family and the villagers would have covered their mouths, lost for words, if they had learned Aunt Julia had earned ten times that amount two years before she retired.

Whatever the case, deep inside me, I knew Njoki's job wasn't the kind I wanted. I had already helped raise two children. I longed for a job that would divorce me from the village.

# Chapter 51

# The Wedding

It was a complete surprise when news of another potential marriage descended on us, again, from Alan's family, a Western-style wedding, no less. The only glitch was that Alan and his parents would miss the wedding. They were already dead.

My family learned of this firsthand. Elithi dropped by our house—a rarity for her. Too busy, the two mothers rarely visited each other. They mainly met at work or church on Sundays. After a brief exchange, Mami realized it was a visit and offered Elithi tea.

"Mbũrũ nĩagwĩka ũhiki mũtheru." ("Mr. Foolish" will do a *clean wedding*.) That meant the two families—the groom's and bride's—had already completed negotiations. It also meant a Christian *white-dress* wedding. The term endures as if African marriages, which are still the majority, were tainted.

My image of *a clean wedding* came from hearing the church chatter. Besides the bible reference, however, none of the Christians had done a *clean wedding* or seen one.

With the news, a greater restlessness fell upon our village, especially upon the women and children; men always took a back seat in social matters. Country weddings then and now were a public affair, like funerals—no invitation needed.

Finally, our first Solai wedding day arrived, with the venue set at Tindaress Primary School in my former classroom, which doubled as a church on Sundays. Because our pastor didn't qualify to officiate weddings, a pastor from Nakuru Town officiated.

Only adults witnessed the couple exchange their vows because those in charge refused to let small children and teenagers in. (There probably wasn't enough room anyway.) We remained at the school's far-out periphery.

On one side of the schoolhouse, women had set up an open-air kitchen where they cooked tea in big pots over campfire-style fires. They stored sodas and buttered bread sandwiches in *itarũrũ* (woven trays) on make-shift tables.

During the service, cooks determined to hear the couple exchange vows left a handful of women to mind the kitchen. Soon, three boys saw their chance, dashed in, and scooped a handful of sandwiches. The trays got disturbed, and some sandwiches fell off. Before the women could turn around, the thieves had sprinted to safety.

"Ĩhĩĩ ichi itarĩ na mĩtugo!" (These lads have no manners!) one woman said.

When those who had left the kitchen returned, the kitchen came to life again. Trays loaded with bread, cupcakes, large tea kettles, and crates of sodas started disappearing inside. We kept vigil and learned tidbits from children brave enough to inch close to the door, or from adults closest to the cooks. From the onset, we waited patiently, eager for a glimpse of the process, a chance we knew we wouldn't get. During the eating, we wished they could hurry and finish cutting the cake; we wanted to see the couple.

Finally, the moment they couldn't deny us came when the couple emerged from the "church," smiling. That one sighting of women singing and throwing rice at them, and them mingling with adults, sealed my claim of having attended my first wedding. Mr. Foolish wore a gray suit, white shirt, and tie. His bride wore a flowing white dress and a net with a hair band decorated like a crown.

I ate nothing; nobody outside did. Nonetheless, a glimpse of the newlyweds felt good enough.

People talked about that wedding for months afterward.

Mr. Foolish's wedding was the only one I witnessed or heard of in Solai. My family had no prospects for such a wedding. David, the only one who could have done such a thing, had gone AWOL.

Similar weddings took place decades later as couples converted to Christianity. But these were mostly by couples already married through traditional marriages. Most had already brought forth children, some of them already grown. They termed the process "*gūtheria ūhiki*" (to clean the wedding/marriage) or "*kwerūhia ūhiki*" (to renew the wedding/marriage vows).

Like Western names, Western-type weddings are part of Christianity. Sometimes, churches, especially the Catholic Church, never allow long-standing members to take part in certain church rituals if they have never been married in church.

There is also a tussle between men and women. The women want church weddings, while many men prefer traditional (or customary) marriages where getting a divorce is simpler, and division of property favors the men, who often hold property titles in their names only.

Sometimes couples settle on "Come we stay," a shack-up union in which they bear children and conduct their union as if it were a marriage. Sometimes, the arrangement is disrupted when death or "divorce" occurs or when a man steps out and gets into another clandestine union. When this happens, it's to the detriment of mainly the woman and the children.

# Chapter 52

# Crime & Punishment

Major Miller introduced rules that employees had never dealt with before he took over the farm. During Kamunge's era, if an employee wronged him, he would either warn the employee or dock the employee's wages. The only exception was when Mŭriŭki, at age fourteen, stole oranges from the orchard, and Kamunge had him charged.

Major Miller never gave warnings or second chances to the rare employee who went out of line. He never used physical violence like the manager at Major Stein's farm, but he punished employees in whatever way he deemed fit or called the police to do it for him.

One day, my brother Simon and two other casual laborers worked at the cows' milk pen about 200 yards behind our homestead. A Tugen man, I'll call Kiplagat, squatted beside the cow he had just milked and took a long swallow from the milk bucket. Major Miller caught him in the act. Kiplagat froze, still hugging the bucket in mid-air. The Major called the other three men.

When Simon and his colleagues reached the crime scene, the thief had rested the milk bucket on the ground while he remained on his haunches, Major Miller bearing down on him.

"I want you to see what will happen if you steal," Major Miller said.

According to Simon, he and the other two workers became nervous. They feared the ex-military man wanted to beat the milk thief.

"Pick up the bucket," Major Miller ordered.

Kiplagat did as told.

"Drink exactly the way I found you."

He hesitated and looked up at his employer, face scrunched as his tears threatened.

"Nasema kunywa!" (I said drink!)

"Semehea mimi, bwana," (Forgive me, Sir.) "Sitarundia tena, bwana," (I'll never do it again, sir.)

"Ulikua unakunywa maziwa; Sasa kunywa." (You were drinking milk. Now drink it.)

Kiplagat's hands trembled along with the bucket.

"Kunywa!" (Drink!) Major Miller raised his voice an octave.

The milker started on his binge.

"Endelea!" (Continue!) Major Miller said that whenever the man stopped and begged for forgiveness.

Kiplagat made gurgling sounds as his eyes bulged.

The bucket swayed.

"Kunywa! Maliza!" (Drink! Finish!)

Kiplagat gurgled, knees shook, and his body swayed, still clutching the bucket.

He struggled to steady himself and failed.

His bottom smacked the ground.

The bucket slipped out of his hands. It tipped over one way. Kiplagat tipped the other.

He convulsed, his body stretched and twitched.

"Please, forgive him, sir," one man said.

"Sir, this man will die," Simon said.

Major Miller stared at Kiplagat, shaking his finger and said, "I never want to hear your name or see you ever again!" He then stomped away.

Simon and his colleagues rushed to help the now ex-employee. They hustled Kiplagat outside the cows' pen. At a patch of grass, they sat him down. One man steadied him from the back, another bent him forward, and the other grabbed his fingers and thrust them into his mouth. A torrent of milk rushed out. Kiplagat heaved until he produced scant, unrecognizable fluid.

After the "treatment," one man helped him walk home.

According to Simon, Kiplagat hunkered down for some days in a cottage he shared with other bachelors. He then disappeared.

Kiplagat's case was an anomaly. We only learned of it because of Simon. The other two witnesses were temporary Tugen men who quit shortly after. I doubt many villagers heard of the incident. But there was more to come.

\*

For decades, during Kamunge's era, men brewed beer as they had always done, long before the invasion. Like Christianity, beer brewing was an important activity and a great crutch for the peasants during the war. After Major Miller became their employer, men continued to enjoy their brew, just like before.

Beer for married adults, especially men, had been part of Gĩkũyũ's ceremonies and rituals and a social drink from time immemorial. By the time of Major Miller's, social upheaval and commercial alcohol had curtailed the popularity of homemade beer.

Older Gĩkũyũ men who drank beer brewed their own for personal consumption with close friends or, on a rare occasion, during marriage negotiations. They preferred clear beer made from water, honey, sugar, and luffa.

Tugen seasonal workers, however, brewed *"busaa"* from maize flour and millet and, much later, after it became a worthwhile business, added yeast (and whatever else) to shorten the brewing period. They not only brewed for their own consumption but also to sell to others in mugs. Busaa drinkers claimed the thick brew contained various nutritional values.

When Major Miller learned of the goings-on, he outlawed home breweries.

From then on, any man who wanted a "man's drink," as they called alcohol, sacrificed half a day's wages to buy a bottle of Pilsner or Tusker at Patel's General Store. Besides the Europeans, Africans never bought takeout alcohol there. If an occasional man wanted a sit-down, commercially brewed beer, he got it at Njeki's Shopping Center. Baba never drank store beers and never intended to start.

New policy or not, a man had to have a man's drink. The traditional brewers ignored the new policy. But busaa brewers took caution. They now hid their unlawful deeds in the wild. They placed their brew drums half-buried in dugouts under overgrown bush canopies, far from home.

Baba used a three-to-four-gallon gourd with a wide opening that he covered with its own cutout top. He tucked the loaded gourd in a catch-all area in his partially lit, windowless one-room thingira and covered it with sacks.

He and the other rule-breakers believed Major Miller couldn't find out about the illicit brew. He never entered the village, let alone men's thingiras. He didn't even trek around the farm like herdsmen, or hunters (who hunted in game parks), or like women in search of firewood. The breweries believed they were safe if blabbers kept their mouths shut.

The brewers were in for a surprise.

One Sunday afternoon, while they enjoyed their brew, two uniformed, lanky constables on foot stopped by, a first for our village.

The two constables ordered every suspect they caught red-handed to sit at a designated spot by the main dirt road between the village and Tindaress River. While the suspects waited, a group collected to gawk at them. Meanwhile, the two constables reentered the village to net more "criminals" in the part they hadn't covered.

The arrested men cursed their bad luck.

After the lawmen arrested every lawbreaker they found, they returned to where they had left their first batch of suspects. They now ordered their catch of five men to hush their pleas for mercy and start marching to the police station, holding their evidence, mainly small containers or mugs.

Two suspects obeyed the order and started inching away, but the other three snickered and refused to budge. They likely became indignant about taking orders from two unarmed constables. The constables raised their voices and waved their tiny batons to shoo the men along. The suspects stood their ground. Without weapons or handcuffs to restrain the accused, the constables found it hard to enforce their authority.

More villagers trailed in to witness the spectacle.

While everyone focused on the standoff, the two formerly obedient culprits mingled and disappeared under the cover of the crowd.

As people jostled to get closer and children hooted, the two constables realized their sure captives had disappeared. They increased their authority over the three left, which led to shoving and pulling between the accusers and the accused. The three suspects roughed up the two constables before they sent them on their way empty-handed.

The rebellious men garnered respect and received a round of congratulations while the drinkers enjoyed their brew in high spirits.

.

# Chapter 53

# Full Extent of the Law

The failure of the two constables energized the brewers.

"This is Major Miller's farm," some claimed. "If he doesn't mind, why should the police butt in?"

Others called for caution and claimed that Major Miller might keep tabs on them because he wouldn't want the police coming in.

"How will he check?" a man asked. "Search in smoky thingiras and around bushes?"

The story dominated the village talk for the rest of the week before it withered. Because Kamunge, Major Miller, or the police had never entered either of the two villages before, the brewers' memories soon faded. They resumed their "wicked" ways, oblivious that the police never entered a white person's private property without the owner calling them.

They were stunned when the law brought the equivalent of a bomb to a fistfight.

A group of General Service Unit (GSU) officers (a SWAT-like unit) in their camouflage fatigues, all the way from Nakuru Town, descended upon the village. Tall, fit, athletic types—unlike the local malnourished police—the officers looked out of place in a place littered with mud-and-thatch cottages and stick fences with frightened natives running around barefoot or in ragged shoes.

I heard a racket in our courtyard, and as I rushed from nyûmba to the porch, there followed heavy footsteps as two officers appeared like ghosts from behind Baba's thingira in pursuit of a fugitive—never mind the fence that separated our homestead from the rest of the village. Whether the men jumped over or bulldozed the fence and Baba repaired it later, I couldn't tell. I never needed to go behind thingira. On reaching our courtyard, the runaway they chased had disappeared. My brother Joseph said he witnessed another officer question and slap a man.

Confused excitement swirled through the village. People cowered indoors. The curious ventured outside for entertainment or the first dip of gossip.

After all that fuss, the GSU officers hopped in their camouflage lorry and left without an arrest. The following day, I heard they came for the three men who had roughed up the constables. Although the military men didn't bother with illicit brew, the incident shook the brewers and the entire village. People suspected a mole, a teetotaler, kept Major Miller abreast of the village activities.

They lay low for months.

After enough time elapsed, addiction seduced the brewers back to their wicked ways. They self-regulated and brewed on different weekends. Because of the staggered supply, a drink was available for anyone who craved one.

Baba brewed only once a month and drank elsewhere on the other weekends. During his dry periods, he left on a Sunday and staggered back home drunk as a wino.

Mami never bothered with Baba's occasional excessive drinking, although his behavior indicated he wished she did. Wherever he went on his drinking prowls, he must have come across women who begged their husbands to return home and even helped them do so. My father may have longed for such feminine attention. But, as a devout Christian, Mami was in a different mental state. She didn't even know his drinking pathways. Several times, Baba reached our courtyard entrance and suddenly "became" too drunk to walk the short distance to his thingira. He sat down or stretched out on a patch of grass. "Is your mother home?" he asked.

Initially, one of us rushed inside, excited, "Mami! Mami! Baba needs help!"

"He'll be all right," Mami would say.

"No, he's too drunk."

"He'll manage."

If we insisted, Mami said, "Your father will get to thingira the same way he got where he is."

Occasionally, Baba caught a snooze right where he sat. When he awoke, he brushed himself off and walked to his thingira. In one instance, he said, "These women!" before he got indoors. After a minute, as he did after his excursions, he called out, "Can I have a cup of tea?"

Although Mami obliged him, she complained she had never heard of anyone who drank tea back-to-back with alcohol.

At another time, after an alcoholic splurge, Baba rested one elbow on the ground; my two siblings and I hung close by in the courtyard. Bitter that his wife never offered him her shoulder to lean on, as some "obedient" wives did, he spoke his mind.

"If I were a young man, I'd get rid of my wife and marry a brand new one," Baba said, flicking the air with his backhand. "If the new wife brings *nyokonyoko* (shenanigans), I'd get rid of her too."

"You'd throw our Mami away?" Gĩthũi asked in such a pitiful voice, his face scrunched, eyes fluttering, ready to cry.

"Which wife have you seen thrown away?" Baba asked him.

At twelve years old, Gĩthũi paused for seconds. He relaxed when he got it.

My father had accepted he was too old to practice tyranny or to maintain a tight grip on his family. But luckily for him, the psychological hold he had on us had taken root.

Meanwhile, his strategy of brewing beer at home once a month and drinking elsewhere at other times turned out to be pure, unwinnable garble.

*

One week, Baba brewed beer, and instead of merely covering the gourd with sacks, he dipped it into a sack, twisted the top, and tucked it in a corner. He rearranged his knick-knacks around it as if it were just another fixture. Of course, he had to take it out when it got ready.

Because he never enjoyed drinking his brew alone, Baba sent for two friends. Meanwhile, he sieved the brew and put it in two gourds—the one he would share with his friends and another gourd for an occasional drink. He put that in his hiding nook.

While Baba and his friends enjoyed their second drink, two constables appeared in the courtyard.

I never learned how many constables dropped into the village that day, but the raid netted four old men, Baba among them. The other brewers, perhaps all agile younger men, either dumped their evidence before the law reached their doorstep or had brewed away from their premises.

Baba hauled his half-full small gourd, evidence perched on one shoulder, while the police walked behind a line of the elderly "criminals."

Afterward, a group of men had a lively banter about the arrest.

"If they arrest me," people reported one man to have said, "I'd trip and drop the gourd. No judge would admit broken pieces as evidence."

When I heard that piece of wisdom, I wished Baba would trip and drop his gourd. But my father was such a stickler for authority.

He and his colleagues spent that Sunday night at the Solai Police Station. The following day, the police drove them to court in Nakuru Town. Baba and two of the men paid their fines. But Mũriũki got hauled to jail. Records had surfaced of him having stolen oranges from Kamunge's orchard when he was fourteen. Mũriũki had gone to steal oranges with other boys. He became the fall guy when Kamunge's gardener grabbed him while the others got away. He was now a repeat offender.

For the beer charge, the white magistrate sentenced him to a mandatory six months in prison, no time off for good behavior. He warned Mũriũki that he would suffer years of prison time and hard labor if he committed a third crime.

# Chapter 54

# Unskilled Thief

I knew about Mŭriŭki's orange theft within the year we moved to our second village. Yet, even with that knowledge, I couldn't resist trying my hand at stealing just because I craved what the law denied me.

During the British occupation, Africans, by law, couldn't grow cash crops or perennials such as fruit. People grew maize, beans, green peas, black-eyed peas, white-eyed peas (njahĩ), and other one-cycle plants for their own families. To ensure people followed the law, every year before planting season, Kamunge and, later, Major Miller, sent a tractor to plow through the peasants' plots to ensure no plants remained after the previous harvest.

Not growing fruits wasn't as hard on us children as on adults. We ate wild fruits and berries on our way from our garden or scavenged when we were out and about. Goatboys ate more fruits when minding their herds in or near the woods. But adults, especially men, hardly ate any fruit.

After the war ebbed, certain fruits like bananas found their way to our weekly market, coming from the native reserve where people owned their ancestral land, and the fruit trees had revived. Because Mami couldn't afford enough ripe bananas to go around, she occasionally bought an entire unripe stalk when she went to

Njeki's Shopping Center. At home, she dug a trench, lined it with fronds, laid the stalk in, covered it with fronds, heaped dirt on top, and buried it for a week or so. We then enjoyed ripe bananas for days, although they remained green. I still preferred the yellow banana, even if I got only half of it. Sometimes, Mami bought a couple of mangoes that had found their way from the coast. She peeled and sliced them and gave each of us a slice.

But nothing could match the bounty at the forbidden orchard.

When we lived in our old fenced village before I entered school, and I babysat my brothers and hardly ate fruit, people talked of an orchard with some mysticism. I concluded it was something for white people, not for us. I had no reason to get near the orchard to satisfy my curiosity, even after we moved to our second village, a quarter of a mile from the colonial house. But boys were always more enterprising than we girls.

Now and then, my brother Joseph mentioned nonchalantly, among us children only, the huge, juicy oranges in the orchard. I soon learned that he and a handful of boys had at least twice indulged in what could have landed them in jail, and also earned Joseph a life-threatening beating by Baba.

The boys went in a pack of threes or fours, cased the grove, and ensured the gardener wasn't nearby. They then scaled the fence to avoid telltale signs if they scooted under or between the wires. Before Major Miller's two German shepherds got a whiff of the thieves' scent and raised the alarm, the boys had tossed the oranges over the fence and clambered to freedom.

After they ate their booty, they got rid of the smell by washing at the river or eating onions or peppers.

Although I enjoyed my brother's sneaky escapades along with the exaggerations, the desire to eat the oranges didn't arise in me. But when Major Miller availed me of the opportunity, temptation got the better of me, and my fortitude faltered.

*

Major Miller required his employees to abandon their gardens after harvest in November until mid-March when they returned to prepare for the next crop. From January to mid-April, the gardens offered no food; some women scavenged wild vegetables along the riverbank, while others went without. In my family, Mami dried enough vegetables when they were in season to cover the lean months. Joseph nicknamed these *kauka* (dry).

Somehow, Major Miller learned of his employees' struggle with scarcity during the lean, unproductive months. To help them, he allocated the ones with large families, like ours, small strips of plots alongside Tindaress River's low bank, east of his house. Because of river deposits, the soil remained damp and fertile year-round, and women needed no manure or rain to grow humongous cabbages, collard greens, carrots, and juicy tomatoes. A handful of women diverted little river tributaries to plant arrowroots, the water hogs, or planted them right by the water.

To get to the plots, we walked east as if going to the colonial compound, turned north between the coffee factory and the compound, rounded the fence, and entered the clearing between Jumatatu Mountain Range and the huge, fenced orchard that stretched behind the residence for about two acres.

A six-foot barbed-wire fence surrounded the orchard; its entrance faced the compound. Major Miller had cleared the land behind the fence for about fifty yards to separate the orchard from the mountain slopes' scrubby area. We followed a footpath in the middle of the clearing, the fenced-off "Garden-of-Eden" in full view to our right.

The first time I passed by, the entire area smelled fruity. The orange fruit trees looked like blooming bouquets of yellow and gold flowers. Further down grew the peaches. The hanging fruits, some strewn on the ground by the wind, made my mouth water. The ground alone held enough oranges and peaches to feed every individual in the village.

Whenever Mami and I walked by the orchard, I feasted my eyes and marveled at the waste. But I had my fill on our way back.

One late Saturday afternoon, Mami and I went to the vegetable garden. She liked to take me on excursions—I suppose for mother-daughter bonding. In the garden, Mami puttered around, pulling weeds and marveling at the bounty of cabbage and juicy tomatoes. I plucked one and ate it. Otherwise, I tagged along and admired the produce, wandered along the calm river, or helped her pick the vegetables.

On our way home, without a prior ulterior motive, I somehow walked behind my mother. I was thirteen, a small thirteen, but old enough for Mami not to keep checking on me. As my eyes traveled about, they stopped and ogled the orchard, the bouquet of oranges a mere twenty-five feet off the footpath. An urge arose within me as if the bounty beckoned. The urge became so irresistible that I had to act on it.

I slowed my steps to put more distance between Mami and me. About fifty feet before we rounded the bend, away from the orchard, I slid the kīondo from my back, set it down, and quickly tiptoed toward the fence. It seemed too high for me to scale. I carefully parted the second and third-tier barbed wires, crawled through, and dashed to the nearest bouquet.

I gathered the front of my dress to deposit my loot. I plucked and deposited one, two, three oranges. As I reached for a fourth one, figuring that for all my trouble, I needed more, I heard a throaty WOOF!

I gasped and yanked the orange. It dropped in midair.

By the second WOOF, I had covered the few steps to the fence. My left hand still cupped my dress, without enough sense to toss the oranges over. I debated how to scoot between the wires without losing my precious oranges.

Another WOOF cleared my mind.

It was the oranges or my limbs.

I let go of my dress, parted the wires, and shoved my leg through.

After my body went through, the next WOOF sounded so close I feared for my other leg.

I yanked it out to safety.

Like every criminal, however, I left evidence by the fence—three oranges, torn pieces of my dress, and blood smears from a gash on my right thigh.

Before I reached where I set my kīondo, I saw Mami ahead, facing my direction, her back erect despite her load, which she guarded by holding the strap across her head on both sides of her ears.

My heart sank. My plan to get oranges without her awareness had backfired. It was doomed from the start. Without planning, I wouldn't have known where to eat the oranges undetected.

When I reached about ten feet from my mother, she shook her head, lips tightened, a remarkable control for my mouthy mother. It wouldn't have reflected well on her if anyone knew her first daughter had become a thief. She then turned and resumed her walk.

By the time we reached inside her nyūmba, and she wiggled her finger at me and waggled her tongue in clipped sentences, her lips controlled, voice lowered so Baba's ears wouldn't get wind of it, I had resolved never to steal again—not from a moral conviction but for my lack of skill.

From then on, if I passed by the orchard, I ignored it as if it were nonexistent, and I quickened my steps whenever I neared the spot where I had escaped.

# Chapter 55

# Fruit Graveyard

A year after botching my orange theft, Joseph and I transferred to Kabazi Primary School on the eastern side of Jumatatu Mountain Range. The climate was more temperate than the western side where we lived. Instead of coffee, European farmers grew cash crops like pyrethrum, flowers, and fruits.

The following year, in grade five, I learned that Major Ward, the owner of Kabazi farm, grew fruits. Boys talked about Kabazi Canners, a sprawling factory in the middle of several orchards that canned fruits for export. The reputable factory sounded more ominous than Major Miller's orchard. Besides the workers, nobody ventured through the tractor and vehicle trails that crisscrossed the orchards. And nobody dared steal fruit in Kabazi. People claimed armed men with guns guarded the orchards.

Nobody needed to steal, anyway. During harvest season, Kabazi Canners discarded heaps of fruits, especially peaches and strawberries, with only the tiniest defects. A dump truck deposited the discards on the bank of the foot and vehicle thoroughfare that turned into the footpath that crossed Jumatatu Mountain Range to Njeki's Shopping Center and other western farms—the path Rose had taken before she detoured to visit us. Perhaps the factory established the fruit graveyard as a place for people to help themselves, or used it as a convenient dump for easier manure collection.

Whatever the reason, during the bounty season, when the school let out on Fridays, Joseph and I walked with others to the fruit graveyard, about a mile from the school.

Like the others, I stuffed my mouth as I piled fruits into my gallon-size pail, which I took to school to draw water for the school garden.

With each of us hugging a full or half-full pail, we headed home in case night fell on us, eating as we went. We continued on the thoroughfare to the bigger Jumatatu Mountain Ridge. We ended up at Gĩtharia's farm, then looped north to reach our old village. By then, we had emptied our pails and walked at least two miles longer than our usual trek home.

Before we crossed Tindaress River to reach our village, we rinsed our pails. Joseph and I feared that if Baba got wind of it, he wouldn't believe our fruit graveyard story, mainly because, having never learned to converse with adults, we never explained things to him. We gave him one or two-word answers. But we would have given Mami the entire yarn. But her opinion counted for little against Baba's suspicions.

Because he craved privacy, he wouldn't have asked around to determine the truth. And he couldn't have beaten Joseph because he had already gone through the rites of passage to adulthood, where a father couldn't discipline his son physically—adult insanity only applied to the weaker humans who got the blunt side of the cane.

And, of course, I wouldn't have expected an assault because, according to Gĩkũyũ tradition, fathers left the discipline of daughters to their mothers. But Baba had overstepped tradition twice. First, he beat Wairimũ-big, his daughter from his first marriage, when his friend's goat, which she and Simon were taking care of, went astray and was eaten by a predator. And, second, when he rained twig-whips on me when I was four years old because of potty infractions.

But even without punishment, if Baba doubted our innocence, it would have gnawed on me for days.

# Chapter 56

# Anger Variation

My parents' anger fell on opposite ends of the spectrum. Mami was short-tempered and acted fast lest her anger dissipate. Because of this, she pinched or whacked a child at the moment of wrongdoing, having forgotten her past warnings or threats. If she couldn't reach her target, she said, "You! Wait until I catch you," while she wagged her finger at the offender. She wasn't into verbal abuse.

I recall a time in our old fenced village when Morry wronged her. When Mami reached for him, Morry dashed away. In frustration, Mami used a despicable practice she had picked up from the village mother-talk.

"No food for you tonight!" she declared.

But what eight-year-old cares about a future event?

Morry may have cared nil about future meals, but he became restless when enticing food smells filled the courtyard. We, his siblings, abandoned our play and eased indoors to wait for our mother to finish cooking.

Morry skulked and stood by thingira's doorway where Mami had cooked that day, and Baba wasn't home. Morry took occasional peeks inside. When Mami finished cooking, she cut ugali into various portions, ladled the collard greens, and handed the loaded plates to eager hands, ready to dig in.

Morry couldn't stand to watch us munch. He walked right up to Mami. "Mami," he said, "beat me and give me food."

Mami looked at Morry with sorry, pitiful eyes and said nothing, lost for words. My mother seemed so helpless; I hated to see her like that.

"Just sit down and eat," she said. She fetched and handed Morry his plate.

Distracted by hunger, I hadn't noticed Mami had kept aside and covered a share of ugali and greens for Morry.

She never threatened a child with withholding food again.

Baba was of a different ilk, like a calm, ripple-less river that a traveler never could tell the depth unless he dipped in his cane. Usually, Baba nursed his anger and banked a wrong to include it in a future beating. But he never waited for minor infractions; he dug his long nails into a boy's head and shook it.

Luckily for us girls, he followed tradition and left our discipline to our mother. He handled the boys' discipline. We knew it was a full-fledged battle if he grabbed any of my brothers. Watching him physically abuse my brothers tortured me and likely left the same negative effect.

But if he snickered or complained, nothing further happened; he left it at that. Other times, he settled for verbal abuse or put-downs.

Unlike his beatings, he dished out verbal abuse across the board. Although the boys still got the bulk of it. Up to their pre-teens, he called them names. He especially liked to call them kondoo! (sheep!) and chura! (frog!). I don't know why he chose those names, but the stress he put on them sounded awful. From the boys' teens, Baba abandoned name-calling. Instead, he started using put-downs like "You will lag like a sloth." For the girls, he used mean comments. Even then, he spared Tabitha—except for a click of his tongue—because she was named after his mother-in-law.

I recall an afternoon when I took a nap. Baba hated day naps; to him, they meant laziness. He called my name, and, of course,

I couldn't hear him. Gĩthũi rushed to nyũmba—where Tabitha and I spent nights before we moved into our own cottage. "Wake up! Wake up! Baba is calling you," Gĩthũi said, shaking me. I panicked and hurried to the porch, still groggy, with not enough sense to shake it before appearing.

"Were you sleeping?" Baba asked from the courtyard.

My mouth stayed shut.

"Why don't you grow food by your bed's footboard?" he said. "And reach out whenever you get hungry, so you won't have to get up and work."

His retorts stung me terribly.

Working hard to grow our food, or whatever else we needed, took so much energy and dominated most of our lives and metaphors.

*

Baba nurtured his animals like one would a child. Besides occasional grains, potatoes, and vegetable peels, Mami fed the goats; he bought them five-pound pink rocks of salt from Maji Moto (Hot Water Springs). He placed one at each end of the trough for them to lick at leisure when they hung in the courtyard.

A goat herder suffered much grief if goats went astray or fed in people's gardens. To prevent such incidents, Baba installed bells around the necks of the lead goats and miniature bells on their kids. He also branded the rumps of goats that lacked identifiable marks so he could easily identify them if his herd mingled with others.

He checked their hooves or coats in case they had ticks and kept a watchful eye when my brothers corralled the goats, sometimes with his help, into their cottage in the evenings. I suspected that if he saw any of us abuse his goats, he would have done the same thing to him or her.

I almost gave Baba a chance to confirm this one late Saturday when I assaulted his goat.

Mami had asked me to winnow beans she planned to leave

slow-cooking overnight.

I sat on a low bench close to the porch, sorting the beans in a woven tray in my lap. Goats romped and frolicked in the courtyard, licked pink rocks at the trough, lounged around, or fussed with each other or their young.

Absent-mindedly, I set the tray down and hurried indoors to fetch a bowl for the beans I sorted. On my return, right on the porch, my heart fell. One young goat buried its snout in the beans, munching as if it had starved for days. Two others were about to join her.

Beans were a no-no for goats. If they ate a generous amount, their bellies swelled, followed by serious diarrhea, bad enough to devastate the strong or kill the weak or the young.

Nonetheless, goats loved forbidden foods.

When they grazed or licked the pink salt rocks, they paused, acknowledged their neighbors, and fussed with their young or the opposite sex. But when those same goats spotted enticing forbidden food—food that harmed them—they rushed in, buried in their snouts, and munched as if they had two sets of teeth—and never raised their heads unless accosted.

I now rushed toward the goat, shooing and flailing my arms, apprehensive that I would alert my father. The goat dashed a few feet away and stopped. But its copycats gave up and strolled back to rejoin the others. Instead of doing the same, the young thief dived in and scooped another mouthful.

A surge of anger took over my body.

I scrabbled for a weapon.

A piece of firewood from Mami's heap nearby made a perfect weapon. I grabbed one and swung it with a lethal merger of energy and anger.

The stick landed smack on the thief's lower back. Its pelvis buckled. It turned into splits. Its hind legs collapsed and stretched. The useless legs swept the ground like a mop while the poor goat dragged its torso.

I froze, left hand over my mouth, right hand still holding the weapon, horrified that with my father's door ajar, he would see his disabled goat while it dragged across the courtyard. Baba would only chastise me—I hoped—because leaving the beans unattended in the presence of his goats amounted to attempted murder.

His voice never came.

My tension eased as the goat mixed with the herd. Oh! I still held the evidence. Someone could make the connection. I quickly tossed the stick back on the heap and remained transfixed, my eyes on the goat.

I dealt with two forces—guilt at what I had done and the desire to disassociate myself. I thought of grabbing the tray of beans, disappearing indoors, and letting time heal my guilt. Nobody would know what happened.

The poor animal saved me the trouble.

When I hit it, it freaked out. It rushed toward its fellow goats for refuge or to seek support. When they saw its deformed state, they got spooked, even the strong males, and all dashed away. In search of a sympathetic companion who would at least spare a pause to look, the victim dragged itself, turning this way and that, hind legs sweeping and tripping over each other. Not a single goat slowed down.

Meanwhile, my father snickered and said, "These goats!" That was his reaction when male goats rushed around the courtyard and fought for a female.

To my relief, in the melee, the goat's hips reset before another human appeared.

I monitored the goat for a couple of days. I noticed diarrhea that left fresh and dry trails down its hind legs. But because of goats' sneaky ways, diarrhea occasionally happened. No one could connect the poor animal's trails to me.

I was off the hook!

# Chapter 57

# Internal Self-Government

As we busied ourselves with the business of living unknown to us, the cogs of the larger society still rolled along. Before we moved from our first fenced village in 1959, we had heard that the Mau Mau freedom fighters were on the verge of losing the war to the British. But without TV, newspapers, or radio, such news came only from the landowner, an occasional letter from Kikuyuland, school, or village gossip.

Back when the colonial government hanged the Mau Mau general Dedan Kĩmaathi on February 18, 1957, people accepted that their heroes had gambled and lost. A malaise had fallen on the village; people wondered what would come next, and they talked in slow, uneasy tones. An occasional woman discussed politics with Mami in her house; men didn't do so with Baba. When he reacted to politics, Baba uttered a clipped dismissive comment or merely snickered—especially after the colonial government snared Mr. Kĩmaathi—as if my father knew all along the Mau Mau lacked the capacity and skill to eject the British. And who could blame him?

When the British invaded Kenya and subdued Baba's community at the turn of the 20th century, he was a little boy. As a young man, the colonial government conscripted him and his younger brother, Mwai, into World War 1. Mwai never came back. Although Baba didn't talk about it, I bet that to him, the idea of the Mau Mau winning over the British was like winning over a god.

Politics confused me; even though I got occasional glimpses of a different life through school, I couldn't imagine my family or the villagers' lives in any other way.

After we moved to our second village, politics took a back seat for about two years as villagers finished building their homesteads and worried about their children's schooling and about producing enough food. A few petitioned the colonial government for permission to repatriate their suffering relatives in Kikuyuland.

During that period, the Ministry of Education abolished the common national entrance exam that pupils took in grade four. Everyone concerned sighed with relief as the Ministry extended community schools to grade seven. We, schoolchildren, dodged a life of six-day farm work, at least, until we got older. But no one connected the changes to the rumored political negotiations.

In time, we heard about Kenya's forthcoming independence and the British returning to their country. Nobody seemed to wonder about the contradiction of the British leaving after they had won the war.

"What about the Indians?" a man asked.

No one answered him.

The Indians had stayed under the radar as they raised their families, stuck to their culture, and ran their retail businesses. They owned the means of production of the country's basic goods—the stores and gas stations, the distribution, and the factories. They treated their customers and workers with disdain but kowtowed before the colonizers. Africans hated the Indians as much as the Europeans. But the Indians hadn't seized their lands or made the oppressive colonial laws, the crux of the grievances, the activists, the freedom fighters, and the masses focused on.

Now, the village know-it-alls, mainly the ones who had trick-led back from Kikuyuland, sounded more knowledgeable about freedom matters. They said our lands would revert to us without further struggle and that the era of servitude would soon end.

Questions rattled in my mind. What did it mean for my family? How would independence affect us? Would Baba get that 25-acre coffee farm after all? After Major Miller gave up the farm?

By the time my classmates and I advanced to grade six, enough political news had percolated and seeped through for us to learn that uhuru, independence, was imminent.

Dedan Kīmaathi was long gone; the moderate, well-known, and accepted Jomo Kenyatta was now the apparent leader.

On June 1, 1963, Kenya attained internal self-government, with Jomo Kenyatta as prime minister.

For villagers who understood power dynamics, the day was a big milestone. The man who owned a radio and the few who listened with him spread the news of celebrations in Nairobi and other towns.

We in Solai, like the country's majority rural community, waited for a sign—something to happen. But when the big day came, people went to work as always. Nothing changed.

Because it was a Saturday, a non-school day, we joined Mami in the garden, disappointed it wasn't a holiday. But it mattered little; I didn't know what to expect. I doubt it mattered to my parents, either. The politically astute adults who witnessed deaths and atrocities that the community had pulled through in Kikuyu-land consoled themselves.

"This is just mock independence," they said. The real independence would come in December. In our household, however, we enjoyed a different type of good news while we waited for "the real" independence.

One day, Baba returned from work with a letter stuffed in his shirt pocket. He called Joseph to read it to him. When my father learned who sent the letter, he called out to my little sister in the courtyard.

"Wairimũ! Go tell your mother to come."

Usually, when a letter came, one of my brothers read it to Baba. Afterward, the reader disclosed the news before Baba told Mami. Before that, nothing had justified my father calling Mami to thingira so she could learn the news firsthand.

Soon, Mami emerged from thingira all smiles, eager to spread the great news.

Her long-lost son, David, had returned from the dead. He was alive and well, despite Baba and her fear to the contrary. He worked as a civilian clerk at Kahawa Garrison, fifteen miles from Nairobi.

David started sending an occasional letter. He didn't mention the aborted American scholarship that my parents blamed for his three-year disappearance.

Meanwhile, nobody dared ask him for an explanation. The family feared he might disown us again. However, when he visited us in 1964, at twenty-five and a half, Baba couldn't help himself. "It's about time you got married," he told David.

David indulged my father the following year and married Pricilla Njeri "Lucy" Ng'ng'a. Afterward, based on reports of his infidelity and bar-hopping, it became clear he hadn't finished sowing his wild oats or bingeing on alcohol.

Sadly, to this day, parents' expectations and push for marriage have burdened some of my male relatives. The parents urge them to marry before they can adequately support themselves, let alone support another person or a family. Some men may need years to handle the responsibilities of marriage.

Granted, these early marriages might minimize children born out of wedlock (many Kikuyu men who bring forth children outside marriage abandon them), but the early marriages also ensure a continued cycle of poverty.

# Chapter 58

# Independence Day

December 12, 1963, a Thursday, the *real* independence arrived, and Kenya became a republic. It was a holiday, a great day, a rebirth for the country, with Jomo Kenyatta as the first president.

However, anyone with a pinch of foresight would have never picked December 12th to solemnize such a sacred day, only thirteen days before Christmas. They should have never picked December, for that matter. Because they did, I want to believe it was an oversight, ignorance, or, heaven forbid, the architects intended to weaken the monumental day.

For over sixty years since the British conquered Kenya, as much as they wanted to squeeze maximum production from the natives, they also, for easier management, wanted to demolish indigenous cultures—the collective strength of a people. They used one of the best psychological tools man has—religion. They introduced and enforced Christianity and allowed natives Sundays off to partake in those rituals.

Besides Sunday, Christmas was the only public holiday people celebrated. Women and children wore new clothes, Christians went to church and sang carols, men drank themselves silly, and there was plenty to eat. This included the once-a-year chapatti and beef, a rarity in those days; we usually ate goat's meat. As an employment perk, the landowner shot a cow or two, had his workers slaughter them, and distributed the meat to all the employees. We ate food with beef for several days.

But for Independence Day, there were no prior preparations or perks. When the day arrived, peasants didn't know whether they needed to do anything special besides stay home. In my household, no one seemed concerned. Except for my two brothers, who went goat-herding, the rest dispersed. Mami cooked a regular meal—a mixture of maize, beans, potatoes, and greens we call mūkimo or mataha, a staple for Agĩkũyũ. (Sometimes people call it irio, a misnomer because *irio* means food.)

Although I wanted to see what freedom meant, especially when I heard there would be celebrations in towns, I didn't expect us to do anything special. After all, what day could surpass Christmas? Nobody wanted to shortchange the special day; they couldn't afford it, anyway. Mami had already bought our new Christmas clothes.

But I was bored. Longing to learn of the news from Nairobi, the official center of speeches and celebrations, or to experience something that proved we were free, I walked about in the village, searching for activity. I encountered a small group of men at a homestead; some stood, and others crouched around a small transistor radio set on a stool.

From where I hung in the periphery, I eavesdropped to get scraps of news. I couldn't just butt in. I teetered between childhood and adulthood—an age where people expected a female to know better and stay out of men's way. The exclusion stung. I envied the men.

"I want to hear it for myself to believe it," one man said.

He meant the announcement about lowering the British Union Jack and raising the Kenyan flag at a park in Nairobi. The park was later named Uhuru Park (Freedom Park) to memorialize the occasion.

(There has been confusion among the younger generations, where some claim former President Uhuru Mũigai Kenyatta [2013–2022] named Uhuru Park after himself. This isn't the case. When he was born on October 26, 1961, his parents—Jomo Kenyatta and Mama Ngina Kenyatta—named him "Uhuru" in anticipation of Kenya's independence, three years before Independence Day. Uhuru Park was thus named because it was the venue where the British handed the country back to its owners, and the Union Jack slid down as the Kenyan flag rose)

Others in the small group around the radios said they wanted to hear Jomo Kenyatta's acceptance speech and address to the nation. Whether they heard anything, I couldn't tell. Because of the Jumatatu Mountain Range, the static was so bad that the news came in spurts.

At its worst, a man stuck his ear inches from the speaker to catch whatever was said. I gave up and returned home, disappointed that the village could offer only a static radio to mark our independence.

# Chapter 59

# Uhuru Celebrations

I don't know what I expected of Independence Day, but I suppose I wanted to see or experience something unusual, something transformational, not just nothing. At least we didn't go to the plantations to pick coffee cherries, I consoled myself. That was what we did full-time during our December school holidays.

That morning, people in our homestead had dispersed, except for Mami. She never ran out of chores to occupy her time. With nothing to do, I sat in her house, bored, wondering whether there was anything tangible about independence.

Unknown to me, however, people who returned from Kikuyuland were no slackers; they had something to energize the village and mark the special day.

On the verge of giving up, I heard a spurt of people singing in Gĩkũyũ. That was unusual. Tugen people were the only ones who sang and danced outside our old village; I knew no other people who did. I went outdoors to listen and determine the source. Then I headed to the main part of the village, toward the main dirt road.

By the roadside, I found a group of about twenty people, half of them dressed in full celebration garb. The apparent leader stood at least six feet with a medium build. He wore elaborate brown and red cloths wrapped around him, a colorful hat with an assortment of pins and the long-valued ostrich feathers stuck on, beads across his chest, wide brass bangles on his wrists, and rattles on his legs.

About ten other men dressed similarly, although not as elaborately as the leader. The rest of the men wore brown cloths across their shoulders over their regular clothes. They decorated their hats with rooster feathers.

Several women dressed in leather clothes, tops adorned with beads, and traditional skirts with tails called mĩthuru (mũthuru in singular). They wore beads, bangles, and humongous bunches of hang'i (earrings) made of red, orange, green, and white beads.

Because their pierced, elongated earlobes couldn't bear the weight, women reinforced the earrings with strings that rested across their heads, ear to ear. Some women wore brown cloths over their skirts or regular dresses. Younger women, born after the era of pierced, elongated earlobes, didn't wear the large, round earrings.

The leader and his female partner, who was as decorated as he was except for a hat, earrings, and rattles, introduced the songs; the entire group echoed them, and two couples sang the chorus.

The group entered the village and meandered through pathways. It grew larger and larger as people joined in, some with rooster feathers stuck on their regular hats. Throngs of children romped behind as the group returned to the main dirt road in front of the village. They inched forward now and then.

Behind the leader and core group, dancers occasionally dashed this way and that, waving green branches as a sign of peace. The leader waved his fly whisk high in the air with the rhythm. Occasionally, he whipped his whisk over one shoulder and then the other.

I watched in awe like the other spectators; most of them, like my family, had never left the farm.

The singers and dancers bobbed their heads and their upper bodies and stomped their feet as they sang about the Gĩkũyũ history, the war, and about Kĩrĩnyaga (Mt. Kenya), the beauty of its snowy three peaks, and their beloved land of milk and honey. Despite the years of servitude they had endured, they sang: Ngai had refused to abandon the children of Gĩkũyũ and Mũmbi—the Gĩkũyũ's primordial parents. The singers punctuated their songs with chants of Uhuru! Wĩyathi! Freedom!

The dance and songs became so robust that one man who used a walking stick—in case his legs failed to cooperate—waved the stick in the air while he swayed his shoulders and bobbed his head.

People who lived closer to the road collected in their front yards or stood by footpaths, some Christians among them. But others like Mami—although I suspect she itched to take a peek if she were closer—didn't. She remained indoors. According to Christianity, such celebrations or dances fell into the African culture category and, therefore, were considered primitive, sinful, and against church rules.

But non-Christians or those who gravitated toward wherever the social wind blew, even if they had never danced, got their dormant senses awakened. They swayed this way and that as they joined the group or trailed behind.

I felt buoyed and wished I could dance. But I was painfully shy. And although I felt euphoric, I still believed the school wouldn't approve of such native celebrations. Besides, I told myself I didn't know the freedom songs, anyway.

I contented myself with gawking from the sidelines, marveling at how the singers could remember all those songs.

By noon, the crowd swelled to the scrubby, uneven road banks, some people rushing ahead to get a better view of the lead group. It is hard to tell whether the lack of room forced the leaders to make their next move or if they planned it.

Instead of letting the spectators settle in one spot, the leaders marched eastward toward the plantation house, about a quarter of a mile away. As I followed, I believed they would reach a certain point and turn back.

But they inched on and on.

The closer to the colonial house the crowd got, the farther back cowards like me trailed.

I remembered grown men whipping off their hats and holding them slightly back in their hands, or the hatless wringing their hands, shoulders hunched as they approached Kamunge or Major Miller. What would happen if Major Miller learned or saw the boisterous peasants in their traditional garb, singing, marching, and their rattles making quite a racket as the men stomped on the ground like warriors ready for battle?

When the crowd passed the coffee factory, the halfway mark, and didn't slow down, doubt faded from my mind about where they headed. Uneasiness clouded my euphoria, and I feared joining the troops to battle. Who knew what could happen? Major Miller could unleash his fierce German shepherds on the crowd, resulting in a melee and likely causing injuries. Or he could fire the troublemakers or their fathers. But I hungered to bear witness, to claim forever more that I witnessed Uhuru celebrations. I inched on from behind among my fellow cowards.

When the celebrants reached the Millers' gateless entrance, the core group slightly toned down their enthusiasm as they readied to cross the gate line. The larger group behind hesitated, their voices lowered. But the lead group proceeded inside for about twenty-five feet. Some wishy-washy remained in between, while the largest group congregated and bellowed their freedom songs at the entrance.

Alerted, the boss emerged from the colonial house about 200 feet away. He strolled toward the small lead group, whose boisterous singing toned down the closer he got.

I stood back, way back from the gate line, watching, ready to take off if the boss unleashed his ire.

Instead, Major Miller stopped at a distance from the lead group. "Karibu! Karibu!" (Welcome, welcome!) he said, waving his hand for them to get closer.

When they reached where he waited, he beckoned the rest of the crowd to enter. People hurried, milling behind the lead group, which was now in a semi-circle, Major Miller in front, slightly on one side.

He said something to the leader, likely instructions on the singing agenda. People at the back slightly elbowed each other to get closer.

"Ni sawa, ni sawa" (It's all right, it's all right), Major Miller said. "Endelea kuimba." (Continue singing.)

People resumed singing, hesitant at first, perhaps to confirm he really meant it.

As the singing gathered momentum, Major Miller said, "Karibu! Karibu!" (Welcome! Welcome!), waving his hand at the cowards behind the gate and the wishy-washy who trailed in between.

He watched the boisterous singing and smiled, which may have been a smirk. He waved, turning left and right to acknowledge his subjects as if he were the one installed in the presidency.

With the other cowards, who would be answerable to husbands, fathers, or themselves, I merely watched, interested in the dynamics instead of enjoying the celebration, resolved not to set a single foot across the entrance, no matter how much Major Miller beckoned. I wondered how the whole thing would play out.

He remained there for less than two minutes, if that, before he turned and headed toward his house. The farther Major Miller got, the more boisterous the crowd got. When he disappeared to rejoin his family, who must have already peeked through windows at the rowdy celebration, it's possible they made disparaging remarks and chuckled about "these poor natives."

The dancers stayed in the compound for about twenty minutes while they sang and threw verbal barbs at *nyakerū* (white people) for stealing their lands. They should hurry, pack up, and return wherever they came from.

I failed to understand the point of their singing—Major Miller understood no Gĩkũyũ. He only communicated with his workers in pidgin Kiswahili.

After all the euphoria, I woke up the following morning expecting to feel different now that we were independent people. Perhaps there would be an announcement. I got disappointed, just like in June, during the "mock independence."

Things remained the same, at least from my perspective. People discussed *Uhuru* like any other political subject. They returned to work and tended to their families and animals. And Major Miller remained the big boss.

# Chapter 60

# The Colonized Post-Independence

After Kenya's independence, peasants on European farms like my family were way down the pecking order. The priority was to get qualified and educated Africans to run the new government. But in a country where the masses lacked formal education, the biggest pool available to tap into was the educated and experienced colonizers, their African loyalists and homeguards, already in those jobs.

Out of pure necessity, the Kenyatta administration gave enemies of the people the first dip of the jobs. Many colonizers, especially the ones in specialized fields and their secretaries, kept their posts while the new government scrambled to educate and train Africans to take over.

Although the new administration strove to improve the lives of its citizens, many of its administrators—out of self-interest or for the sake of a peaceful transition—ignored the history of the Mau Mau and the atrocities committed by the colonizers and their loyalists.

Meanwhile, politicians and technocrats tackled the monumental challenges of managing the transition government and establishing a new constitution in a multi-ethnic Kenya, composed of micronations (tribes) that, before the British, had governed themselves under their own customs and legal systems. The new administration fell back on the colonial constitution framework and tweaked it to give it an African flavor.

The situation worsened when Kenyatta died in 1978 and his Vice-President, Daniel Toroitich arap Moi (1978–2002), took over. People alleged Kenyatta had appointed Moi as his vice-president to ward off opposition, especially because he was non-Gĩkũyũ. When Moi assumed the presidency per the constitution, he subsequently "won" every election and entrenched himself. His administration turned into a ruthless and murderous 24-year dictatorship.

A former elementary school teacher with an eighth-grade education, Daniel T. arap Moi was also a former colonial member of the Legislative Council of Kenya (LegCo), modeled after the Westminster system. Moi was ill-equipped to rule over a multi-ethnic population. To his credit, he improved the lives of his own ethnic group through education, training, job and business placements, and other developments. He also merged his ethnic group's various subgroups (from the most progressive Nandi to his own pastoralist Tugen tribe) into one Kalenjin tribe, which is now the third-largest tribe in Kenya.

The 39-year stretch of Kenyatta's and Moi's administrations provided ample time for the former colonizers, loyalists, and their descendants to diminish or bury their colonial-era crimes. The populace focused on bettering themselves or weathering the dictatorship, while the former enemies of the people aged and retired. Their adult children continued to ensure the embarrassing atrocities of the Mau Mau era stayed buried.

And because the major burden of suffering brought by the Mau Mau revolt fell mainly on the Gĩkũyũ tribe, other tribes and those who had campaigned for multi-racial independence through the colonial constitution saw no benefit in honoring the Mau Mau troubled period.

For these reasons, a sizeable number of writers and politicians in Kenya, academics included, side-stepped, ignored, or underplayed the Mau Mau history. When people aligned with the Mau Mau independence aspirations wrote books, those in power sidelined them or actively frustrated or jailed the authors. The distortion made the colonizers and their cohorts' abhorrent legacy seem insignificant.

In the 21st century, however, patriotic writers and the Kenyan civil society have made strides in unearthing and documenting Kenya's colonial history and the high price natives paid to attain independence. Writers like Maina wa Kĩnyattĩ have even gone further. They have covered not only the colonial era but also the post-independence period.

The government of Mwai Kĩbakĩ (2002–2013), the third president of Kenya, made efforts to commemorate the Mau Mau's vital contributions to Kenya's history.

Will those freedom fighters and their descendants get the full credit they deserve? I don't know. But I would guess not. However, the patriots who abandoned their families to fight for their country and sacrificed their lives for a free and humane Kenya would be appalled by the unpatriotic and outright corrupt leaders that Kenya has to endure.

Although people who experienced savage colonial activities have died off, and time has dulled the memories of their descendants, any Gĩkũyũ person who experienced the Mau Mau era atrocities, directly or indirectly, has a wound that time alone cannot heal.

Meanwhile, just like the slaveholders in the Americas, many loyalists eased from a colonial system into an independent Kenya without a pause. They enjoyed independence and secure jobs, businesses, privileges, and other benefits that, for six decades now, have accrued to their descendants.

# Chapter 61

# Colonizers post-Independence

Post-independence, the Kenyatta administration gave the former colonizers two options: become Kenyan citizens or leave the country within two years. Some left because they loathed the idea of an African government ruling over them. Others feared a backlash, expecting they would suffer from the same inhumane policies and crafty tactics that they had subjected the Africans to. But many more Europeans stayed. Entrenched in Kenya, they had no family or friends to return to in England.

The government gave similar options to the Indians and their descendants. The British had imported the older generation to help build the Kenya-Uganda Railway. After Kenya's independence, Indians automatically became British subjects. They had three options: return to India, remain in Kenya, or move to England.

Between dim prospects in congested India and a Kenya led by an African government, many Indians liquidated their businesses and moved to England; some moved to Canada. A few, mostly older and still nostalgic about their country of birth, moved back to India. The rest, rich and too entrenched, remained in Kenya.

*

Major Miller and other majors in the area did not budge. Neither did Mr. Patel, who owned the Patel General Store, where we bought the few household supplies we did not grow.

For the people in Kikuyuland, it had been a total commotion since the British eased their grip on the country. Most Mau Mau members laid down their arms and emerged from the forest and other hideouts. The government released people from detention camps and dismantled the "secure" villages, and families searched for their lost relatives or a word about the dead ones.

The main challenge came from people who had been displaced and wanted the government to return or replace their stolen lands; many could identify their former lands. The government refused. If, after generations, the government had grabbed land from one and given it to another, total chaos would have ensued.

Resettling people became such a monumental task that, sometimes, only the passage of time and fading memories could ease.

My parents and other villagers who worked and lived on European farms longed for a sign that independence would improve their lives. Like my father, the older ones did not expect much for themselves; they looked forward to whatever the new government decided, hoping their children would have a better life.

As time passed, we noticed no changes, not any we could articulate anyway. No "fruits of independence," villagers said. The peasants still toiled in the fields as before, but Africans could now join the Kenya Farmers Association (KFA) and sell their surplus maize directly rather than through Major Miller.

The only glitch was that the few individuals who could have sold directly to KFA didn't know the mechanics involved, lacked transportation, and didn't have enough maize to sell wholesale. They continued selling through Major Miller until the new government came to their aid.

In the early 1970s, the government began to buy British-owned farms. Whatever government resettlement agency organized the purchases, it then structured each farm as a cooperative that sold land shares in installments, first to former employees and then to others. As soon as members paid off their share, the cooperative allocated them about a two-and-a-half-acre plot.

Because managers ran the cooperatives, similar to homeowners' associations, the new small landowners started selling maize through their own co-op.

In my area, people learned that Major Miller had more than paid himself for his involvement. When KFA paid him, instead of taking the cost and a little profit for himself, he paid the villagers only half of what he received per bag. That's what he deemed the Africans were worth.

# Chapter 62

# Benefits and Challenges

To smooth the changeover process, the government offered free education to students at the University of Nairobi, the Kenya Government Secretarial College in Nairobi and Mombasa, and others, provided they worked for the government for three years after their education.

In addition, the Ministry of Labor created the Department of Kenyanization Service Bureau with the assignment to scout for qualified Africans, issue work permits, and phase out replaceable foreign nationals. The Department phased out the ones they termed "dead woods" without delay and replaced them with qualified Africans who had been held back during the colonial era.

Skilled Africans in towns, including clerks, could get jobs with little effort. Those who had gone overseas to universities couldn't graduate fast enough to return home to serve their country. For those who had married while overseas, depending on their degrees, the government enticed them with job offers and free passage for their family and personal effects.

Because these sources couldn't fully satisfy the government's immediate needs, it kept some Europeans in senior posts, including the military, the police, the judiciary, and even moderate-skill jobs like secretaries. Under the colonial setup, secretarial jobs—

occupied by women trained in Pitman's shorthand, office procedure, and typing—came under the managerial category. And because of the former African colonial loyalists' administrative experience, the government appointed some of them or their educated adult children to major posts.

To have former enemies of the people work in the new government irked the Gĩkũyũ masses to no end. They believed Mau Mau freedom fighters and their political supporters—individuals who had spent years campaigning for the country's independence (not assimilation into the British colonial system)—should have had first consideration in jobs.

But people overlooked that most of the Mau Mau rank-and-file had minimal formal education, or none. A sizeable number of the leaders had reached standard eight and passed well in Kenya African Primary Education (KAPE)—better educated than most of today's Kenyan high school diplomas. However, they lacked school fees to join the few premier high schools set aside for Africans. Although the men were intelligent and skilled in military tactics and command gained in World War II and later at home, they lacked the skills, temperament, and experience needed to run the transitional democratic civilian government.

If the government had explained the bind they found themselves in, especially President Kenyatta, who had clout from every tribe in Kenya, it's likely most people would have begrudgingly understood. But I doubt anyone in the new government dared to admit that.

Perhaps the government expected the issue to fade away. But Mau Mau members never let up. They refused to accept that the British and their collaborators, their archenemies, could play any role in the new government. A subset of them refused to recognize the new Kenyatta administration and refused to lay down their arms. The staunchest in the group remained hunkered down in the forest around Mt. Kenya.

To the Mau Mau, besides the employment issue, which was detestable enough, Kenya's leadership had fallen into the wrong hands. They believed they should have been the architects of the new administration.

Jomo Kenyatta, the new president, thought otherwise. He had been a political activist most of his adult life. He and others had long pushed for the British to return the stolen lands and for equal rights based on the "fairness" of the British constitution, in other words, a multi-racial government.

The community had sent him to London to present the natives' grievances to the London Colonial Office and parliament. When his attempts to gain recognition from British officials failed after they ignored and snubbed him, Kenyatta furthered his education in anthropology and economics and started another family. Meanwhile, he continued his activism and gave speeches at Hyde Park, which enhanced his oratory skills and collaboration with others—including Julius Nyerere of Tanzania and Kwame Nkrumah of Ghana—who sought independence for their own countries.

When Mr. Kenyatta returned to Kenya, he assumed the chairmanship at the Kenya African Union (KAU). He became even more politically active through newsletters, rallies, and meetings with the colonial authorities (when they didn't rebuff him).

At the onset of the war, Kenyatta's activism led the colonial government to sentence him and his cohorts to seven years of hard labor, a fact that Kenyatta let no one forget.

Besides, Kenyatta had another argument to support his presidency that people had taken to heart.

Reports said that the British colonial government had offered to designate the landlocked Central province (now Kĩambũũ, Mũrang'a, and Nyeri counties) as the home of the Gĩkũyũ people, the troublemakers, and to grant them independence, as the Boers did to the Transkei homeland in South Africa in 1976. The British would keep ownership of the rest of Kenya.

Kenyatta and his group turned down the offer, reports said. They insisted they wanted the entire country of Kenya to be free and for people to be treated equally.

Despite Kenyatta's impressive record, it failed to appease the Mau Mau faction. The idea of assimilation had been a big fallout for them. They refused to embrace Kenyatta—he wasn't one of them. The masses also snickered at his relationship.

During his stay in England, between 1931 and 1946, he married a white woman. The two had brought forth a son. Mr. Kenyatta had left his ex-wife and son back in England, although he invited them to Kenya for his inauguration. Besides the Mau Mau members, Gĩkũyũ people frowned on this union for years.

When Mr. Kenyatta settled into his presidency, he became tired of the complaints. "Did you want me to stay alone and parlay with prostitutes?" he asked at several of his rallies.

The community dropped the matter, unable to fathom their new president visiting houses of ill repute.

But the Mau Mau fighters' resentment smoldered.

Aside from the stolen lands and the poor treatment their fellow natives endured, they couldn't forget how the colonial government had conscripted them to World War II under the pretense of offering them jobs and money to open businesses after they returned from the war.

The veterans watched as thousands of their colleagues died fighting someone else's war. When they returned home, the colonial government paid each of them one month's salary, allowed them to keep one change of military uniforms—which the military replaced with an inferior material before release—and issued them insignias bearing the image of King George VI with instructions to wear the "prestigious" symbols so their communities would respect them for fighting for the Crown.

The colonial officials also warned the African veterans not to indulge in politics or spread propaganda about the war they had fought. If they did so, the officials warned, the police would arrest them and treat them like German and Italian enemies on the front lines. With that ominous warning, the colonial government discarded those veterans, many of them crippled physically or psychologically or both. They became jobless and landless.

In contrast, the white veterans, including the German and Italian war prisoners, received honorary medals, land, and seed money to resettle and run their new farms or businesses. Some got employed in government departments.

Meanwhile, with time on their hands, the discarded Gĩkũyũ veterans learned of the KAU splinter group that had become dissatisfied with the slow-paced constitutional campaign that Kenyatta and the KAU group advocated. The veterans joined the splinter group and formed the Kenya Land and Freedom Army (KLFA), which, over time, morphed into Mau Mau.

Even though Kenyatta's group and the Mau Mau disagreed on strategy, they never collided because they both, with some variations, aimed for the same goal: a fair and just independent Kenya.

As the activism heightened, however, the colonial government struggled to contain the Africans.

In October 1952, when Gov. Baring declared a state of emergency in the country, they dubbed moderate Kenyatta a member of the Mau Mau, although he wasn't. He considered them hotheads.

The officials dismantled Kenyatta's group, arrested and threw him into the notorious Lokitaung and Lodwar detention camps in arid northern Kenya for seven years. (Bildad M. Kaggia, one of the chief architects of Kenya's independence, was released last, after nine years) The group included Fred Kubai, Kũng'ũ Karũmba, Bildad M. Kaggia, Kariuki Chotara, Warũhiũ Itote

(General China), and non-Gĩkũyũ activist—Paul Ngei from Kamba land.

Other prominent political activists and a handful of their supporters, like Achieng Oneko from Luo land, included hundreds of other Gĩkũyũ people—journalists, writers, publishers, clerks, and business people, who were detained in various detention and concentration camps.

Despite Kenyatta's record, the Mau Mau members saw him as part of the elite who sought change through the colonial constitution instead of dismantling the colonial system entirely. They hated that Kenyatta had rubbed shoulders with colonizers when he went to the colonial office and the British parliament in England to negotiate and *plead* for independence, while the Mau Mau fought for it.

And now, this new administration expected their members to return to their devastated communities and their families—dead or broken up or missing or scattered—and carry on with their lives. It was an outrage, they said.

At his rallies, President Kenyatta threw occasional political tantrums or zingers at the Mau Mau. He claimed the "dissidents" had achieved their goal of driving the colonizers away. They should rejoice that Kenya became independent. Instead, they turned against the African government, just as they had in the colonial era. "The dissidents should be ashamed of their disloyalty," he said.

# Chapter 63

# The Weakened Mau Mau

Despite the Mau Mau's splinter group hunkering down in the forest, they negotiated from a weak hand. Weary of war, the majority had already bowed out after independence. And, before independence, when some of their leaders were captured, they had turned traitorous in exchange for their lives.

To weaken the splinter group even more, the colonial government had long eliminated Kenyatta's one potential opponent, the Mau Mau leader, Dedan Kĩmaathi. And Bildad M. Kaggia, Kenyatta's colleague in detention and one of the other capable people who would have given Kenyatta political grief, had already bowed out because of respect and consideration of Kenyatta's advanced age and longer political activism.

Knowing his administration had the upper hand, Mr. Kenyatta didn't shy away from condemning the Mau Mau and calling them "imaramari" (terrorists), even to foreign presses, whom, for years, the colonizers had fed stories on the evils of the Mau Mau.

As David Anderson quotes in the *Histories of the Hanged*, at a political rally, when a reporter asked Kenyatta about his thoughts on Mau Mau, his quick reply was unequivocal:

"We shall not allow hooligans to rule Kenya," Kenyatta had replied.

"Mau Mau was a disease which has been eradicated and must never be remembered again," Kenyatta would write later.

The issue remained a thorn in his administration's underbelly for many years. Finally, Kenyatta's administration blinked first and stepped toward a resolution. If the splinter Mau Mau group came out of the forest and surrendered, the government promised no legal action and would allocate them land to settle on.

On the surrender day, men and a few women in ragged clothes and dreadlocks, with sober manners and expressionless faces but with alert, bloodshot eyes, walked out of the forest, waving green branches—Gĩkũyũ's traditional sign of peace. They packed Nyeri Stadium as arranged by their emissaries. President Kenyatta— flanked by his cabinet—thanked the group for their sacrifice and welcomed them home.

Did Kenyatta keep his promise?

With the group now scattered, he had let out air from the proverbial balloon. The ex-freedom fighters had immediate family matters to confront.

The Mau Mau members who had dug in had been away for years. It included the initial core group—Mau Mau Karĩng'a (the patriots—independence or fight-to-death proponents). The group also included others who had chosen sides to avoid the colonial government's detention, while others joined the freedom fighters to help the cause, sometimes against their families' wishes.

How were the returnees going to rekindle the severed or shredded relationships? Some found smaller families, their relatives having been lost in the war rubble or through death; others found larger ones from rapes, and others were rejected by their families. The families blamed their relatives for embracing the Mau Mau cause and couldn't get over their abandonment issues. They also didn't want to deal with impoverished, worn-out,

PTSD-prone husbands or fathers who left them during the turmoil, their time of dire need.

Despite easing the pressure from the ex-freedom fighters, Mr. Kenyatta's administration still had to deal with the country's outstretched hands—people craved change.

The government struggled to keep its word. They resettled some who were known and easily identifiable. A few got posts in the government. But the rank-and-file, most with not a single year of formal education, who couldn't maneuver the bureaucracy to prove their involvement or get someone higher to vouch for them, had a hard road ahead. They got stuck at the end of the line for years.

Meanwhile, the other tribes accused Kenyatta and his Gĩkũyũ people of nepotism and tribalism, claiming he was allocating free land to his own tribe.

Of course, the government had only so much land to dish out. Most Mau Mau members received no compensation or recognition. They leaned on their families or community. The issue stretched out decades beyond Kenyatta's death in 1978.

As late as 2016, I received a first-hand account from an applicant about a piece of land intended for some then-elderly Mau Mau members or their descendants. They had registered decades ago and attended occasional meetings, but were still waiting for their promised land.

I suspect the ones who hadn't received their shares died off, and there is no telling—with changing administrations—how far their determined descendants pursued or will pursue their entitlement.

# Chapter 64

# The Thaiyas

A month after independence, when I entered grade seven in January 1964, I focused on my last year at Kabazi Primary School. If I passed the national exam, I had three options: high school, a nursing school, or a teacher's training college. And if I failed, I needed to brace myself for a deplorable backup—joining my parents on the farm. Oh, how it grated on my mind. I hated to think about it. But I planned to pass and attend a boarding high school, my number-one option.

Since I failed grade four at Tindaress Primary School and moved to Kabazi Primary three years earlier, I had promised myself that if three or more pupils passed the national exam, I would be one of them. In our grading system, #1 was the highest score. I teetered between #5 and #10 in our yearly school exam. I was #3 one year, with only two boys beating me. As the only girl in class, that was a big deal.

We sat two at a desk. I shared mine with Gerald Wangunyũ Thaiya, whose parents owned the canteen.

When the colonial government declared a state of emergency in 1952, the following year, in early 1953, the Thaiyas joined the exodus to Limuru, Kĩambuu, one of the Kikuyuland districts. Hungry and ragged, they returned to Kabazi in the late 1950s and moved back into the same house they had occupied before leaving.

Mr. Benson Thaiya now worked as an overseer for Major Ward while his wife worked at home and in their garden and ran their canteen.

From our second term in May, when it rained, Joseph and I, and a few other pupils, sheltered in the canteen's porch. The canteen was a 14' x 12' rectangular stick-and-thatch shack, with a door facing the street to the west and another facing north, which led to a small, standalone circular kitchen where Mrs. Thaiya made coffee.

If Wangunyũ, my desk-mate, accompanied us from school, he invited Joseph and me into the kitchenette.

We warmed ourselves by the fire pit or charcoal brazier and left when the rain stopped. Sometimes, Mrs. Thaiya gave us black tea but never asked us to help, even if multiple customers placed orders and Wangunyũ was busy elsewhere.

Mrs. Thaiya invited me to spend the night if it rained too long. "It's too late for a girl to walk all the way to Solai," she would say.

The Thaiyas' home was about a mile away. They walked up on a footpath that meandered through undergrowth and bushes before it leveled off into grassy open land. The distance doubled if they used the public road, then turned east on the private road leading to the village and to Major Ward's residence.

They lived in a three-bedroom, L-shaped, stone-block house on higher ground, away from the village. The living room came between two bedrooms—one for Mr. and Mrs. Thaiya and the other for the girls. Off the veranda, one end was the boys' bedroom, while the kitchen with a western-style fireplace came at the opposite end. Through the windows or the veranda, one could enjoy a panoramic view of the sprawl of land dotted with trees and hills and the village below.

Major Ward first built the house for one of those abusive white farm managers. The manager bailed out. His type didn't like owners like Major Ward, who were married to their farms and loved to snoop around to check on things. The managers preferred hands-off or absentee landowners so they could deal with the natives as they wished.

When it rained heavier than usual, sometimes Joseph arrived home after dark because he waited until the rain ebbed. He hated to spend the night. He preferred the freedom at our house where he could talk, make jokes, and, always hungry, complain to Mami when she took too long to cook.

The Thaiya children didn't enjoy such freedom with their mother. She never expected such free talk or boisterous behavior. They acted calmly, addressed each other like adults, and spoke matter-of-factly, even in the parents' absence.

In the kitchen, no child complained of hunger, unlike my siblings, who whined to Mami. A child waited for food until Mary, their adult sister, announced it was time to eat.

Our supper comprised either a mixture of maize and beans or ugali and greens, cooked in a big pot on three masonry stones placed under the curvature of the fireplace. We paid little attention to the mantel and the surrounding area, blackened with soot. Mrs. Thaiya warned us not to let the fire embers get out of control to prevent the soot-laden chimney from catching fire. I doubt it ever occurred to them to get the chimney swept.

Mr. and Mrs. Thaiya spent their evenings in the living room, a step up from the veranda. Mrs. Thaiya cooked their tea and supper on a charcoal brazier while she sat on a bench. Mr. Thaiya sat at the dining table with his chair turned toward the brazier, a cigarette smoldering in the ashtray or between his fingers. Everyone in the family called him Mũthee–Mzee in Kiswahili—a respectable old man. The children called their mother Mami, and Joseph and I called her Mama Wangunyũ. The two traded stories, mainly Mr. Thaiya's, dotted with chuckles, laughs, or sometimes cigarette-induced coughs.

The Thaiyas seemed more "affluent" than us; they lived in a stone house, owned a canteen, and could eat bread anytime they wanted, or so I thought.

One Saturday, we went on a school field trip to Lake Victoria port in Kisumu, a distance of about 420 kilometers round-trip, where I boarded a sailboat for the first time. Wangunyũ and his sister carried a bottle of Coca-Cola and a whole loaf of bread each. Besides our breakfast of ugali and greens, Joseph and I ate and drank nothing else the rest of the day. We didn't have money to buy sodas, loaves of bread, scones, or my favorite—a concave golden pastry—and we felt embarrassed to carry mataha or mũkimo (a healthy mixture of maize, beans, potatoes, and greens).

The more I got used to the Thaiyas, the more I noticed their quirks. The children endured harsh rules, a poor diet, and living conditions just like in my family, if not worse. For example, although our diet was lacking at our house, we still ate a variety of foods. During the time I spent at the Thaiyas, we only ate two types—ugali and gĩtheri (a mixture of maize and beans). And in the girls' bedroom, we slept on the floor, on concrete, without a mattress. Since I was little, Baba had always made cots and then beds for us.

And even if we feared our father, it paled compared to how much they feared theirs. If someone heard steps or a cough and said, "Muthee is coming," the entire family lowered their voices. The household treated him and his wife like a colonizer and his memsahib.

But Mwangi, their first son, who attended Mang'u Boys—one of the few premier boarding high schools at the time—enjoyed the status of being the only child, as my brother David had. The rest of the children could as well have been a sideline for their mother. Mrs. Thaiya stocked dry maize, beans, and maize flour in the granary, brought or asked someone to fetch vegetables from the garden, and supplied cooking oil, tomatoes, onions, and salt. It was up to Mary, the adult daughter, to cook. After that, Mrs. Thaiya devoted her energy to her husband's comfort.

She even filtered family conflicts before they reached him. If the children needed something, including school supplies, they had to tell their mother first so she could approve it before bothering their father. According to Margaret, about my age, her mother approved only half the time, and their father never learned of the other half.

Occasionally, Mrs. Thaiya appeared at the kitchen door. "Shhhhh, Mūthee is unhappy today," she said, finger on lips. She never said what the source of his unhappiness was. In seconds, every mouth clamped shut. When she left, and we opened our mouths again—from the biggest to the smallest—we spoke in low voices the rest of the evening. No child dared enter the living room until they guessed the worst was over.

When I left in the morning for school, I never expected the matter to stay alive after the previous evening's hushing. I admired how orderly their home was until Margaret updated me decades later.

According to her, it wasn't over until their mother said so. In Mr. Thaiya's absence, if his anger concerned the children, Mrs. Thaiya indulged in a rant and warned or whipped whoever was supposed to have stressed him.

Although Mr. Thaiya didn't beat his children, he did so by proxy through a complaint, getting angry, issuing ultimatums—and his wife would act on them—or using unusual punishment.

One day, before I knew the family, he caught Mary, his then-teenage daughter, stealing a cigarette from his packet. He gave her cash and sent her to the store to buy a pack of Marlboro cigarettes. In the yard, he ordered Mary to sit on the ground, gave her a match, and told her to smoke. He raised his voice when she dilly-dallied. She then smoked, coughed, cried, apologized, and begged for relief. Mr. Thaiya gave up only when she threw up and heaved as if she were having a heart attack.

The couple seemed to lead a blissful life separate from their children. They conversed and treated each other like newlyweds. Unlike Baba, who owned goats, beehives, and a garden to attend to besides his job, Mr. Thaiya did nothing besides his overseer job, not even helping at the canteen. And while Baba drank moderately sugared tea, beer, and snorted tobacco (which he quit when his nose became itchy), Mr. Thaiya was a teetotaler; he enjoyed heavily sugared tea and chain-smoked real store-bought cigarettes.

He rode on a bicycle, still wearing his long black coat, a gray hat, and store-bought shoes. After work, he stopped at the canteen. If he missed his wife there, and whoever she left in charge didn't know her whereabouts, Mr. Thaiya cycled home or to their garden. Apart from work, he never stayed in a place unless his wife was there.

More often than not, he found his wife at the canteen and waited for her while he discussed politics and other current affairs with male customers. Women never ventured into the canteen— they were rushing home to cook for their families—unless it was a market day on Sunday.

After Mrs. Thaiya closed the canteen at dusk, the two walked home, she carrying the supplies she needed to cook their supper while he pushed his bicycle.

With a quiet demeanor, I fell in sync with the rhythms of the Thaiya household. Our friendship flourished not only among us children but also between our mothers. Once in a long while, they visited. Other times, they sent children to deliver something to each other.

"I feel about Beth the same way I would a blood sister," Mami told me once.

Both she and Mrs. Thaiya had a brother and no sisters.

Without friends in Solai, where I could have sleepovers or spend time on my own, I enjoyed my sporadic stays at the Thaiyas, where the children treated me like one of them. I spent the night even on that fateful day when my family needed to stick together.

# Chapter 65

# The Fateful Day

Signs that parents have more children than they can manage or provide for include poor food, cramped or sub-standard housing, and ragged clothing; parents getting frustrated or angry when children ask for money for basic needs; a parent, usually a mother, turning one child into a surrogate parent; and other basic behaviors.

Occasional babysitting is fine, family helping family. Parents cross the line, however, when they prevent their older children from visiting family or friends or attending activities because those children must care for their younger siblings. It's even worse when parents force a child, mainly a daughter, to take a baby sibling along as a parent would.

My family, like many families in my youth—and some nowadays—fell into this category. Mami had reached a stage where she had no full-time babysitter because my sister Tabitha and I, who she had relied on before, now attended school.

Bless her heart that she didn't suggest one of us drop out of school to babysit. She did the best next thing. She left my little sister, Wairimũ, almost seven, and my brothers, Mũrĩithi, almost five, and Njomo, nearly three, at home to fend for themselves.

After all, nothing harmful had happened in our village, and definitely not in one's courtyard—at least not yet.

My siblings played with the others in the courtyard. If they got hungry, they dashed inside the house and grabbed a fistful of whatever Mami left for them. Occasionally, as all children did in that era, they quarreled but always settled their disputes.

One day after school, I spent the night at the Thaiyas. Joseph didn't report to school the following day. Concerned about what happened to him—we didn't miss school—I hurried home after school.

I sensed our household's trauma the minute I entered our courtyard. Several people sat on the jutting boards of our granary. They wore drawn, sober faces, indulging in an occasional withered comment now and then. Yards away, close to the porch, sat my mother on a three-legged stool, a time she should have been busying herself with preparing supper.

When I reached closer to her, her face looked haggard; her body slouched as if she had been sick for days. I looked at her listless eyes to pick up clues on the source of her pain.

"What's wrong?" I asked her.

"Family tragedy," Mami said softly.

She struggled to say something else. Her voice failed her. She blinked her eyes to stave off tears, covered her mouth with one hand, and staggered toward the side of her house, Baba's thingira to her right.

When my siblings and I were little, each of us had fallen sick, and Mami had worried one of us could die. But I never saw such collective sadness around our homestead.

Perhaps one of my siblings would enlighten me.

I entered nyūmba.

My siblings sat around a dormant fire, including Joseph, the oldest in the group.

"What's the matter?" I asked.

"It's Njomo!" Mũriithi blurted out.

"Where is he?" I asked, looking around.

"He died!"

"Died? Do you even know what dying is?"

"Yes, they put him in a hole," Mũriithi said.

I looked around again. Joseph nodded.

I plopped down on a low bench, lost for words. Njomo had hardly caught the sniffles that young children had a habit of suffering. Except for a baby Mami gave birth to at the hospital, who didn't make it home because of hospital negligence, Njomo's death was the first in our family since my birth.

Despite not having a meal since the previous evening, the hunger pangs that gnawed at me on my way home had disappeared. I sat with my elbows on my knees, hugging my cheeks, wrapped in my helpless sadness, wondering what had happened, but without the courage to ask for details—that I couldn't handle yet—from people who had suffered through telling it.

# Chapter 66

# Search for Njomo

Mami told me the story the following day, breaking down every so often. She had left my three siblings at home with food she told them to eat it when they got hungry.

At one point, before they ate their lunch, my sister Wairimũ, just shy of seven years old and the oldest of the three, noticed Njomo's absence from where they played, between the granary and Elithi's house. She and Mũrĩithi set out to search for him. They searched anywhere and everywhere they could.

The school crowd from Tindaress Primary arrived home first and started helping their younger siblings. By the time Mami arrived, Wairimũ and Mũrĩithi dragged their bodies, worn out from walking, their puffy red eyes drained of tears, their mouths incapable of speech beyond stammers of apologies for Njomo's disappearance.

Mami consoled her distraught children but didn't get alarmed; the situation didn't sound serious. We may have lived in squalor, but our village was safe, we all believed. At the time, she hadn't noticed that the children hadn't touched the food she had left them.

Before she started looking for Njomo, she sent Tabitha, Gĩthũi, and Morry to the maize mill near Kabati (gwa-Kĩmutoruthi) to grind flour for ugali that evening. She then left to look for Njomo in homes she suspected he could be.

Joseph—the one person we needed around during matters that called for quick action—arrived from school just as Mami's search proved futile, and Baba arrived home. Joseph told Mami and Baba to stay home while he took over the search. He mobilized young men in the village; others who heard the story joined in. Joseph and his group visited every household with children. They searched in backyards, around fences, and under eaves, thinking Njomo may have gotten tired and fallen asleep.

They found no sign of him. He had disappeared without a trace.

The search party moved to the grassland across the dirt road behind our homestead. Baba suffered alone in his thingira while he waited for the agile men to continue the search. Knowing the potency of his intuition, however, I believe he already feared the worst. A handful of women dropped in to help Mami keep vigil.

For Njomo, three months shy of three years, to have gone that far, he would have had to toddle about ten yards from our courtyard to a four-foot-wide pedestrian gate, walk another seven yards through scrubby grass before reaching and crossing the wide dirt road with ragged banks before he reached the scrubby grassland with a bush or thicket high enough to conceal him.

The road started from the cows' pen and meandered through grassland northwest through thickets and trees to end up at a small coffee farm we called Quarry because it was next to the farm's quarry. Cows, goats, and pedestrians used that road, along with the occasional tractor, lorry, or Major Miller's Land Rover.

It seemed improbable that a toddler could walk alone that far. But the men fanned out and continued their search. They combed the area through shrubs and mounds big enough to conceal a child. They found no sign of Njomo.

At the hint of dusk, Joseph, who had covered twice the ground the others had, couldn't contain himself; he itched to break ranks.

"We haven't searched the cows' pen," Joseph said. In the cows' sprawling sleeping enclosure, the herdsmen had already separated nursing mothers from their calves to hoard the milk overnight for milking in the morning. About two hundred cows chewed cud or dozed, set for the night.

"The cows' pen?" some searchers protested. "No. That's not likely."

"Perhaps the cows trampled on him," Joseph said.

"We're wasting our time out here," one man said.

The men made suggestions and traded opinions.

"The child may still be in the village," another man said; a handful of others agreed.

Joseph refused to wait for opinions to play out. Like one driven by an invisible force, he broke out and hurried toward the cows' pen. He first came to the cow dip—a twenty-five-foot deep and fifty-foot-long trough that jutted from the cow's pen.

Once a month, Major Miller had his cows dipped in poisonous water to kill ticks and fleas that clung to the animals' skins.

Before every dip, the pen minders cleaned the dip of floating debris and replenished the poisons. Herdsmen would then lead the cows and calves in a single file, whipping the stubborn ones that refused to proceed through a narrow, wooden-fenced pathway. It was a total commotion of mooing, ducking, and sprinting by the cows determined to skip the dive. None did.

When a cow reached the end of the narrow path, a point of no return, it jumped into the murky water and waded through until it reached the shallow end and onto the garbled concrete, where it shook the water off and proceeded to the open country. They munched on grass or shrubs while they waited for their fellow divers.

After the last cow finished its dive, two herdsmen rounded and shooed the animals to the day's pasture.

The dip always looked damp and hazy because of its low roof and murky water, with occasional mirages or shimmers. With the encroaching dusk, the dip looked hazier when Joseph reached there.

He first walked around the vicinity of the dip and found nothing. Then he sidled alongside the short wall, from the shallow to the deep end, while he gazed down below. Three-quarters along, he saw what looked like a billowing brown rag. He squinted and looked some more.

Disturbed by what he saw, he stepped out from under the dip's eaves. "Hey! Hey! Let's check in the dip!" he called out to the search party, who were still strategizing their next search. Two men broke off and hurried toward Joseph.

Meanwhile, he scrambled for a stick long enough to reach the water below. Finding none, he climbed into the enclosed wooden pathway. At a corner, he saw the extra-long brush the workers used to prod novice calves that struggled. He threw the brush over and climbed out as the men got closer.

"What is it?" the men asked from yards away.

"I saw something. I want to check it," Joseph said, still holding the long brush.

The men closed in.

"That's just debris," one man said.

"It looks like a cloth!" Joseph said.

"I see something!" the other man said. "Let's check."

Fearing Joseph was too excited and might end up in the dip, one man asked him to hand over the cattle prod. The man nudged the floating debris to the shallow end while Joseph bent over, gawking and inhaling the poisonous fumes.

His heart pounded faster the more the debris neared the shallow end. Gradually, a drenched rag-doll-like mass took shape, face down.

One man struggled to turn the "rag-doll" face up.

Joseph was already wailing, striding on the shallow-end garbled concrete to get to the "debris."

His racket alerted the rest; the group rushed toward the dip.

The people who kept vigil at home heard Joseph's howls and rushed to the fence while the younger people dashed toward the noise. Soon, Mami learned the worst news that she would never wish for another mother. She keened, fell, and fainted.

The family laid Njomo to rest the following day on the strip of land between the dirt road and our backyard garden by a tree behind the fence.

I missed the event. I regretted I spent the night at the Thaiyas on such a cloudless day. David missed both Njomo's birth and his death. Both events happened when he had divorced the family.

But my brother Simon attended the funeral. He had sensed the tragedy from where he worked at Teremŭka's farm, three farms away. Simon had inherited Baba's strong intuition. During Njomo's search and recovery, he had experienced a dread he couldn't explain. Alone in his cottage, a thought crossed his mind to talk to his neighbor so he could ease his mind. He decided against it. Instead, he went to bed early to shake it off. He tossed and turned before he fell asleep.

He dreamed of mourners congregating around a grave. He could identify his family members, but he couldn't tell who they mourned. Whenever he approached a mourner and asked who had died, the person stepped aside and dissolved. When Simon kept to himself, observing, afraid to proceed, the person would reappear. In frustration, Simon jostled his way through to reach his family members. Just before he got to them, he woke with a start.

He didn't sleep another wink.

"Nipatie ruhusa ya siku moja Bwana" (give me a day off, sir), he asked the white manager as soon as he arrived at the work site. "Wazazi wangu wako na maafa" (my parents have a tragedy).

"Maafa gani?" (What tragedy?) the employer asked.

Simon kept quiet. Without a ready lie, he feared being accused of voodoo worship if he told the truth.

"*Rudi kwa Kazi,*" (Go back to work).

"Tafathali Bwana, nitarundi kesho." (Please, sir, I'll return tomorrow).

"Ukienda, hakuna mshahara leo." (If you go, there'll be no pay for you today).

"Ni sawa Bwana" (That's all right, sir).

Simon walked for two hours and arrived home to find mourners around Njomo's grave, the exact image he saw in his dream.

After the funeral, Mami walked like a zombie. Sometimes, she talked and, in another minute, she clammed up and became listless.

Baba seemed dumbfounded. He tried to putter around the courtyard but gave up and returned indoors; he didn't know what to do at home on a weekday. He returned to work after two days.

We never learned whether Major Miller said anything when he heard about Njomo's mysterious death. But nobody bothered to ask. Even we children already knew African lives were of no consequence to owners of the farms; the colonial government never investigated those deaths.

We peasants were just a bunch of helpless people. We anguished, weathered whatever caused us grief—without getting visibly debilitated—and kept on going.

# Chapter 67

# The Psychic

Like Baba, my siblings and I returned to school two days after
the burial, without my venturing close to Njomo's grave then or
ever. The cow dip, where I had stood and marveled at calves
swimming without prior training, was about a hundred feet from
our footpath to school. I never went close to it again until February 25, 2024, while working on this book.

(Now, the dip is in a private property whose owner likely
doesn't know its history. He has cultivated all around it. The roof
is long gone; the only guardrails are brush and creepers, except
for the deep end that gives a full view of the entire structure. Because of rainwater, the abandoned dip still has a shimmering puddle at the bottom. It's scary to look down below, and one can't
help but wonder why cows needed such a deep, dangerous structure.)

Back in 1964, my acute sadness lasted a week before it turned
into a gnawing heaviness. But Mami's melancholy continued despite burying herself in her work. As we went about our business,
none of us mentioned Njomo. It saddened me that his name had
become taboo. Would I ever hear of him again? After his unexpected death, we forgot about him, or so I thought.

In about a month, however, instead of sending one of us children to take Baba his evening mug of tea, Mami started taking it
herself.

My siblings and I suspected my parents were up to something. We eyed each other whenever she left. I noticed she had stopped her shuffling walk and started eating again. She seemed both energized and distracted.

Then, bam!

"Someone killed Njomo," Mami announced one evening.

We merely looked at her over the fire without asking how she knew.

"Someone threw him into the cow dip," she said.

"Why would someone kill a little child?" one of us asked.

I thought grief had gotten the better of my mother.

"Yes, someone killed him," she said.

Oh, well, whatever.

*

One Sunday, I heard voices in Baba's thingira. My mother came outside once to visit the outhouse way behind nyũmba, close to the fence. When she returned indoors, I thought of an excuse to hang near thingira and eavesdrop. I decided against it—it would have been too obvious.

That evening, none of us children gathered the courage to ask Mami what she and Baba were up to. We all kept our thoughts to ourselves, which now seems strange that we never discussed family "secrets" with one another, even as adults.

During that week, I heard rumors that my parents were investigating Njomo's death. They had even involved Waigwa and Wairimũ-big, my half-siblings. I suspect my mother confided in a friend, who then spread the news. By then, my parents had already solicited help from a psychic. Because they conducted their activities in Baba's thingira, it became hard for me to confirm. I listened for any tidbits or slip-ups from Mami. But my big-mouth mother never made a single slip-up.

I later learned a psychic had sneaked into our homestead on three Sundays. I got a brief glimpse of him once. Average build, at least 5'10". He wore a brown suit and a white shirt. Besides the one sighting, I learned nothing else about the man or where he had come from.

The psychic rendered his verdict on his last visit. From then on, Mami spread the word to her friends and us. She started with us that very evening.

"Mũriithi murdered Njomo," she said. "The psychic saw it in his mirror."

David Mũriithi Gathatwa was our neighbor, who moved to the homestead formerly occupied by Kamunge's cook's family. (Because of confusion with my brothers' names—David and Mũriithi—I'll refer to him as DM Gathatwa.)

"Why would he kill a small boy?" one of us asked.

"DM Gathatwa is jealous of boy children," Mami said. "He can't stand that an old couple like me and your father bore such a handsome boy."

Mami told us the story as if the psychic were an eyewitness. She and my father harbored no doubt.

I don't know about my siblings, but having already disliked DM Gathatwa, I accepted our mother's word without reservation.

A year after we moved to our current village, I was crossing Tindaress River from our old village one late afternoon when I noticed the back of a naked man washing upstream. It surprised me that a man would wash there during the day. When the man turned his head, I recognized DM Gathatwa. He dashed to what I believed was for cover. I went on and crossed the river. Soon, he appeared on the opposite bank, headed to the crossing, wearing shorts and holding a stick. Already halfway on the other bank, he couldn't catch me. I ran home and told Mami.

"If he doesn't want to be seen naked," Mami said, "He shouldn't bathe in the river, close to a crossing."

According to Mami, the next time she saw DM Gathatwa, she warned him never to touch her children.

In Njomo's case, after Mami and her friends spread the word. Hush-hush rumors swirled across the two villages about the murderer among us. No one argued or challenged the story.

If DM Gathatwa heard the rumor, which was likely, he didn't dignify it with an explanation. However, he avoided my parents as one would lepers. In everybody's eyes, that proved his guilt.

With no way to punish DM Gathatwa, Mami issued her final verdict.

"Ngai will avenge Njomo right here on this earth," she said, poking her index finger toward the ground.

Afterward, the matter fizzled and died.

My parents could play judge and jury, but they lacked the legal power of executioners. Their busyness, however, helped Mami get out of her funk and get on with the business of living.

*

Decades later, when I asked about Njomo's tragedy, my brother, Morry, and sister, Wairimū, expounded on the story.

They heard that DM Gathatwa sneaked into our courtyard, enticed Njomo with sweets, carried him with the pretext of taking him to Mami's work, and tossed him into the cow dip.

Wairimū-big, who attended two of the psychic's meetings, added another tidbit. She said DM Gathatwa had come for lunch. After he enticed Njomo, he took him to his house and fed him food spiked with disabling poison. When Njomo lost consciousness, DM Gathatwa rolled him with a cloth and dumped him in the dip.

I suspected that after the psychic showed my parents the "image" he *saw* in his *mirror,* which Wairimū-big swears to this day, they filled in the other details with an occasional prompt from him.

I don't know what to believe. I still wonder how Njomo ended up in that cow dip. If someone threw him there, a plausible scenario, why did he do it? And nobody saw him?

# Chapter 68

# The Avenger

When Mami declared Ngai would avenge Njomo's death, it was as if she permitted us to stop grieving. But I remember feeling sad that if I died, people would forget me just like they forgot Njomo.

Meanwhile, years chugged along before something untoward happened. But when tragedy struck DM Gathatwa and his family, it left a trail of bodies. It started when DM Gathatwa's youngest daughter fell ill. Her mother rushed her to Nakuru General Hospital. Not long after, the little girl returned home in a box.

The following year, their next-youngest daughter fell ill. The mother followed the same hospital routine. But this time, she caught a disease in the hospital, got in the box, and her daughter returned home motherless.

From then on, DM Gathatwa lost interest in life and became a hermit. As a teenager, his oldest daughter (Wanjirũ-no relation) helped him raise the remaining two girls.

In time, Wanjirũ DM Gathatwa (Wanjirũ DMG) became of age. She fell in love with Mũthee Waigwa, my half-nephew. As a little girl during Njomo's tragedy, she likely didn't know the heinous accusation that had swept through the village about her father. Or if she had heard of it, she and Mũthee decided to ignore it. The couple married and had two children before divorcing.

Meanwhile, her father, DM Gathatwa, battled high blood pressure and diabetes. When he died, no one could tell what killed him first—heartbreak or the two diseases. But the family's tragedy didn't stop there.

*

DM Gathatwa had a younger brother, Kaguamba Gathatwa, who never went to school because of a lack of school fees. As an adult, Kaguamba embraced his peasantry; he worked all day long until the sun set on him.

When the government bought farms from the former colonizers, set them up as co-ops, and sold them piecemeal on installment plans, first to former farmworkers and then to other landless people, Kaguamba bought himself a share. He homesteaded his family, grew their food, and raised chickens, goats, and two cows for their milk.

The one downside was that, without education, Kaguamba had developed an aversion to banks. He couldn't trust them to keep his money safe. He also didn't trust his thin mattress or the hole in his backyard.

After this became an open secret, his wayward, good-for-nothing son had a habit of appearing like a ghost. The father feared that while hiding his cache, his youngest son could appear. Or the rogue could poke around, which he may have already done before he learned where his father kept his prized bundle.

(Incidentally, the son, unlike his two brothers, had dropped out of school because, he claimed, his father didn't go to school, and he had turned out okay. In his warped reasoning, he forgot to factor in hard work.)

After Kaguamba ruled out the bank, his mattress, or his backyard, he had only one option. He became his own banker, the bank manager he trusted without reservation. He stuffed his bundles of shillings in every pocket or fold of his oversized clothes. If he went goat-herding, or to tend to his coffee bushes, or to milk his cow, the money went along with him. The only time the two separated was at night, when he locked his room door.

Kaguamba kept on living; a tightwad, his shillings multiplied.

One morning, he went to milk his cow in the usual enclosure. When he took longer than expected, his wife got impatient. She sent their grandchild to tell the grandfather to hurry up with the milk for their morning tea. The girl found the bucket knocked down with less than a cup of milk left. Meanwhile, the cow fidgeted for someone to let her out of the enclosure.

"He would never leave the cow tethered," the wife said to her grandchild, "and the milk unattended." She raised the alarm.

People put together a loose search party. The group went door-to-door to the adjacent plots, although Kaguamba wasn't one to visit people's houses. There was no sign of him.

The searchers now concentrated on the family's two-and-a-half acres.

They started walking around the milking enclosure. They came to a drag wake through grass and weeds. It led to the coffee bushes where they found Kaguamba or what remained of him, his body strewn between two coffee bushes, his oversized stuffed jacket and trousers gone. On a closer look, the men noticed two blows to the back of his head, and blood was already crusted. With no trace of the wayward son, the searchers easily guessed who had committed the heinous crime.

When the police caught up with the culprit in town, clad in a trendy outfit, he had lived like the wealthy in the months it took him to deplete his father's life savings. When they questioned him, he claimed cows had trampled his father.

"How would you know that?" the police asked.

"You just told me my father is dead," the Rogue said.

When the police hurled him to court, and the gavel came down, the Rogue got life.

Unfortunately, a life sentence turned out too long a wait for fate. The man met with a mysterious death in prison. People claimed inmates had no use for anyone who preyed on family.

Did Ngai avenge Njomo?

Who knows the workings of the invisible?

# Chapter 69

# High School Prep

When I started school, education meant the ability to read and write. As I progressed, it dawned on me that education was my lifeline to a better life. It didn't matter that I couldn't imagine that life or know what to say if an adult asked me, "What do you want to be when you grow up?" But I focused on that endgame like Christians focus on heaven.

Meanwhile, I glimpsed such a life through Madam and her scooter, Rose and her confident attitude and friendship, the Ministry of Education's actions, and my determination, which was the sum that prodded me along.

During the August holidays, while we were in grade six, my brother Joseph helped me see even further. He, the busybody in our family, had established himself as our village "librarian." He hunted for and brought home beat-up, sometimes coverless, old novels and comics. (The two or three comics failed to impress me; the images and stories were too alien for me.)

After he read a book, he passed it on to me. I read about cowboys and love stories. One book was titled "The Guilty Are Afraid" by Hadley Chase.

Those beat-up free books opened my mind and expanded my thinking beyond my village.

Meanwhile, adults had snickered that independence had not changed or improved our lives. It had not occurred to my classmates and me to credit independence with the changes in our education system. Nonetheless, after independence, we pupils focused on high school.

In our last term in grade seven, teachers started an after-school prep program twice a week, where we studied math and English. Instead of an occasional sleepover, I started spending the two nights at the Thaiyas. Although Joseph didn't like it, he started doing the same. Teachers shamed pupils who missed a session, as if they didn't want to attend high school. They also became more attentive to our general questions—a courtesy they hadn't extended to us before.

As the pioneer class, our teachers fussed about the exam as if they were getting tested. Looking back, I now realize they felt the pressure of their school competing with older, established national schools whose students had taken and passed the national test for decades.

A month before the exam, the school held a session in which two teachers advised us on what to expect in our upcoming exam and on our choice of high schools. They required each of us to choose three high schools.

As we completed our forms, papers rustled while the teachers hovered. Eager to answer any questions or make suggestions, they peered at our choices to ensure they aligned with our abilities. They passed on their nervousness to us, and the heaviness hung in the classroom as if we were taking the actual exam.

To avoid mistakes, I first wrote my three choices on scratch paper. One teacher approached me before I transferred the names to the official form.

"Include a day school as a backup," he said. "I expect you to get into a boarding school, but it's easier to get admitted into a day school."

I hesitated, caught between the teacher's advice and my gut feeling to place my future in boarding schools, which had been my focus since I started school. I didn't know there were day high schools before the teacher gave us the overview. He told us about the various schools and read their names.

To make matters worse, the day schools were all in town. Where would I stay? I wondered. But I kept my concerns to myself. Not used to airing my thoughts to an adult besides Mami, I had never gone against an authority.

It pained me to scratch my third boarding school choice and instead insert Menengai High School, a former Indian school—until independence, less than a year ago—in Nakuru Town.

After we completed our school selections and the teachers ensured our forms were in order, they collected them and left. I put everything out of my mind. Not once did it occur to me to wonder how Baba would pay my school expenses for boarding or day school, let alone for Joseph and me.

# Chapter 70

# The Plantation Escape

We took the national standardized Kenya Primary Education (KPE) exam in late November 1964. After the exam, I felt immense relief. In the schoolyard, my classmates and I asked what others had done. Every one of us underplayed their performance, even the few who scored top marks in class. Pupils preferred to spring a surprise when they passed.

I, the only girl in class, stuck to my mantra—if some pupils pass, I'll be one of them. I knew I had a good chance of passing. How well? I had no clue; I had struggled in some sections.

When we left Kabazi Primary School for the unknown, we bid emotional goodbyes to each other, unaware that I would never see or know what happened to 99% of my classmates.

I spent a relaxed December, knowing the exam was behind me.

When school opened in the first week of January 1965, before our exam results came out, anxiety crept in. I hated to see children leave for school while I accompanied my mother to the plantations to pick the last scant crop of coffee cherries in the extreme heat.

But we didn't wait for long. In another week, the KPE exam results came out.

Joseph got the news first. He dropped everything and trekked over Jumatatu Mountain Range like a marathon runner headed to Kabazi Primary.

On his way home, he could have tripped and hurt himself as he hurried down the mountain. When he arrived, with a receptive audience, he talked and talked.

"This is the greatest day of my life!" he said. "And it's the best day for you, too!"

"Whaaat?" I asked.

"We conquered it! We passed!" Joseph said.

When he said, "We passed," even before I learned my score, an eruption started from my chest and swept through my entire body. I tightened myself, wrapped my arms around my body, and shut my eyes to let the news sink in.

When I relaxed, I got tempted to gyrate in a happy dance. Instead, I joined my brother, who spoke too fast, tripped on words, and hand-gestured. We talked over each other as if competing to see who could tell the story faster and better. To say the results elated my brother and me is an understatement.

*

The exam came in sections—math, English, Kiswahili, history, geography, and others. A pass was marked in three letters—ABC—or a combination of them.

Joseph passed with B+B+B+, and I received BBC.

None of us mentioned that he had done better than I had. I wasn't concerned. My result was good enough.

I could already imagine myself stepping away from the life waiting for me on the farm.

Seated at her usual bench by the firepit, Mami made little fanfare. But she spoke easily, her face aglow, and seemed pleased.

"It turned out just as I expected," she said.

I didn't need to spread the news. Joseph and my mother would carry it through the village far better than I could.

Baba heard it secondhand from Mami. He wasn't home when Joseph returned. Whatever passed between them, I do not remember him saying much to us. Perhaps he did. But I never expected much from him in moments like these.

I didn't need it.

I had stepped off the plantation merry-go-round.

And I was not getting back on.

# Acknowledgments

Thanks to Carol Perkins, Mary Thorne Kelley, and my editor, Isabella Furth. Your input and support are greatly appreciated.

And thanks to you, the reader or listener, for spending time with my words. Words are meaningless if no one reads or hears them.

Peace and love.

# Afterword

Thank you for spending time with my words and for walking with me through these pages that carry the people, places, and moments that shaped my early life. I am deeply grateful you chose to read this book.

If, along the way, you found echoes of your own beginnings, discovered that roots can travel wherever life leads, or recognized the quiet strength it takes to endure change, then this journey has been shared in the truest sense.

If you feel moved to share your reflections, a brief review can help carry this story to other readers.

Wanjirũ *Warama*
WanjiruWarama.com

Scan Here to Stay Connected:

www.ingramcontent.com/pod-product-compliance
Lightning Source LLC
Chambersburg PA
CBHW020434130626
46549CB00001B/136